D1485454

BLOOD, DREAMS AND GOLD

Other titles by this author:

Twilight of Truth: Chamberlain, Appeasement and the Manipulation of the Press (1989)

My Dear Max: The Letters of Brendan Bracken to Lord Beaverbrook (ed.) (1990)

David Astor and the Observer (1991)

Thinking the Unthinkable: The Economic Counter-Revolution, 1931–1983 (1994)

Sudan: Darfur and the Failure of an African State (2010), also published by Yale University Press

BLOOD, DREAMS AND GOLD

THE CHANGING FACE OF BURMA

RICHARD COCKETT

YALE UNIVERSITY PRESS
NEW HAVEN AND LONDON

Copyright © 2015 Richard Cockett

All rights reserved. This book may not be reproduced in whole or in part, in any form (beyond that copying permitted by Sections 107 and 108 of the U.S. Copyright Law and except by reviewers for the public press) without written permission from the publishers.

For information about this and other Yale University Press publications, please contact:
U.S. Office: sales.press@yale.edu   www.yalebooks.com
Europe Office: sales@yaleup.co.uk   www.yalebooks.co.uk

Typeset in Adobe Garamond Pro by IDSUK (DataConnection) Ltd
Printed in Great Britain by TJ International Ltd, Padstow, Cornwall

Library of Congress Cataloging-in-Publication Data

Cockett, Richard.
  Blood, dreams and gold: the changing face of Burma/Richard Cockett.
    pages cm
  Includes bibliographical references and index.
  ISBN 978-0-300-20451-3 (cloth : alkaline paper)
  1. Burma—History—1948– 2. Burma—History—1824–1948. 3. Burma—Politics
and government. 4. Burma—Colonial influence. 5. Civil war—Burma—History.
6. Authoritarianism—Burma—History. 7. Social change—Burma—History.
8. Interviews—Burma. I. Title.
  DS530.4.C63 2015
  959.1—dc23
                                                                  2015017634

A catalogue record for this book is available from the British Library.

9 8 7 6 5 4 3 2 1

CONTENTS

ILLUSTRATIONS

Plates

Maps

ACKNOWLEDGEMENTS

THE RESEARCH FOR THIS book was carried out mainly while I was South-East Asia correspondent for *The Economist* newspaper from 2010 to 2014. To cover the region, I lived in the lush, wealthy city-state of Singapore, but I was quickly drawn to Burma. When I started the job the country was about to hold its first general election of the new democratic era, but as this event was boycotted by the main opposition party of Aung San Suu Kyi, none of us journalists took it too seriously. However, during my next couple of trips to Burma in 2011 it was clear that something genuinely momentous was happening there. Hence, I would travel regularly back and forth over the following years between Burma and home in Singapore – the one caught in time, the other in the vanguard of the Asian century. It was exciting to explore and discover a country that seemed to be opening up so quickly, especially against the backdrop of the Middle East's Arab Spring rapidly turning to winter.

This work is based on the people I spoke to and the information I gathered during those many trips, sometimes to the most remote parts of the country. A lot of the pleasure in travelling around Burma was about meeting the Burmese, Karen, Kachin and other ethnic peoples in this extraordinarily diverse country. Many are quoted in this book by name; it was one of the advantages of my timing that many people were able to speak at length about their experiences under military rule for the first time, once Big Brother finally started leaning back a bit. These men and women were all generous with their time and uncommonly hospitable.

Others I talked to, but who are not necessarily named in the text, include: Alan Saw U, Ariyawuntha Bhiwunsa, Aung Kyaw Zan, Aung Naing Oo, Cheery Zahau, Devi Thant Cin, Jason Eligh, Glenn Kyaw Nyunt, Han Sein, Hkalam Samson, Hkanpha Sadan, Hkun Htun Oo, Hla Maung Shwe, Ho Wa Zan Gan, Richard Horsey, Hpunggan Hkun Nawng, Htay Oo, Iftekar Ahmed Chowdury, Ja Seng Hkawn Maran, Khin Lay, Khin Moe Samm, Stephanie Kleine-Ahlbrandt, Derek Mitchell, Myint Thein, Myo Win, Nang Voe Phart, Naw Rebecca Htin, Nay Win Maung, Nbyen Dan Hkung Awng, Ngun Cung Lian, Nyantha Maw Lin, Pe Myint, Léon de Riedmatten, Moses Samuels, Sammy Samuels, Set Aung, Shwe Maung, Edmund Sim, Soe Win, Tony Stern, Tan Khee Giap, Tejobhasa, Thant Myint-U, Tin Oo, Mathew Walton, Wang Dong, Win Htein, Win Kyaw Oo, Ye Htut, Zang Xiaomin, Zha Daojing.

I was also lucky to benefit from the wisdom and experience of several experts on Burma, and indeed Asia, over the course of my writing. I learned a great deal from my constant conversations with them. I thus wish particularly to thank Romain Caillaud, Farah Cheah, Joseph Fisher, Hla Hla Win, Tom Kramer, Simon Long, Michael Montesano, Nay Chi Win, Robert Pé, Mael Raynaud, Ben Rogers, Kantan Shankar, Irene Slegt, Soe Thein, Ashley South and Hans Vriens. Needless to say, though, any mistakes and misjudgements are mine alone.

I also owe a particular debt of gratitude to an old friend, Dominic Ziegler, who also happened to be my editor back in London throughout my time in South-East Asia. He never seemed to panic as I disappeared for days on end in a country with medieval communications, and at least appeared to be genuinely happy when I reappeared again. He is a model editor.

I would like to thank the team at Yale University Press who saw the book through in such a professional manner, as they did the last time around. Phoebe Clapham commissioned it, Heather McCallum took it over and steered it through to the end, while Tami Halliday was a very dedicated editor. It's reassuring that one publisher, at least, still cares so much about the books that it produces.

Finally, this book owes a great deal to my wife Harriet Paterson. We did a lot of travelling around Burma together, with our son, and she helped to interview people in Yangon. An expert copy-editor, she also improved the manuscript considerably towards the end. It was a joint endeavour, and all the better for it.

Hammersmith, London, 2015

PREFACE

The Burmese mosaic

BY THE END OF the first decade of this millennium, Burma stood virtually alone. Its isolation was more pitiful than splendid: its leaders secretive and despotic, its citizens semi-feudal and desperately poor. Amongst neighbours the country bore comparison only with North Korea, for its benighted people and its vicious regime. No Asian tiger this – the ruling generals had recklessly ignored the technological and economic innovations that had transformed so much of the region over the previous decades and instead led this beautiful and once-prosperous country on a race to the bottom. A police state oversaw a ruined economy, widespread hunger and political prisoners locked in dog kennels.

This was tragic for Burma, even more so as this trajectory could not be blamed on external circumstances. The military regime had set a course towards ruin long before western economic sanctions started to bite in the mid 1990s. True, the military officers who ruled the country from 1962 had been dealt a bad hand by the British colonialists as they departed in the 1940s, but independent Burma's new rulers only compounded the manifold problems left to them. This was national self-immolation.

In this book I will tell the story of how a proud imperial people, the Burmans, built an empire and then in turn were humiliated and conquered by a European empire; how the colonialists exploited the territory for their own ends; and how a ruling junta of generals then tried to eviscerate all traces of foreign influence after independence to build a pure Burman nationalism in their own image. I will show how this disastrously misconceived policy came to leave the country largely isolated by 2010, and how the government then surprised the world with an apparent change of course – including the release of the world's most famous political prisoner since Nelson Mandela, the Nobel peace prize winner Aung San Suu Kyi. Lastly, I will examine these reforms to try to judge how far they may undo the past and point towards a modern Asian nation.

I have tried to tell Burma's story through the country's physical geography, its cities and villages, rivers, mountains and jungles, and the seemingly infinite variety of people who live there. Military rule cut off many of these people and places for decades from the rest of Burma, let alone the world, but most of the country is now accessible to the reasonably persistent tourist. This is, in a sense, a work of modern anthropology, of rediscovering ways of life that have almost vanished elsewhere, and of encountering the remnants of those many communities, such as the Anglo-Burmese of Moulmein and the Indians of downtown Yangon, that the military governments tried to drive out altogether. They have instead clung on, and must be involved in building a new Burma. In this sense Burmese studies are gloriously tactile – you can still see, touch and talk to Burma's living history. These are the tesserae, the small but glistening fragments of the Burmese mosaic.

There have been many books written about Burma before, of course, journalistic, impressionistic and scholastic. I point the reader towards the best of these, or at least the ones that I have found most useful, in the bibliography towards the end. Most of these works, however, focus just on particular aspects of Burmese politics, history, ethnography and culture, and often over a fairly limited time frame. This book attempts to do something different. I want to give an accessible account of modern Burma in a single volume, blending interviews and reporting with historical and political analysis. Where necessary, I have referenced the facts and figures that I use in the book. Most of the interviewees were happy to be quoted, but sometimes I have had to disguise them, for obvious reasons. I state clearly when this is the case.

I have organised the first part of my book, "The plural society and its enemies", around the three distinctive forces that have shaped contemporary Burma: British colonialism, Burman nationalism and the struggle for autonomy of the country's minority ethnic groups. All too often these forces have been galvanised in violent reaction against each other, shattering the mosaic. I start off with a consideration of the colonial era, not because I think it is necessarily the most important aspect of Burma's recent history, but because the remnants of this era – the ghostly edifices of downtown Yangon – are what hit the contemporary visitor to the *de jure* capital of the country most forcefully.

It is the contention of this book that ultimately Burma will never enjoy a peaceful and prosperous future until all these three forces can be reconciled, at which point an entirely new nation must arise out of the detritus of the old. For the fact is that throughout its history as a post-colonial country Burma has never worked, it has never been at peace. At this most profound level, the country is still struggling to exist. There is no golden age to which all of its peoples can refer back, only a splintered, bitterly contested history on which few can agree. In Burma one person's golden age is another person's memory of misery and oppression.

But the prize for reconciliation is great, for within each of these mutually antagonistic forces lies an abundance of commercial, intellectual and cultural capital. If they could be united and incorporated successfully, then Burma should easily reclaim its former position as one of Asia's leading states. At the moment, the parts overwhelm the whole.

Chapter One explains the founding and the consequences of colonial rule in Burma through the old littoral entrepôts of Yangon (formerly Rangoon), Mawlamyine (Moulmein) and Sittwe (Akyab). Chapters Two and Three give an account of the rise of Burman independence, nationalism and the generals' military rule, focusing mainly on the new capital of Naypyidaw and the former royal capital of Mandalay.

I place Burma in its regional context, to show that its experiences were often commonplace, such as colonialism and the reaction against it. Many in the West seem to expect that a reformed Burma, under the guidance of opposition leader Aung San Suu Kyi, must surely develop into a liberal western democracy. It is much more likely, given their shared histories, that Burma will become like Malaysia, Singapore or Thailand – authoritarian states with stunted democracies dominated by the politics of ethnicity and religion. Yet it could be so much more.

Chapters Four and Five tell the story of the many ethnic groups of Burma, sometimes called "hill peoples". They mainly live on the peripheries of the country and have spent the past sixty years or so locked in conflict with the Burmans of the central lowlands, the majority ethnic group that make up about 60 per cent of the country's population. Chapter Four, "Under enemy occupation", is an account of the Kachin. Chapter Five is principally about the Karen and the Shan, but it also focuses on the scourge of drugs and how this has overwhelmed the lives and aspirations of all the ethnic groups who live along Burma's eastern border. The division between the minority ethnic groups and the Burmans remains the principal fault line in the country's modern culture and politics, as it has been ever since independence. Not just because of the terrible violence inflicted on the hill peoples by the Burman military, but because the continual fighting was used by the military to justify its dictatorial control over all aspects of Burmese life, and to squash those students and democrats who challenged its rule.

In the second part of the book, "Reform, to preserve", I explore the pressures on the country's military rulers to change since the uprising of the National League for Democracy and other opposition groups in the late 1980s. In particular, the final three chapters assess the apparent volte-face in the policies of the military regime since 2010 and attempt to answer the tantalising question of why, after so many obdurate decades, the generals decided to undertake more far-reaching reforms than ever before. Within the space of just a few years the vast majority of political prisoners have been released, a lively free press has burst forth and an American president has visited.

The last chapter, "Burma's future and the ghosts of the plural society", shows how much of the early optimism for the reforms is now fading as the processes of democratisation and modernisation risk being derailed by the eruptions of ethnic and religious violence – the ghosts of Burma's past. On one level, the new era of partial democracy has been a triumphant vindication for those thousands of political activists who had to suffer years of torture and imprisonment to force such a change. But on another level, the country now has to live with the unintended consequences of that change.

ON NAMES AND PLACE NAMES

EVERYONE WHO WRITES ABOUT Burma, now also called Myanmar, is confronted with the unusual issue of what to call the country. In 1989, the ruling military junta officially changed many of the country's place names, and that of the country itself (from Burma to Myanmar). Confusion has reigned ever since. Most people in the country now call it Myanmar, but Burma is still mainly used outside the country, particularly in Britain and America.

Changing the place names was a political decision, part of a programme of 'Burmanisation', and the full context of this is described in Chapter Three. For reasons that I make clear in the text I have chosen to remain with the country's former designation as Burma. I also use the original "colonial-era" names to describe those towns, cities and other places that I write about during that period, for the sake of historical authenticity. This is a list of the eight administrative regions (of fourteen) that were changed in 1989:

Arakan to Rakhine
Irrawaddy to Ayeyarwady
Karen to Kayin
Karenni to Kayah
Magwe to Magway
Pegu to Bago
Rangoon to Yangon
Tenasserim to Tanintharyi

A very good and full explanation of the name changes, and a useful introduction to the toponymy of Burma in general, can be found at http://webarchive. nationalarchives.gov.uk/20140402150947/http://www.pcgn.org.uk/ burma%200907.pdf.

To clarify a further potential area for confusion, the word Burman is used here to describe the largest ethnic group in the country. Depending on the context, Burmese either describes all the people of Burma (that is, the Burmans as well as the Kachin, Karen and the hundred or so other ethnic groups who live in the country), or is simply used as the plural of Burman.

Burmese personal names are equally resistant to customary Western notions of how they should be rendered. Usually, Burmese names cannot be separated into a family name and a given name; they function only as a whole. Honorifics are also something of a problem. They are often used in Burma, most commonly U or Maung in front of a man's name, and Ma or Daw in front of a woman's name (thus Aung San Suu Kyi is often referred to as Daw Suu Kyi). I have chosen not to use them, except in circumstances where it would be difficult to identify them without the honorific. Nu, for example, the first prime minister of independent Burma, is always called U Nu.

ACRONYMS

ASEAN	Association of South-East Asian Nations
BDA	Burmese Defence Army
BDF	Burma Defence Force
BIA	Burma Independence Army
BSPP	Burmese Socialist Programme Party
CIA	Central Intelligence Agency
DSA	Defence Services Academy
HI	Humanity Institute
IFC	Irrawaddy Flotilla Corporation
IMF	International Monetary Fund
KIA	Kachin Independence Army
KIO	Kachin Independence Organisation
KMT	Kuomintang
KNLA	Karen National Liberation Army
KNU	Karen National Union
MIS	Military Intelligence Service
NDF	National Democratic Front
NLD	National League for Democracy
PAP	People's Action Party
PBF	Patriotic Burmese Force
PMF	People's Militia Forces
PSRD	Press Scrutiny and Registration Division

SNLD	Shan Nationalities League for Democracy
SLORC	State Law and Order Restoration Council
SPDC	State Peace and Development Council
UMEHL	Union of Myanmar Economic Holdings Limited
USDP	Union Solidarity and Development Party
UNDP	United Nations Development Programme
UNESCO	United Nations Educational, Scientific and Cultural Organisation
UNODC	United Nations Office on Drugs and Crime
UMNO	United Malays National Organisation

PART ONE

THE PLURAL SOCIETY AND ITS ENEMIES

Map 1. Burma.

CHAPTER ONE

"A world at its zenith": Rangoon, commerce and colonialism

UNIQUELY FOR A CONTEMPORARY Asian metropolis, it is a religious monument that still dominates the skyline of Yangon, Burma's biggest city and former capital. Vertiginous plate-glass skyscrapers long ago vanquished Bangkok, Kuala Lumpur, Seoul and Singapore, but in Yangon the shimmering golden stupa of the 99-metre-tall Shwedagon pagoda continues to draw the eye from all vantage points. Deservedly, every tour of the city starts here, and if you are going to visit only one building in Yangon, or the whole of Burma, it has to be the Shwedagon. "A golden mystery upheaved itself on the horizon – a beautiful winking wonder that blazed in the sun", is how Rudyard Kipling, poet laureate of the British Empire, described it on first sight, and the Shwedagon remains as much a wonder today as it was in Kipling's time. Beyond being Asia's most graceful religious monument, it is surely the most treasured. There are 22,000 gold plates on the Shwedagon. Every Buddhist pagoda has a tapering, conical structure at the top known as a *hti*, or umbrella, usually encrusted with gemstones, but the six-metre *hti* of the Shwedagon is a thing of fable. The whole structure is believed to hold about 85,000 jewels, and at the very pinnacle is a single 76-carat diamond.

The Shwedagon probably dates from around the fifteenth century, although the Burmese claim that it is over two thousand years old. Whichever is true, this is no lifeless, ancient monument, merely to be cosseted and admired from a respectful distance. Quite the opposite. The Shwedagon is constantly being restored, refreshed, regilded and rebuilt; it is an organic structure, still the central shrine of the very vital and lively Burmese tradition of Theravada Buddhism. Thus, every five or six years most of the pagoda is cleared of the millions of tiny pieces of gold leaf that have been pressed on it by pilgrims and worshippers. The wood beneath is inspected and, if necessary, repaired. The gold that is scraped off is moulded into pure golden Buddha images.

The *hti* is replaced regularly as well, if at rather longer intervals. The present *hti* is the fourth, and was hauled to the top in 1999. The three previous ones are preserved at the foot of the pagoda. The two older *htis* are encased in stone tombs, but the third one is still visible in a metal and glass shelter; it was donated to the Shwedagon by the penultimate king of Burma, Mindon, in 1871. And like the old king himself, except on a more modest scale, every year thousands of Buddhists donate their own gifts to decorate the *hti*. Rings, bracelets, pendants and necklaces of ruby, sapphire, jade and diamond, are winched to the top in a little wooden sleigh, to sparkle and shine over the sacred site. Jewels are popular now with the faithful partly because there is no room left within the vast Shwedagon complex to build their own pagodas or pavilions, or to contribute a statue of the Buddha, as they would have done in the past. There are already about 150 smaller, separate pagodas and six thousand Buddha images jostling for space around the main pagoda. Doing a good deed, such as honouring the Shwedagon, is a very pragmatic way to improve one's life in Burmese Buddhism: it is called "making merit".

At the base of the Shwedagon pagoda are the eight stations celebrating the days of the week (Wednesday has two); here worshippers come to honour their own birthday by pouring water over the small statue of the animal that represents their day. The most famous visitor is Aung San Suu Kyi; she comes to the Tuesday corner, by the south entrance, and gently douses a lion.

It is just as well that the Shwedagon is so organic since, apart from the demands of Buddhist tradition, it has had to survive numerous tremors and storms. In fact, the first *hti* was toppled by an earthquake. The Shwedagon has also had to survive the predatory instincts of invading armies. After subduing the city that they called Rangoon in the mid nineteenth century, British soldiers tried to carry off the exquisitely carved, 24-ton Singu bell, as booty, but they dropped it into the Yangon River while trying to manoeuvre it onto a waiting ship. It was subsequently dredged up by the Burmese and has now been restored to its original position close to the Shwedagon pagoda. Legend has it that one golden Buddha image taken by the British, the *Su Taung Pyay*, had to be sent back to Burma by Queen Victoria because she dreamt that it was giving her headaches. The queen's migraines cleared up, apparently, once the Buddha was back in Rangoon.

However, although the Shwedagon dominates Yangon, much of the city that we see today is hardly a Buddhist city at all; it is, in fact, primarily a creation of commerce and colonialism. To this day, the two worlds of the Shwedagon and the Western commercial city feel remote from each other, as much spiritually as geographically. They are isolated in their own worlds by the vagaries of history and politics. Whilst the pagoda and its immediate surrounding are lovingly maintained and embellished, the old colonial city, by contrast, is mostly crumbling and forlorn. Down by the old docks, barely a couple of miles from the magnificence and serenity of the Shwedagon, Yangon is dilapidated, dirty and distinctly unloved. Until recently, Burmese tour guides scarcely bothered to take their charges into the downtown area, of whose history they were almost entirely ignorant, and concentrated instead on the Shwedagon and Yangon's other Buddhist temples and monasteries. They assumed that the rest of the city, the part built by the Europeans along the shores of the Yangon and Bago rivers, must be of little interest. And, on the whole, until very recently they were probably right.

Yet, scarcely a century ago it was just the reverse. Back then the Shwedagon was certainly admired, even if haughty Europeans were reluctant to remove their shoes to visit it, but the real attraction was downtown Rangoon. The capital of the British colony of Burma, it was a thriving mercantile capital to be compared with Kolkata, Singapore, Penang and Shanghai. It was one of the most modern, cosmopolitan and exciting cities in the East, "a world at its zenith", as the poet Pablo Neruda described it in 1927 when he was Chilean consul there, "a city of blood, dreams and gold".

Nowadays, although there have been decades of decay and neglect, enough survives of the area to evoke that city of dreams and gold, a metropolis that drew to its narrow, filthy streets such a number and profusion of the world's races and religions that it quickly produced an entirely new form of society, the precursor of the modern globalised world. That is why it is the best place to start an account of modern Burma, because today's rulers are still grappling with the consequences of what took shape in Yangon well over a century ago, a direct product of British colonial rule.

Churchill's great adventure

Europeans started arriving on the shores of what became Burma as early as the sixteenth century. The Portuguese, in particular, played an occasionally signif-icant role in the various wars of conquest and reconquest, which raged across the Burmese heartlands in the centuries after. But it was the most successful of the European colonialists, the British, who had the most decisive influence on Burma, building the modern city of Rangoon and eventually shaping the country into the territory that we know today.

The British were initially drawn to the country during the early nineteenth century because of its close proximity to British-controlled India, then admin-istered from the Bengali city of Calcutta. Theirs was a gradual conquest of Burma, completed in three stages as the century progressed. Border disputes between British India and the Burmese kings at the court of Ava, the royal capital just outside Mandalay, led to the first and most important Anglo-Burmese war in 1824. This was not, like many colonial wars of the time, a hopelessly one-sided confrontation between a small but modern army and a large but medieval one. Rather, it was a genuine clash of empires, between the two most militarised, ruthless and ambitious forces in the region. The Burmese had recently completed their own imperial conquests of Assam and Manipur in north-east India, having previously conquered the independent kingdom of Arakan (now Rakhine State) on the Bay of Bengal. Just as these victories had brought the Burmese perilously close to the borders of Britain's eastern empire, so they had also invested the Burmese generals with a great deal of faith in their own abilities, and the martial prowess of their army. They were confident that they could fight the British and win, just as they had seen off the Arakanese, the Thai army and many others.

In the end the Burmese were defeated, but only after two years of hard fighting at a cost to the British imperial forces of about 15,000 British and Indian lives, a high figure for the times, alongside tens of thousands of Burmese dead. The British forced the court of Ava to sue for peace and the Burmese were

subsequently forced to cede the province of Manipur, as well as their own provinces of recently conquered Arakan and the Tenasserim Peninsula (then called
Tanintharyi), a sliver of land on the Andaman Sea stretching down to the west
of Thailand pointing towards what is now Malaysia. Thus, the British gained
their first toehold in Burma. Languid, tropical Moulmein, a small port at the
top of the Tenasserim Peninsula, became the first capital of British Burma.

Trade disputes with the court of Ava then led, in 1852–3, to the conquest
of the rest of Lower Burma, the region of the country that comprises, roughly,
the Irrawaddy Delta, littoral Burma and what was then the smallish port of
Rangoon and its environs. Originally founded in the eleventh century as a
fishing village by the Mon people, Rangoon had in turn been conquered by
the Burmese kings of Ava only in the mid eighteenth century.

Finally, in 1885, the British launched their assault on the Burmese heartlands in Upper Burma, attacking Mandalay, the latest (and last) of Burma's
many royal capitals. As was to be the case so often, on this occasion the
remnants of the once mighty Burmese kingdom fell victim to great power
rivalry and commercial avarice. This was the heyday of Victorian imperialism,
and the British wanted to deny Upper Burma to their greatest imperial rival,
the French, who had been pressing into Indochina, conquering the territories
that now comprise Vietnam, Cambodia and Laos. But politicians and officials
in Calcutta and London were also seduced by the merchants and financiers of
Rangoon into thinking that only the conquest of Upper Burma could open
the door to neighbouring China and the vast trading opportunities that, they
claimed, lay beyond in the Middle Kingdom.

So, just as the desire to force the free trade of opium on the Chinese had
led earlier British governments into war with China, the 1842 annexation of
Hong Kong and the start of the "century of humiliations", so now the prospect of doing still more business with China helped to seal the fate of Burma.
As one British merchant put it, "Supposing that the entire commerce of
south-west China and independent Burma were added to that of British
Burma, we may conceive what a vast opening there would be for the merchants
of Great Britain." In Rangoon merchants were calculating that "the Chinese
provinces neighbouring Burma contained approximately 103 million inhabit-
ants and that such a vast population was hardly touched by European

commerce." This was a prize, so the argument went, that the British could not afford to let slip from their grasp.[1]

If these were the real motives driving the British, a pretext for invasion was provided by the mad, bloody and exasperating reign of the last king of Burma, Thibaw. His father, Mindon, had ruled relatively well, acting with an admirable degree of tact and diplomacy as British imperialists took ever-larger bites out of his kingdom. Having sired 110 children during his reign, including forty-eight boys (and thus possible heirs), he also left a court riven by factionalism. Soon after Thibaw succeeded him in 1878, most of Mindon's other children were rounded up and imprisoned. The following February, they were massacred over the course of a few days, strangled or wrapped in carpets and bludgeoned to death so as to avoid the spilling of royal blood. The dead included thirty-one of old King Mindon's sons.

These murders, although not unprecedented in the annals of the court of Ava, caused outrage among the British and other Europeans in Burma and beyond. King Thibaw always denied direct involvement in the deaths, but from that point on his court was dismissed as a den of vice, barbarism and insanity. Thibaw's often eccentric and maladroit behaviour did little to help, and his half-hearted courting of the French and refusal to grant British merchants all the trading concessions that they demanded finally provoked the British into action.

The man who eventually ordered the charge in 1885 was Lord Randolph Churchill, then Secretary of State for India. The third son of the 7th Duke of Marlborough, he was a scion of one of Britain's most exalted aristocratic families and almost as grand, impetuous and regal as a Burmese king. Churchill was still only in his thirties in 1885, but already one of his country's most famous politicians. An aggressive Tory imperialist, he leapt at a chance, provided by yet another trade dispute with the Burmese, to send the Burma Field Force up the Irrawaddy to bring King Thibaw to heel. Unlike the first Anglo-Burmese war, this really was a one-sided affair, with the Burmese forces surrendering after their first clash with the ten thousand or so British and Indian troops under the command of General Henry Prendergast. Soon after, Thibaw was forced into exile in India, where he died in 1916. This was a novel form of forced imperial king-swap, for the British had earlier exiled the last

Moghul emperor, Bahadur Shah Zafar, to Rangoon. Burma's Muslims still commemorate him every year on the day he died; his tomb is near the zoo.

The hasty invasion of Upper Burma and the toppling of the monarchy was Lord Randolph's very own contribution to the British subjugation of Burma, and it was to have lasting repercussions. The usual custom at the time was for the British to rule the empire through the good agency of local princes, tribal chiefs or maharajahs. This system has come to be known as "indirect rule", or in the parlance of the time "the establishment of a native prince under British advice". Lord Randolph, however, was adamantly for the wholesale annexation of Upper Burma in order to bring the whole country under direct British rule. Many British MPs and officials opposed this, mainly on grounds of cost. Lord Randolph's own boss, the Conservative prime minister, the Marquess of Salisbury, at least fretted about it, but in the end Churchill got his way.

Thus, on top of foreign invasion, the Burmese had to witness the exile of the king, the dismantling of the monarchy, as well as the council that advised him, the *Hlutdaw*, and the destruction of most of the other ancient institutions and practices that had sustained the royal kingdom. This outright suppression of their monarchy, customs and identity provoked in turn a furious reaction from the defeated Burmese, who embarked on what amounted to a guerrilla campaign of resistance against British rule. The British met violence with more violence, eventually deploying as many as forty thousand British and Indian troops to defeat the rebellion, only finally snuffing out the last resistance in the mid 1890s.

This left such a legacy of hatred and bitterness among the Burmese that it evoked extremely visceral anti-British feelings even among the first generation of Burmese independence leaders about forty years later. Burma was well known for being one of the most dangerous places in the empire, and although the British blamed this on the criminality and poor character of the Burmese, there is no doubt that this *dacoity*, as the British called it, could more readily be explained by plain anti-British sentiment. At the top of Burmese society, the abolition of the monarchy also left a dangerous vacuum, one that the military dictators of more recent times were to exploit to the full.

Worse still, the newly conquered Burma did not become an independent British colony, as other such territories did. Rather, it was absorbed for administrative purposes into Britain's Indian empire, to be ruled as just one of so many "Indian" provinces from the viceroy's offices in Calcutta (and after 1911 from New Delhi). Thus, the once proudly independent Burmese empire had become merely an addendum to somebody else's empire, so heaping administrative humiliation on top of military humiliation. As we shall see, being placed under Indian rule created some, at least, of the deadly tensions and fissures in Burmese society that still govern the country's politics to this day. Such was the price of Lord Randolph's capricious colonialism, as his son, Sir Winston Churchill, was one day to find out.

Rangoon, the pomp and circumstance . . .

The new capital of British Burma, moved from Moulmein after the second Anglo-Burmese war, was to be Rangoon. The colonial city was freshly laid out, a couple of miles south of the Shwedagon, by colonial architects in 1853. So complete was the physical separation between the heart of the old indigenous Burmese culture around the Shwedagon and the new imperial city, that as late as the 1920s residents remembered tigers prowling the forested areas that divided the two parts of the city. The new downtown, with the smaller Sule pagoda at its centre, was built largely on swampland bordering the Rangoon River, using millions of cubic feet of earth excavated from the north of the city to shore up the foundations.

Most of what the visitor sees today of the colonial city south of Bogyoke Aung San Road was built in the ninety or so years after 1853. The strict grid pattern of roads here is in marked contrast to the rest of the city: an attempt, perhaps, by high-minded Victorians to impose order on what they viewed as the sinuous, superstitious society that went before. Many of the finest buildings that the British built to administer the new colony remain, although most are in various stages of decrepitude. The famous Pegu Club, a gentleman's retreat where British officials enjoyed the eponymous cocktail and pocketed their snooker balls, is today on the point of collapse, inhabited only by stray animals, ragged children and weeds. Nonetheless, enough of the past survives to convey an impression of how grand and enticing imperial Rangoon must have appeared in its heyday.

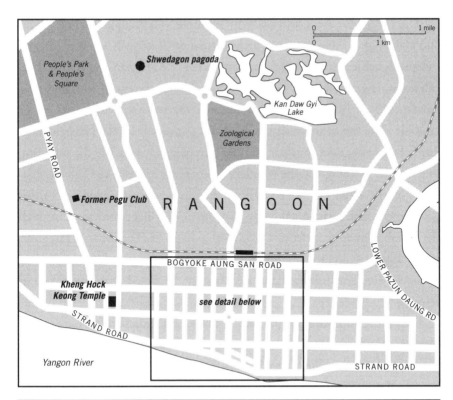

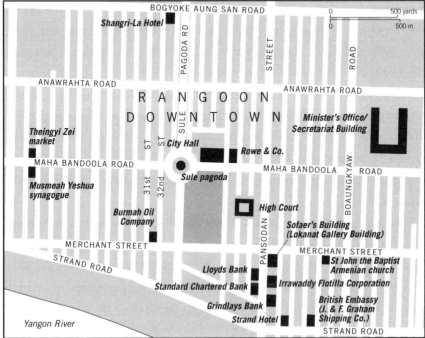

Map 2. Rangoon: The colonial centre.

The vast government secretariat, for example, still occupies a whole block, and makes up in sheer size for its architectural mediocrity. It was here that the independence leader General Aung San (father of Aung San Suu Kyi) and his cabinet were gunned down by assassins in 1947 on the eve of winning independence from Britain. Now cordoned off, the secretariat has been left to crumble since the entire government moved to the new capital Naypyidaw in 2005. Still being used for their original purposes, however, are the imposing High Court building and the wonderful City Hall, opposite the Sule pagoda. Most of the afore-mentioned official buildings were designed by British government architects, notably the Scotsman John Begg, but for City Hall the British allowed themselves a little local indulgence. The contract was given to the Burmese architect Sithu U Tin and the result is an exotic blend of European functionalism and Burmese fantasy, bedecked with peacocks and serpents.[2]

Even more impressive are the finance houses and commercial headquarters that remain clustered around Merchant and Pansodan Streets. Better than anything else these showy, intricate facades evoke an era from before the Second World War when Burma was the wealthiest country in the region. The country has abundant natural resources, and British (mainly Scottish) and European trading houses made fortunes in oil, rubber, tungsten, lead, silver, jade and much else. Oil had been extracted from the plains alongside the Irrawaddy River for centuries before the British arrived, but it was a Scotsman, David Cargill, who mechanised production and turned the country into an oil exporter. He founded the Burmah Oil Company, a cornerstone of the colonial economy, later absorbed into BP. The Burmah Oil Company enjoyed a monopoly on Burma's oilfields until 1901 when Standard Oil also started to operate. Eventually, Burma was producing over 1 million tons of crude oil a day.

Not only was the colony famous for "black gold", but for "brown gold" too, since Burma had the most extensive reserves of teakwood in the world. But it was not just the quantity of teak that mattered but the quality. Burmese teak was highly prized because among its other fabled properties, of strength and durability, it seemed to be resistant to termites – the Royal Navy, for example, would use nothing else for the decks of its warships. Companies like the Bombay Burmah Trading Corporation (known in London as Wallace Brothers) set up large, intricate forestry and trading networks across Burma and Thailand to exploit teak. Its headquarters occupied one of the best addresses in Rangoon – Strand Road, the main street that ran along the docks. So large were its operations that at one time the company employed a herd of six thousand elephants to drag the huge logs from steep hillsides down to the Irrawaddy to be shipped off to Rangoon and beyond. The renowned Burma Forest Service was founded to protect the country's reserves of teak, and over time this became one of colonial Burma's most influential and respected institutions. As well as teak there was also the Asian staple, rice. By the inter-war years intensive cultivation had turned Burma into the world's biggest exporter of rice, a lot of it grown among the verdant emerald green wetlands of the Irrawaddy Delta.

Most of the British Empire's leading banks, both British and Indian, arrived to service these fantastically lucrative businesses. By the beginning of the Second World War most of these banks had large operations in Burma, and they commissioned new buildings to reflect their self-importance. The Chartered Bank of India, Australia and China, now just Standard Chartered, set up in Burma in 1862 soon after its founding in London. Largely involved in financing agriculture, the bank outgrew several premises before buying a big plot of land facing onto Pansodan Street. Completed in 1941, its headquarters were a scintillating blend of art deco and Burmese. When it opened, the building was considered to be one of the most up-to-date structures in the East. Apart from its brand new vaults especially made in England, it also boasted the city's first underground parking lot. The original interior is still well preserved, as are the old working methods of the employees. Here, little seems to have changed since the bank was nationalised by the Burmese military government in the early 1960s. Fans suspended from the ceiling still whir noiselessly over polished teak counters as tellers shuffle reverently through small pieces of paper.

Opposite Standard Chartered on Pansodan Street was another imperial stalwart, Grindlays. Its headquarters were built in 1930 and still boast a magnificent art deco portico above a gold-painted doorway. Next door were the lavish headquarters of the famous Irrawaddy Flotilla Corporation, set up in 1865 to provide inland transport on Burma's numerous rivers. Before the Second World War it operated about six hundred vessels, the biggest such company in the world (or so it claimed). The general manager resided in a commensurately sumptuous mansion just north of the downtown area, now the residence of the British ambassador. The headquarters on Pansodan Street, with its classical columns and recessed entrances, still house the staff of the state-owned inland waterways department, working at the same teak desks. Among other prominent offices still standing is that of the Burmah Oil Company on Merchant Street.

All in all, by the eve of the Second World War the downtown commercial quarter of Rangoon thus included some of the most luxurious and architecturally distinguished buildings in the East outside of the Bund in Shanghai. Likewise, the city boasted the latest in contemporary steam trams as well as early "motorised wagons", vehicles that quickly began to replace the "coolies" hauling all the merchandise off the docks and up to the warehouses behind Strand Road. Modern department stores opened; the most famous was Rowe & Co., often called the Harrods of the East. Its neo-Baroque building, on the corner of Mahabandoola Road, had fallen into ruin, but has since been restored to its former glory, courtesy of one of Burma's domestic banks – the first of the old colonial structures to get this sort of makeover. Operating a network of stores throughout the country, Rowe's boast, as one customer recalled, was that there was nothing in the world that could not be bought from them. As one impressed Burmese resident has written of this era:

> Cinema houses, bearing such names as the Palladium, Excelsior, Globe, and Carlton, were a great attraction for the inhabitants. Trams and buses . . . plied the city. Living in Rangoon meant that one was exposed to the cosmopolitan features of the city and had access to all the amenities of modern-day living – thanks to the presence of an alien ruling class who made sure that this little corner of earth lacked nothing that they were used to in their own country and, in many ways, offered more.[3]

Regular trains headed out to Mandalay and Moulmein from one of Rangoon's most spectacular constructions, the 1877-built railway station. Unfortunately, this was one of the few colonial buildings that did not survive. It was blown up by the retreating British to deny it to the advancing Japanese in 1942.

The blood and dreams

Such was the well-heeled and well-ordered European part of the city. Neruda's "blood and dreams", however, were to be found in the teeming streets running up from the docks, beyond the pompous edifices of colonial finance and officialdom. Here the city begins to resemble Glasgow, in its time the second city of the empire after London. The likeness is no coincidence. Scottish firms predominated in exploiting Burma's natural resources; Scottish money accounted for much of Rangoon's growth, and so Scottish architects did most of the building. Thus, the Irrawaddy Flotilla Corporation, for example, actually had its headquarters in Glasgow, as did the major trading company J. & F. Graham Company, whose head office in Rangoon on Strand Road is now the British Embassy. Just as Scottish architects took charge of an unusually large amount of the official government building, so they also had a hand in the design of the domestic tenements that are still numerous in the downtown area. They closely resemble the old tenements, now mostly demolished, of Glasgow.

These backstreets are still much as they were. The ground floor of the typical Rangoon tenement is invariably a small business of some kind, stretching far back into dark recesses. A narrow staircase rises steeply to four or five upper floors. Nowadays, the balconies of the family apartments spill laundry, plants, antique electric wiring and brand-new satellite dishes. Once grandiose Corinthian pilasters crumble beneath layers of ancient paintwork, whilst the roots of climbing plants dig deep into the colonial facades. A particular shade of mint green was very popular, or very cheap perhaps, a decade ago, and is now flaking into the streets everywhere. Also in vogue are ornate metalwork cages enclosing the balcony space, designed as much to prevent people falling out as to stop the city's innumerable pigeons from flying in.

At head height all along the pavement hang bulldog clips or small handbags dangling from strings. They are waiting for mail. A water seller yanks on one and a bell rings in a flat far above. A shutter opens and a head peers down. The water seller gestures with a fat plastic bottle in the road. "Maybe tomorrow", says the inhabitant with a wave, and the water man pushes his barrow on down the street. One difference between the Glaswegian tenements and those of Rangoon, is that the streets of the Burmese city are narrower to afford shade even when the sun is at its height – scarcely a problem for Glasgow.

But the resemblance to Scotland's biggest city ends with the masonry. For still crammed into these slender, shabby buildings are the remnants of what used to be one of the most cosmopolitan societies in the world. Soon after its foundation the new Rangoon had sucked in so many people that the resident British colonialists, despite laying out and ruling the city, only ever made up a tiny fraction of its population. Like the rest of Britain's imperial cities operating under the official "open door" trading policy, Rangoon welcomed traders, labourers, priests, stevedores, adventurers and more from all corners of the globe, regardless of race, colour or religion, all looking to make their fortunes. And as long as they accepted the basic structures of British political and economic hegemony, usually enforced here with a fairly light touch, they were allowed to trade, sell or hustle pretty much as they liked. Just as importantly, for many of them, they were also allowed to practise their religion and keep their cultures as they liked too.

For the hundreds of thousands of immigrants to Rangoon the city was therefore a remarkably liberal and tolerant place. Integral to the planning of the new city, land was specifically allocated to Hindus, Armenians, Muslims, Jews, Baptists and others to build their sites of worship under the official policy of religious neutrality. The British and Europeans, in fact, kept themselves very much to the relatively small "white" enclaves in the city – the officers' clubs, swankier hotels and the Merchant Street banks and trading offices. They had little day-to-day contact with the vibrant, multiracial society that exploded all around them. And since colonial Burma was administered as part of Britain's Indian empire, the vast majority of newcomers to Rangoon, and to Burma more generally, were consequently Indian – or rather the disparate peoples, Hindu, Muslim and more, who made up British India. There was nothing to stop the influx. Indeed, it was encouraged by the British colonialists. They needed the "coolie" labour to build the new colony and its cities as well as the administrative and professional skills that the Indians had learned in helping them to run

British India. Eventually, as the American anthropologist Ruth Fredman Cernea has written, the British clubs in Rangoon such as the Pegu and Gymkhana became merely "islands of Britishness in the great Indian sea, to which the imperialists might withdraw when they felt a personal, social or ritual need."[4]

Indians, usually desperately poor, were arriving in Burma at the rate of about eighty thousand a year by the late nineteenth century. By 1931, the Indian population of Burma as a whole passed one million, out of an estimated population of just over fourteen million. Chittagonians, from Bengal, made up about one-quarter of this immigrant population, and many of them were Muslim. Most of the poorer bearers, sweepers and dock labourers who worked in Rangoon came from Orissa (now Odisha), a province next to Bengal, and nearby Chota Nagpur. Tamils came from Madras to work in the rice paddies in the Irrawaddy Delta. The highly entrepreneurial Gujaratis arrived in droves. The Nepalese came too. All these people identified themselves by their ethnic group – Bengali, Punjabi – just as their descendants do to this day, generations after their forbears first made the journey to Rangoon. Even today, the political concepts of India, Bangladesh and Pakistan don't mean much in downtown Rangoon; the bloody break-up of Britain's Indian empire in 1947, felt so intensely in South Asia, seems to have had little bearing on personal and community relations.

So many of the South Asian immigrants settled in the colonial capital that by 1940 over half of the city's population was from the subcontinent. As the Indians could move freely between Rangoon, Burma and India itself, all one territory under British rule, so the Indian community was very fluid. Many single males came for a while, earned relatively good money, and returned to India. Nonetheless, increasing numbers began to settle permanently in the Burmese capital. According to the 1931 census, already 39,949 Indians born in Burma were living in Rangoon, constituting 15 per cent of the whole Indian population of the city.[5]

As one Burmese woman, Wai Wai Myaing, remembers of this era, "Upon arrival, a visitor coming into the Rangoon harbour by seagoing vessel . . . would see a predominantly Indian population; the dock coolies in simple loincloth and turban, gharry wallah, and Sikh policemen in their trademark headgear."[6] Rangoon today still feels much more like Kolkata or Chennai than its South-East Asian equivalents of Kuala Lumpur or Singapore.

Most of the tenements and other buildings in the city were built by Indian labourers, not very lovingly known as the "Bengal sappers". They were often employed by Indian-run companies, and usually worked in terrible conditions. About one-tenth of them worked as bonded labour, virtual slaves with no sanitation, medicine or decent food. Indeed, apart from anything else this relatively sudden influx of impecunious newcomers clearly overwhelmed attempts by the British authorities to maintain the appearance, let alone the substance, of an orderly European city. As one British police inspector put it, "Conditions of labour in Rangoon were a disgrace to any civilised and allegedly democratic country."[7] Beyond the confines of the European quarters, by the late nineteenth century, before the clearing of the area just behind the docks in the 1920s and 1930s for the banks and other offices, downtown Rangoon had become a byword for squalor and disease. The 1891 census report noted the high mortality rate of the Indian immigrants: "Crowded together in insanitary lodging houses, they swell the death rate of our chief town . . . living in the veriest hovels in the suburban swamps, with the most disgusting filth piled up in heaps or fermenting in pools at their very doors."

Clearly, things didn't improve a great deal with the passage of time. The travel writer Norman Lewis was equally dismayed when he visited the city in 1950, albeit at a time when the city was struggling to recover from the devastation of war:

> These massive columns [of the British colonial buildings] now rise with
> shabby dignity from the tangle of scavenging dogs and sprawling, ragged
> bodies at their base. Side lanes are piled up with stinking refuse which
> mounts up quicker than the dogs and crows can dispose of it. The covers
> have been taken off the drains and not replaced. Half-starved Indians lie
> dying in the sunshine.[8]

There are no people dying in the streets today, but the open drains are still much in evidence. Yet, for all the hardship and squalor, the incomers helped to create one of the most dynamic entrepôts in the world. The period of maximum migration coincided with, and was partly responsible for, an era of "astounding economic progress", as one historian of colonial Burma has described it. The value of exports in 1900, for instance, was fivefold what it had been in 1870. By 1927, it was more than twenty times that. Many immigrants might have started out in poverty, but by the inter-war years many had a higher standard of living than in most other parts of Asia. Thus, the thousands who endured the terrible sea passage to Rangoon, to be greeted by such fetid circumstances when they arrived, were still likely to enjoy better conditions than in the country they had left behind. These immigrants were not only escaping extreme poverty, but also the famines, floods, cyclones and other natural disasters that blight those lands bordering the Bay of Bengal.

Driven on by the classic immigrant's desire to better oneself in a new country, many Indians became extremely wealthy in Burma. Besides the notorious *chettyar* moneylenders, of whom more later, these were men like Abdul Karim Jamal, who was knighted by the British in 1920. He arrived in Rangoon from Kathiawar in India with his father in the 1860s, aged just six. His father began to build up some businesses, but Sir Jamal, as the Burmese liked to call him, vastly expanded them. He was called the King of Rice, in honour of his role in the export of that commodity, but he also had extensive interests in oil, teak and tea. Sir Jamal was a Memon Muslim, a philanthropist and a millionaire, and even had an avenue named after him in Rangoon.

There were many other rich Indian merchants in Rangoon as well as in Moulmein, Mandalay and elsewhere. If the white British colonialists very clearly composed the most privileged and racially exclusive stratum of Rangoon society, the richer Indians were not that far behind. They even had their own Monday Afternoon Club, modelled, of course, on a British gentleman's club.[9]

The enormous influx of South Asians gave Rangoon its unique flavour, but as well as the Bengalis, Punjabis and Orissans, approximately thirty other races and nationalities came to make the most of booming Rangoon. Like in the British-run Straits Settlements on the Malay Peninsula – Penang, Singapore and Malacca – the Chinese came in their thousands, settling just to the west of the Indian community behind the port, between what is now Shwe Bontha and 25th Street. They were mainly small traders. According to the (imperfect) census of 1931, there were 200,000 Chinese in Burma by that date, the largest proportion of them from Yunnan province just over Burma's north-east border. Chinatown begins on 24th Street, and on the corner of 18th Street and Strand Road is the most impressive of the several Hokkien temples, Kheng Hock Keong. It is over one hundred years old, but well maintained; in the mainland Chinese style this historic building is being constantly "improved". The Chinese influence in Burma was to become pervasive by the 1980s and 1990s, but started early.

There was also a thriving Jewish community in Rangoon, at its height numbering as many as 2,500, who began arriving in the 1850s. Mostly immigrants from Baghdad, many Jews came to Rangoon via the already well-established Jewish community in Calcutta. Others were from Persia and a few from England. Most of them were merchants, attracted particularly by the commercial opportunities in teakwood and rice. At one point, in 1910, Rangoon had a Jewish mayor. There were smaller numbers of Jews scattered throughout the main trading ports and towns of colonial Burma; Bassein, now called Pathein, in the delta, also had a Jewish mayor.

One of the most successful Jewish traders from Baghdad, Isaac Sofaer, designed and built the Sofaer Building, in its time the most prestigious office block in Rangoon (now the Lokanat Gallery Building), and used green tiles specially imported from Manchester to adorn the entrance. As befitting the elevated status of Sofaer, the governor-general himself opened the building, which still stands next to the old Irrawaddy Flotilla Corporation headquarters. Sofaer died in 1926. His son Abraham left and pursued a career in Hollywood, where he featured in the first television season of *Star Trek* as well as another children's favourite, *Lost in Space*. International tenants of Sofaer's included the Reuters news agency, a renowned German photographer called Philip Klier, a Greek leather merchant, and one of the city's most sought-after barbers, the Filipino M. D'Cruz. There was even a Viennese café.

The richest Jewish families, the Solomons, Sofaers and Cohens, owned large residences both downtown and out beyond what were then the suburbs, summer houses clustered around Inya Lake and farther. They employed scores of servants, among them Bene Israel and Cochin Jews (Indian Jews, who prospered under British colonial rule in India), Hindus and Muslims. The Solomons had a famous ice and bottling factory, and first brought Coca-Cola to Burma. The Baghdadi Jews mostly spoke Arabic among themselves and English to everyone else.

The Jewish quarter was more or less concentrated around 31st Street, and Sammy Samuels, a scion of one of the most prominent Jewish families, still has his offices there. Slight and fresh-faced, Sammy was born in 1980 and was raised and educated in the city. He is a Burmese citizen (Aung Soe Lwin is his name in Burmese) and runs a travel agency called MyanmarShalom, which, among other things, runs bespoke tours of the country's Jewish heritage for tourists, mostly from America. Sammy's great-grandfather arrived in the mid nineteenth century from Baghdad, taking the overland route across India and then by sea from Kolkata. He was principally a teakwood trader, and his descendants have been closely associated with the centrepiece of Yangon's Jewish community, the magnificent Musmeah Yeshua synagogue, a few blocks round the corner on 26th Street.

The original wooden synagogue was erected in 1854, but burned down. It was rebuilt in brick and iron in 1893–6 in the Sephardic style and is now tucked away behind a row of paint shops. In stark contrast to the immediate neighbourhood, this handsome building, its soaring interior embellished by wonderful teak beams and a Burmese marble floor, has been beautifully restored. The only synagogue in Yangon, it is also an extremely unusual example of the genre anywhere as it owes so much to the geographic origins of its architect and most of its former congregation in Baghdad. In a normal synagogue, for example, everyone faces the same way, towards Jerusalem. Here, in contrast, the fine old teak-and-rattan benches are arranged in squares down each side of the synagogue, so families could commune with each other during prayers, a Middle-Eastern tradition. The more prominent families of the Jewish community had their own squares in the synagogue, and also an adjacent teak box in which they could leave their own prayer books. Most impressive, though, is the small shrouded room at the front of the synagogue where the *torahs* were kept, encased in silver standing caskets two feet high. They were crafted in Baghdad in the early 1900s. Each family kept its *torah* here; there used to be 126 of them. Now there are only two left, reflecting the post-war exodus of the Jewish community. There was also a Jewish school, for about two hundred pupils, near to where the present-day Park Royal Hotel stands. Isaac Samuels, Sammy's grandfather, was a longstanding trustee of the synagogue, and made his own son promise that he too would do the same.

Until his death in 2015, Moses Samuels, Sammy's father, could be found on most days proudly showing surprised tourists into the synagogue, just as he also kept an eye on the Jewish cemetery on 91st Street. Isaac Samuels was one of the last to be buried there.

There was also a strong Baha'i community in Rangoon, followers of the Baha'i faith who originated in north-east Persia. On one particularly monsoonal morning I sat down (round a very fine, highly polished teak table, of course) with members of the Baha'i National Spiritual Assembly to discuss the origins of the Baha'i and its connection with Burma. The faith was founded in 1844 by Bab, the first prophet-herald, who was martyred only six years later in Tabrit. The second prophet, Bahaulah, was exiled from the land, and wandered successively from Baghdad to Istanbul and finally to Acre in Palestine, now Akko in Israel, where he died. The world headquarters of the Baha'i is in Haifa, Israel, and the links between the Baha'i and the Jews have always been close, especially in Rangoon.

Bahaulah wanted to spread the faith, and in 1876 two Baha'i missionaries, Jamal Effedi and Sayyid Mustafa Rumi, arrived in Rangoon. Such was the prestige of the new colony at the time that Burma was only the third country chosen for such missionary work, after Turkey and Egypt. The two Baha'i were evidently very persuasive; Tin Kyine, chairman of the assembly, told me that in its heyday there used to be 47,000 Baha'i in Burma. To this day there are still about thirty thousand, with two thousand in Yangon alone. The Baha'i run six nursery schools, most of which are in Yangon, and also have study centres throughout the country. Most of the Baha'i were converted from Buddhism, and all members of the national spiritual assembly today are ethnic Burmans, giving the Baha'i a large measure of protection from the ethno-nationalism of the Burmese authorities. Again, Tin Kyine avows that the Baha'i get along very well with the Muslims, Jews and Christians of Yangon, helped perhaps by the fact that the Baha'i are distinct in having no hierarchy, no formal religious services and no temples of worship. They can thus stay very much in the background. As Tin Kyine puts it, with surprising conviction, "Everyone's blood is red, and we love everyone."

There was also an influential Armenian community, numbering five hundred or so. Armenians had long served as advisers to the defeated Burmese kings, but stayed on under the British. The famous Sarkies brothers left their mark. They were renowned for founding a chain of hotels throughout South-East Asia. Their first was the splendid Eastern and Oriental (or E. & O.) in Penang, followed by Raffles in Singapore and then the rather more modest Strand Hotel in Rangoon. This was built in 1901 to a Sarkies design by a Rangoon-based Turkish-Armenian contractor. The hotel faces on to the docks, and was restored to at least some of its former glory in the 1990s. Generations of pampered European colonialists charted their leisurely progress east through the portals of the Sarkies hotels. Noël Coward was one of several English writers to enjoy the Strand during its heyday. In fact, he derived his most famous line from his stay in Burma:

> The toughest Burmese bandit can never understand it.
> In Rangoon the heat of noon is just what the natives shun,
> They just put their scotch and rye down and lie down . . .
> But mad dogs and Englishmen go out in the midday sun.

A block behind the Sarkies' Strand Hotel, appropriately enough, is the Armenian church of St John the Baptist, erected in 1862 and consecrated by the Reverend Aviet Chaytor on 17 January 1863. It may look virtually derelict from the street, but underneath the battered, corrugated metal roof is a beautifully preserved teak interior, lovingly swept and dusted by the Catholic Burmese caretaker, Stephen. He lives on the site with his wife and small daughter, in a small hut partly constructed out of the rubble left behind by a Japanese bomb that landed on the church hall in December 1941. Little has changed since that day. Stephen helped me pick out a few fragments of blue and white porcelain from amongst the debris that still lies strewn across the ground, the remains of a shattered pre-war tea set.

By the beginning of the First World War the Germans had arrived, as had the Japanese. A Japanese shipping line was operating a direct service to Tokyo and Japanese ships were also capturing more of the lucrative trade between Rangoon and Calcutta. More Japanese ships were entering Rangoon's port than those of any other nation. In the late 1930s, the Japanese were increasingly interested in gaining intelligence from Rangoon to prepare for a possible invasion. By the beginning of the Second World War, so rumour had it, there was an abnormally high number of Japanese dentists in town, and at least a few of them were spies. There were certainly front organisations and companies for Japanese intelligence, such as the Daitoa shipping company.[10]

By that time there was also a distinct American presence in Rangoon, mainly composed of the buccaneering pilots who flew with the famous Flying Tigers out of Rangoon airport. The semi-official American Volunteer Group, as they were formally known, flew in support of Chiang Kai-shek's embattled nation-alist army struggling against the Japanese invasion of China; their main job was to protect the Burma Road, the supply route that ferried tons of equipment from Rangoon one thousand miles to the nationalist stronghold of Chongqing. The airmen frequented the Silver Grill, a restaurant and nightspot owned by an Armenian called Pete Aratoon.[11] According to one account, the airmen held the most raucous, and most alcoholic, parties in town; apparently they thought little of "using one of the smaller servants as a volley ball".[12]

The plural society

So extraordinary was the diversity of this Rangoon community that a famous phrase was coined specifically to describe it – "the plural society". Now widely misunderstood, the phrase was originally devised to explain the specific phenomenon of downtown Rangoon (as well as Dutch-administered Batavia, now Jakarta) by the British colonial civil servant turned academic John Sydenham Furnivall. An expert on both the British in Burma and the Dutch in Indonesia, Furnivall wrote several lengthy studies of colonial political economy. Furnivall is almost unknown today, but his books were highly influ-ential in their time, and he remains a guru figure to many scholars of South-East Asian history. Early on in my travels to Burma, one such, an American, advised me firmly: "You can't understand Burma if you don't know Furnivall." He was right.

Furnivall arrived in Burma in 1902 as a colonial administrator for the Indian Civil Service. He lived in Burma from 1902 to 1931 and married a Burmese woman, after which he took up an academic post at Cambridge University until 1941 lecturing on Burmese language and history. He returned to the country in 1948 to advise the newly independent Burmese government, with very mixed results. He founded the Burma Research Society, one of the first bodies to undertake systematic, Western-style empirical research on the country, and was partly responsible for inculcating the values of Fabianism (English-style gradualist socialism) into the first generation of Burmese independence leaders.

This is the description of a plural society from *Colonial Policy and Practice*, his most important book, published in 1948:

> In Burma, as in Java, probably the first thing that strikes the visitor is the medley of peoples – Europeans, Chinese, Indian and native. It is in this strictest sense a medley, for they do not combine. Each group holds by its own religion, its own culture and language, its own ideas and ways. As individuals they meet, but only in the market-place, in buying and selling. There is a plural society, with different sections of the community living side by side, but separately, within the same political unit. Even in the economic sphere there is a division of labour along racial lines. Natives, Chinese, Indians and Europeans all have different functions, and within each major group subsections have particular occupations. The plural society has a great variety of forms, but in some form or other it is the distinctive character of modern tropical economy . . . The plural society arises where economic forces are exempt from control by social will.[13]

Just as each group has held to its own religion, so in economic terms today's Yangon has retained many of those distinctive features of Furnivall's "modern tropical economy", often to the point of absurdity. This is another startling consequence of Yangon's fifty years of economic isolation: Burma's biggest city is run by a cottage economy, dominated by small family-run businesses divided along ethnic lines. Thus, Furnivall's "particular occupations" are still decided largely by ethnicity and street; the mass-retailing, supermarket model of selling goods largely passed the city by, until in 2011 the standard-issue, air-conditioned Asian mall began to pop up here and there.

Take 32nd Street, for example, which runs south several blocks from Bogyoke Aung San Road behind the Shangri-La (formerly Traders) Hotel to the docks. This street is devoted almost solely to paper-related businesses. Indeed, each block of the street specialises only in one particular aspect of the paper business. Furthermore, each ground-floor shop, with a frontage of only six feet or so, is its own self-contained manufacturer, making most of the products they sell on the premises – setting, printing, binding and selling are all completed in one long thin space. Every shop is thus its own boutique, family-owned enterprise.

Almost every business has an ancient British, German or Japanese cutting and printing machine. I glimpse an unlikely publisher in the recesses of a dark, long, narrow shop, dressed only in a *longyi*, his bare torso revealing tattoos worthy of a yakuza member. Another nearby book binder has a smaller business yet – Mr White grins at me from a tiny stool on the pavement, where he is making primary-school textbooks by hand on an upturned box. "Free primary school!", he announces with delight, stitching covers onto the pages, sealing the thread ends with a lighter and trimming it all with giant scissors. "Japan government give money to our Myanmar government, now school free for all children. Good!" He makes 120–150 books per day and sells them for 150 kyat, around fifteen cents. Alongside the primary readers, he sells ciga-rettes, to diversify his client base perhaps.

The street behind him stretches away into an infinity of small one-stop publishers. At the front lie the products on flimsy tables: Chinese martial arts thrillers alongside Orwell and *Huckleberry Finn*; back copies of beauty maga-zines and ageing textbooks on impossibly obscure subjects. A lorry trying to squeeze down the narrow street promises "One Stop Paper Selling" on its side, advertising Korean Art Paper, Canadian Newsprint and Indonesian Wood-Free Paper.

Down one block of 32nd Street shops line the road selling lacy mauve wedding stationery. Another block is devoted almost exclusively to churning out pulp fiction, the next to risograph machines, with some businesses printing and others busy repairing the machines. Most shopowners are of South Asian descent here, both Muslims and Hindus. Farther down towards the docks, 29th Street is also something of a publishers' enclave. Here is the home of the Pyigyimundyne Pitaka Press, started by the grandfather of the present owner, an elegant Burmese woman in her sixties. When I visited a few years ago, the premises were old, dusty, cramped and enjoyably inky – Dickens in the tropics. At the back was a sizeable printing press, with boxes of fresh paper piled up beside it, ready for use. I picked one of her publications off a shelf – *English through Burmese Eyes and Ears*, by H. Kluseman, B.A. (retired) and U Lu Pe Win, M.A., published 1957. The binding was stitched by hand, with thin, yellowing paper. The book was still for sale.

The Chinese seem to have a monopoly on sewing-machines. All down one side of an adjacent street, one after the other, are slim shophouses displaying ageing sewing-machines, for sale or repair. Bengalis, by contrast, do sunglasses, ropes and, all down Ken Ze Dan Street, paint and cement. Some shops offer just enamel and grout. Another street sub-specialises in bicycle repairs, another in air-conditioning units, and so on. Looking for fishing nets? Seven Gujarati-owned shops on 26th Street between Merchant and Mahabandoola Roads. Wire-mesh? At least ten shops, one after another, on 27th Street, between Merchant and Mahabandoola. The gold, diamond and assorted other precious-stone shops line Shwe Bontha Street.

Even the few covered markets remain sub-divided by ethnicity and trade. The biggest and most spectacular of them is Theingyi Zei, directly across Mahabandoola Road from the synagogue. There are several cavernous, Edwardian-style structures, each with their own specialities. The largest of these, so crowded with produce and people that it is almost impossible to walk down the aisles, sells almost exclusively textiles and cheap, Chinese plastic toys and household goods. Here the traders haggling under the harsh light of the low-hanging neon strips are almost all Burmese.

The eastern building, though, is all Indian. Here curries and spices, garam masala, cumin and the pungent flash of lime pickles hit the nostrils and eyes. One of the stallholders, William Oo, is sorting cashews in a wide flat basket on his knees. He is a Muslim who went to a Catholic missionary school. "My father and grandfather worked in this market before me. My grandfather came from Madras and married here in Myanmar. I live in the same apartment he lived in. I was brought up by priests and nuns in the school." He says he learned a lot from them. Did he, as a Muslim, mind going to a Christian school? "No, of course not. We all have [the] same God. Only the prayers sound different." It is hard to imagine three or four generations living off this tiny stall over the decades, selling no more than a few spices, currants and cashews, the produce stalked by glistening cockroaches.

There are electric dyes in lime green, pink or turquoise, there are remedies for diabetes next to cinnamon bark, there are fresh water shells waiting to be ground down into traditional medicines. In the labyrinth of interconnecting passages and alleys mangosteens, spiky durian, gigantic jackfruit, palm fruit, hairy rambutans are all on sale. It is mango season and formidable market women shout each other down over their most prized fruit. An elegant woman waits as a number of fat black crickets fried with chilli are counted off into her shopping bag; she adds long lilac-coloured aubergines and fat asparagus spears. You could simply shut your eyes and find your way around by smell: the over-ripe fruit, the sharp shock of wet fish gradually heating in the sun, fragrant soap cut from the block by weight.

Lazy Moulmein

Furnivall's plural society prevailed in many of Britain's imperial trading posts. To the early idealists and propagandists of empire such as Sir Stamford Raffles and Sir Francis Light, servants of the East India Company and founders of, respectively, the trading settlements of Singapore and Penang, this was the greatest benefit that British administration could bestow on its territories. By developing sleepy old fishing villages into "freeports", where anyone could come and trade under the benevolent but watchful eye of British administration, these cities became thriving, wealthy entrepôts, vital staging-posts along the seaborne arteries of the rapidly expanding imperial trading system. These ports were the physical embodiment of the doctrine of free trade, an idea enthusiastically forced on many supposedly backward peoples by several generations of British adventurers and officials, often at the muzzle of a cannon. As well as Rangoon, colonial Burma's other two main ports, Akyab (now called Sittwe) in Arakan State and Moulmein (now called Mawlamyine) in Mon State, were further examples of the genre.

Even more so than Rangoon, Moulmein, the first capital of British Burma until 1852, still captures the essence of the nineteenth-century plural society

– just as it also retains a rich collection of colonial-era buildings. Rudyard Kipling, again, popularised the town when he stopped off here for a night on his way down the coast from Rangoon en route to Japan and afterwards England. He was there just long enough to visit the Kyaikthanlan pagoda, perched on a ridge looking out over Moulmein towards the Thanlwin River, and a few other sites. When he got back to England, his vantage point at the pagoda inspired the first line of his most popular poem, *Mandalay*. Famously, the poet never did get to visit Mandalay itself, but the poem very successfully evoked the allure of the exotic east for Victorian imperialists. And judging by Kipling's journal, most of that allure lay in Moulmein itself: "I should better remember what the pagoda was like had I not fallen deeply and irrevocably in love with a Burmese girl at the foot of the first flight of steps. Only the fact of the steamer starting next noon prevented me from staying at Moulmein forever." Yet, Kipling undersold the town in his last stanza when he wrote that he was ". . . lookin' lazy at the sea . . ." from his pagoda. The suggestion of tropical torpor is misleading, since Moulmein was and remains a furious bustle of activity, despite having been even more cut off from the world than Yangon over the past fifty years or so. It is Burma's hidden gem.

Moulmein is still laid out just as the colonial-era plural society demanded. Around the main market, along the banks of the river where the jetties protruded, remain the principal immigrant trading communities. These are predominantly Chinese, plus the many peoples who came from South Asia, still numbering some eighty thousand, I am told. They mainly occupy the north end of Lower Main Road, close to the market. Here are the mosques, including the biggest, the Kaladan, built in grey-green brick and dating from 1846. A few buildings farther south towards the market is the smaller Moghul Shia mosque, the only *shia* mosque in the town – "from Iran", one worshipper proudly tells me. In all, there are nine mosques in Moulmein, including the very impressive Soorti Sunni Jamai.

For the non-Muslim South Asian community there are about fifty temples, and these all advertise themselves as catering to the faithful from the various individual regions where the immigrants originated. Thus, on Old Pagoda Road, leading up the hill away from the river, is a Gujarati temple (1956), standing a few doors down from a Hare Krishna temple (1915). Likewise, says

Mannish, a slender young man who looks after the Gujarati temple, there are temples for the Bengalis, the Hindustanis, Tamils, Punjabis and Sikhs. As in Yangon, people describe themselves in these terms, rather than as Indians or Pakistanis, or even Hindus or Muslims.

Mannish looks slightly baffled when I ask him whether there are any tensions or animosities between the various communities. "We are all friends", he assures me, gesturing towards the mosque right next door to his temple. "We all go to the same schools and then everybody works in the market together." His temple might be Gujarati, he says, but all Hindus from other temples can worship there. "There is only one god", he says. But many tongues: he himself speaks Hindi, Gujarati, Burmese and English. Multi-lingualism was virtually a necessity in the plural society, and became a natural attribute for many, simply in order to communicate with the ample variety of nationalities that might live on the same street. One Jew, Jacob Moses Cohen of Rangoon, is recorded as having spoken Arabic, Burmese, Hindi, Urdu and Bengali, as well as English.

Just behind the main market in Moulmein, now a hideous modern concrete construction, is the large ethnic Chinese community. Down a warren of little alleys and side streets are the main Chinese temples, the oldest being the beautiful Kyant Tate, dating from 1852. The interior boasts a perfectly preserved teak ceiling, all painted in traditional red. One of the elders at the temple, Aung Myaing, says that there are still seventy thousand ethnic Chinese in Moulmein, many of them originally from Penang. He says that, like the Indians, the Chinese identify themselves regionally, and express that through more than thirty Chinese temples in the town. Thus, there are three Hokkien temples, including Kyant Tate, the biggest, as well as those from Quandong, Hochin, Hainan and elsewhere. All the Chinese are traders in the market, he says.

And just as region, religion and commerce trumped nationalism with the immigrants from China and India, so too with the Europeans. The white settlements were all along Upper Main Road, far enough away from the market and the sordid world of commerce for propriety's sake, yet close enough to keep an eye on the trade. As the administration of the new colony moved to Rangoon in 1853, there are only a few government buildings left.

The most prominent is the British prison, built on the standard panopticon design, dating from 1908 and still very much in use. Kipling's pagoda looks directly down onto the prison yards – if he had come to Moulmein a few decades later his famous poem might have turned out rather differently.

What do remain in Moulmein in profusion are the vast establishments of the European missionaries: their churches, convents, schools and domestic houses. The most important missionaries for Moulmein's, and for Burma's, subsequent history, were the Baptists, and on the corner of Upper Main Road and Dawei Jetty Road is the country's oldest Baptist Church, built by the American Adoniram Judson, the first Baptist missionary in the country. He was blown off course on his way to India and was forced to take shelter in a coastal settlement called Amherst, about fifty miles south of Moulmein. There, he founded his very first church, but it was in Moulmein that the Baptist mission flourished. The 1827 church itself is fairly ordinary, but it is the red-brick missionary school across the road that really gives a sense of the ambition and self-confidence of the colonial-era missionaries. Built in 1864, this elegant four-storey building, giving out onto a courtyard with an equally grand set of columned buildings on the farther side, was the missionary school, and the fact that the Government No. 6 High School that occupies the site today has room for over two thousand pupils tells its own story.

As the first capital of the new British colony, Moulmein is where most of the British who put down roots in the country settled, including the maternal grandmother of George Orwell, who himself lived here briefly during his time as a colonial policeman in the country in the 1920s. Over the decades many British married local Burmese – or Mon – women, and on the roads leading off Upper Main Road towards the river were many of their substantial mansions. Moulmein was thus home to the largest Anglo-Burmese community. They were the commercial aristocracy of the town, staying on even as most British and Europeans moved on to Rangoon after the second Anglo-Burmese war.

Glenn Kyaw Nyunt, born in 1945, and his wife Catherine, born in 1947, told me their story, fairly representative of the Anglo-Burmese experience. His father Cyril Cusak was Anglo-Burmese; her father, Eric Nelson, was also Anglo-Burmese and fought with the Chindits, the Allies' Special Forces in

Burma, during the Second World War. He was with a Royal Engineers demo-
lition squad and specialised in blowing up bridges. After independence in
1948, most of the Anglo-Burmese stayed behind, even as most of the British
were leaving. Family legend has it that Eric Nelson was picked for the victory
parade in London in 1946 but his wife refused to let him go, fearing that he
would never come back. Typically for his time, he then got a job helping to
run a Scottish timber merchant that had a lot of sawmills in the area. The
Anglo-Burmese ran all the timber, oil and mineral companies in Moulmein,
comprising most of the region's exports. On Glenn's side, his aunts ran a
famous private school. Glenn and Catherine both agree that there had never
been any friction with any of the Muslims, Hindus, Gujaratis or anyone else
living in Moulmein. "There is no conflict. Old Moulmeinis only think about
working and how to make money . . . and how not to have problems with the
government", says Catherine.

The plural society and its enemies

Cernea, the chronicler of Rangoon's Jewish community, has written of the
"silken web" of Baghdadi Jews throughout the region, connecting the Rangoon
Jews to their kith and kin in Kolkata, Shanghai, Hong Kong, Karachi, Surabaya,
Dacca and all the other major trading posts that made up the British Empire
(for the most part) at its zenith. But it was the same for all the other races of
Rangoon, Moulmein, Akyab, Mandalay and elsewhere; each community saw
itself as part of a much bigger ethnic whole, and leveraged those connections for
commercial, financial and political advantage.

These silken webs were remarkably far-reaching and durable. Of course,
they have frayed under the relentless hostility of Burma's xenophobic military
rulers, but they remain, ready to be taken up again to the country's advantage
if only they were to be given the opportunity. But that depends on how, or even
whether, the modern Burmese can learn to accommodate these people again.
For there was a fatal flaw in Burma's plural society. Refreshingly civil and
tolerant as it sounds to a modern ear attuned to the bloody sectarian strife
between Jew and Muslim, Shia and Sunni, Hindu and Muslim, the plural
society embraced pretty well everyone except the indigenous Burmese. For

whereas the British and the millions of immigrants flourished in the commercial havens that they created, the Burmans found themselves forced to the margins of their own towns, administratively, physically and culturally. Indeed, Furnivall's original description of the plural society is very different from the way pluralism has come to be understood in the West. Rather than referring to a rainbow of ethnicities choosing freely to live together, Furnivall used the term almost pejoratively, to criticise the imposition of immigrant races on indigenous societies in the name of commerce and free trade. For him, and other critics, the bustling, ambitious immigrants forced aside or even destroyed the traditional structures of indigenous society, be it Arakanese, Burman, Mon or other. And although this coercive system took root mainly on the coast, in the port-cities of the British and Dutch seaborne empires, the plural society gradually stretched into the interior of countries like Burma as colonial rule expanded during the second half of the nineteenth century.

By nature and history the Burmans were agrarian and feudal, with commensurate values. The new commercial society of colonial Burma was alien to them. At best, they were passive onlookers, at worst resentful victims. The Burmese themselves, for instance, had no control over immigration from the Indian subcontinent until the emergency Burma Immigration Act was passed in 1947, on the eve of independence. Furnivall, for one, chronicles the exclusion of the Burmans from the economic and political life of their own country in some detail.

Indians, in particular, took over most of the jobs that the Burmese could not (or would not) do. Colonial Burma was proud to have one of the first nationwide phone systems in Asia, an innovation that the Burmese still talk about to this day. The Burmese postal and telegraph systems, however, were managed from India, so it was cheaper and simpler to employ trained Indians to manage and run the system than it was to teach new Burmese operators from scratch. As Furnivall comments, "The telegraph department became an Indian preserve . . . so likewise did the telephone system, and up to 1930 or later one could not use the telephone in Burma without a knowledge of Hindustani." Trained Indians filled many of the positions that the British created to run colonial Burma, all the clerks and administrators, even many of the police, thus putting them in positions of power over the Burmese.

Take the renowned Irrawaddy Flotilla Corporation (IFC). To the British who ran it, this inland ferry service was a byword for efficiency and comfort, but, as the historians Christopher Bayly and Tim Harper have described the company, it was also "naked in its racial exclusiveness".[14] Most of the managers were British or Anglo-Burmans and almost all of the employees were Indians from Chittagong (then in Bengal, now the main seaport of Bangladesh). The IFC enjoyed a monopoly over transport on the Irrawaddy, convenient for the shareholders but not so fortunate for the local Burmese; the relatively high prices excluded many of them from travelling on their own sacred river. Even if they could afford it, they were likely to be "subtly excluded from its cabin-class accommodation".

For all the railways and bridges the British so energetically built, few Burmese were employed on these projects and fewer still trained as engineers. In 1895, for instance, an engineering school was opened to train employees for the Public Works Department, but almost all the openings went to Indians or Anglo-Indians.

Increasingly, as all the jobs in this fast-developing, relatively prosperous colony went to outsiders, so the Burmese found themselves as minorities in their own towns – and nowhere more so than in "plural" Rangoon. By 1900, only about one-third of the population there were Burmese, and this was bitterly resented. Although the richer families lived perfectly comfortably in prosperous, leafy suburbs such as Kemmendine, they were fully aware of their subjugation by the white ruling class, as well as their segregation from the surging mass of humanity that had taken over the port and its environs.

Thus, not only did the Burmese have the racism and injustice of white colonial rule to contend with, they also faced being trampled on by other, more privileged, colonial subjects. The composition of the municipal council of Rangoon, when it was incorporated in June 1883, tells its own story. Burmese representatives held five seats, but Europeans, Eurasians, Jews, Parsi (descended from Persian Zoroastrians) and Chinese had one each, while Hindus and Muslims had two each. British conquest and hegemony was one cross to bear, but the Burmese found themselves often outnumbered and outgoverned in their own cities by everyone else as well.

Particular anger was reserved for those Indians and Chinese who made money acting as middlemen between themselves and the British, and the most hated of all were the Indian moneylenders known as *chettyars*. In a largely rural Burmese society, the alien commercial imperatives of the plural society rubbed up disastrously against existing peasant culture. In the pattern of the plural society, the *chettyars* were a small group of people specifically from Chettinand in what is now Tamil Nadu, who carved a niche for themselves as small-scale rural financiers in British India in the early nineteenth century. They subsequently followed the British into Ceylon, Malaya, the Straits Settlements and then beyond into French Cochin China (now Vietnam) and Cambodia. But it was in Burma that they became most active (the colony accounting for about two-thirds of all their operations in 1929–30), and most controversial.

The *chettyars* engaged in a whole range of financial activities in Burma. They took deposits, honoured cheques and dealt in gold; they were essential financiers in the rapid growth of Burma's prosperity. But it was for their money lending that they earned the undying enmity of the Burmese. They fanned out across the Irrawaddy Delta lending money to poor rice farmers to buy seed, pay labourers, repair dykes and much else, claiming their land as collateral. This worked well in the good times, but when the crops failed, as they often did, or prices tumbled on the world market, the Burmese could not pay the loans back and thus had to forfeit smallholdings that might have been in the same family for hundreds of years. The *chettyar* would then sell the land on at a profit, often to a speculator, and so on. This process accelerated dramatically in the wake of the Great Depression, which hit Burmese rice exports hard, until eventually by 1938 almost half of the land in Lower Burma was owned by absentee landlords and exactly a quarter by the *chettyars* themselves.[15]

As one economic historian of Burma, Sean Turnell, has written, "The alienation of much of the cultivable land of Lower Burma, a tragic and seminal event in the political economy of Burma, would also prove to be the equally tragic climax to the story of the Chettyars in the country. Exposed to the understandable anger of indigenous cultivators and the demagoguery of Burmese nationalists, they become easy scapegoats not just for the current distress, but the foreign domination of Burma's economy." Significantly, even the British came to recognise the harm caused by the moneylenders. Lord Mountbatten, the British and

Allied supremo for South-East Asia during the Second World War, argued that the British should try to stop, or at least curtail, what was regarded as *chettyar* exploitation when they took back the country from the Japanese in 1945. Reflecting on the fact that the Japanese had forced most *chettyars* to flee after they took Rangoon in early 1942, Mountbatten acknowledged that in so doing "a great burden of debt must have been lifted from the shoulders of the Burmese cultivator and I should be very sorry to think that its re-imposition would synchronise with our return."[16] Significantly, although many Indians did return to pick up their previous lives once the British returned in 1945, after independence in 1948 the *chettyars* were specifically not allowed to continue their former activities in Burma by the new Burmese government.

A poisonous legacy – the Rakhine and Rohingya

The Burmans were not the only indigenous group to suffer. Others, like the Arakanese, in the west of the country in what is now Rakhine State, experienced an even greater degree of marginalisation in their own land. Their own sense of victimhood remains to this day, with disastrous consequences for the non-Arakanese, principally the Muslim Rohingya, who have tried to live among them. The festering antagonism between the Rakhine and the Burmans, on the one hand, and Rohingya on the other, still carries enormous political consequences for the future of Burma.

The epicentre of this conflict is the city of Sittwe, the tropical capital of western Rakhine State. Originally called Akyab, it was once the capital of the prosperous and independent-minded kingdom of Arakan, founded in 1531, a centre of trade on the Indian Ocean. But all this came to an end when Arakan was conquered by the Burman kings in 1785. Oppressed by the Burmans, who took twenty thousand Arakanese captives back to the new royal capital of Amarapura, Arakan was then the first province to be overrun by the British, advancing eastwards from Bengal at the start of the first Anglo-Burmese war. St Mark's Cathedral, the oldest Anglican church in Burma, still stands in Sittwe. Under British rule Akyab, with its excellent riverine port on the Kaladan, yet also facing onto the Bay of Bengal, quickly became an even more important trading post than it had been in the past. And so, like Rangoon, it consequently sucked in thousands of immigrants looking for work and opportunities, eventually becoming the fourth largest city in colonial Burma.

The *British Gazetteer for Akyab District* published in 1917, compiled by R. B. Smart, the district commissioner for Akyab, records how this influx radically changed the demography of the city and the rest of the state, and in so doing created Akyab's own plural society. In 1872, there had been just 2,655 Hindus (of Indian origin) but by 1911 there were 14,454. In 1872, there had been 58,255 Mahommedans (those of Indian Muslim descent, also called Chittagonians from Bengal); in 1911, there were three times that many. The population of the native Arakanese, however, had increased only from 171,612 at the census in 1871 to 209,432 in 1911. The result, concluded Smart, was that "The Arakanese are gradually being pushed out of Arakan before the steady wave of Chittagonian immigration from the West." In Akyab town itself Smart estimated that "no less than 60 per cent" of the population were "natives of India". By the end of the colonial period there were eighty five mosques in Sittwe, more even than in Yangon (seventy) and Mandalay (sixty).[17]

Yet, Smart was not entirely sympathetic to the plight of the Arakanese. He wrote that "the reason [the Arakanese] cannot withstand this pressure is that they are extravagant and hire more labour than is necessary rather than do a fair share of work themselves." Whatever the truth of this, it is a fact that although by the early twentieth century Arakan had become a centre of Burma's booming rice-exporting business, all ten steam-power rice mills were owned by Indians, except for one, owned by a Chinese. Smart also recorded that although there were still "a few Arakanese artisans left", chiefly gold- and silver-workers, "the Indian appears to be gradually ousting the indigenous handicraftsmen here as elsewhere." This apparent over-running of the indigenous population, whether the Arakanese in Akyab or the Burmans in Rangoon, created enormous resentment towards the incomers and the whole colonial system that was responsible for the migrations. Furthermore, as many of the immigrants were Muslims, so this resentment became focused on Islam as a faith as well as those who practised the faith.

There had been Muslim immigration to Burma before the British arrived, but that had been relatively small-scale and generally accepted. As seen above, for example, the British were recording numbers of Muslims in the mid 1820s in Arakan who had clearly been living there for several generations. In fact, Muslim traders had been settling in Arakan and elsewhere along the Burmese coast for a long time. One Muslim group had worked and fought directly for the Arakan kings, later moving inland to work at the court of the Burmese kings. Their descendants still live near Mandalay today.

But the large-scale immigration of Muslims under the plural society was of a different order, and this continued well into the twentieth century. The people who call themselves Rohingya, originally classified as 'Chittagonians', undoubtedly had roots in Arakan before the British arrived – and some of them have showed me landholding documents to prove it – but thousands more came into Burma with the colonial state.

Tellingly, Burmans of the early phase of colonialism did not distinguish in their language between Europeans and Indians; they were all just called *Kala*, meaning foreigners. Later, as British colonialists appeared in greater numbers, they earned their own sub-division of *Kala*, *Ingaleit Kala* (English Kala). They were also called *thosaung Kala*, or "sheep-wearing Kala", a reference to their strangely thick woollen clothes. The British were fully aware that their new Burmese subjects regarded them as largely indistinguishable from their Indian subjects. Later, the word *Kala* came to be used pejoratively against Muslims specifically.[18]

Furthermore, it should be remembered that the Arakanese resentment against the influx of immigrants, over which they had no control, came on top of their earlier subjugation by the Burmese. Along with the Chittagonians, the imposition of the plural society in Akyab also meant an unwelcome influx of their enemy the Burmese as well. The ancient and independent kingdom of Arakan, the reference point for most modern Rakhine nationalists, had been conquered by the Burmans but never completely absorbed into the central Burman kingdom. It was only in the nineteenth century that the Arakanese felt the full force of "Burmanisation". For as well as the unwelcome influx of Muslims recorded in the *British Gazetteer* of 1917, the number of Burmese in Arakan had risen from 4,632 at the time of the 1871 census to 92,185 in 1911, all drawn by the chance of making money in the thriving port.

Thus, the Arakanese, in their own minds, were cursed doubly by the plural society. They had to endure the mass immigration of Muslims and Burmans.

Ignored by the colonial authorities, these resentments easily tipped over into racism and bigotry, particularly against Muslims from Bengal, or just "Bengalis" as resentful Arakanese – and Burmans alike – came to label the Rohingya, or any Muslim, as they largely still do. The Burmese might have shared the Arakanese hatred of Muslim mass-immigration under British rule, but the Arakanese also hated the Burmese as well, and this has coloured the politics of Rakhine State and Burma ever since.

A spokesperson for what was then the Rakhine Nationalities Development Party (now the Rakhine National Party), a resolute and opinionated school-teacher called Shwe Maung, talked me through it all in the party's dusty, dilapidated headquarters on the main street in Sittwe in 2013. Like the Kachin and other ethnic minority groups persecuted by the Burmans, he argued, "To be a genuine union we have to be a federal state . . . for five thousand years we [the Arakanese/Rakhine] had sovereignty, and after 1948 we agreed to be part of the union [of Burma], but that was our big mistake." He was only slightly less prejudiced against Burmans than he was against Muslims, particularly the Rohingya. Indeed, Rakhine nationalists like Shwe Maung regard themselves as still under assault from both quarters: "We are the victims of Muslimisation and Burmese chauvinism . . . under this twin squeeze we became poorer and poorer and less well educated."

The fact that at least some of the so-called Chittagonians (or Rohingya) can trace their roots back in Sittwe to well before the British arrived does not impress the Rakhine. Uninterested in the nuances of the situation, the Rakhine just want them out of the way – and preferably out of the country. One self-styled Rakhine intellectual to whom I talked in Sittwe, a former democracy activist and teacher called Aung Kyaw Zan, talked of the "influx-virus" of Muslims and how, if left alone, they will breed to overwhelm the Rakhine. "It's a disgrace, and inhuman", he thundered. "They don't accept family planning."

CHAPTER TWO

The generals' revenge

THE IMPOSITION OF THE plural society shaped Burma's anti-colonial struggle in particular ways that continue to influence the country today. In a popular Burmese phrase, the enemies of Burmese patriots were the three Ms, "missionaries, military and merchants", reflecting the most onerous aspects of colonial rule. And if the missionaries and military were firmly identified as Christian Europeans, mainly British, the merchants were almost always, in the imagination as much as in fact, Indian, and often Muslim as well. Hundreds of thousands of Hindus emigrated from India too, but they tended to mix into Burmese society rather more easily. The existence of separate Muslim laws under which they lived their lives meant that Muslims were a more obvious, and political, target.[1]

The slogan of the first significant Burmese nationalist movement, the Dobama Asiayone ("We Burmans"), was "Burma for the Burmans". The struggle against British rule from the early 1920s took, from the beginning, two forms: against the relatively small number of British rulers and officials, and against the millions of their Indian and other colonial satraps. In some respects, the campaign to vanquish white colonial rule was relatively pacific compared to the violence that began to be visited on the Indians. Anti-Indian riots broke out in 1930 in the Rangoon dockyards and again in 1938, during which hundreds of Indians were killed throughout the country. The British colonial authorities set up a Riot Enquiry Committee that published its report in 1939, attributing the main cause of the bloodletting to incitement by the pro-Buddhist Burmese media.

The recent outbursts of savagery in Sittwe against the descendants of many Muslim and Indian immigrants, starting in June 2012, show how old, festering prejudices can be exploited to trigger what became wholesale ethnic cleansing. In many ways, the aggression against the Rohingya Muslims in 2012, which left scores dead, was unfinished business from colonial days. Many analysts probing into the causes of the recent bloodshed came to the same conclusion as the committee of enquiry of 1939, that, in part, it had been inspired and organised by the more chauvinistic and extremist outlets of the Buddhist media. These were newspapers in the 1930s, but now it's more likely to be Facebook and online chatrooms.

"Trespassers" of every kind

Having been excluded from what they regarded as an imposed, alien society for so long, it is perhaps hardly surprising that there was such a reaction against it by those – the Burmans and Arakanese – who had been shoved aside. Indeed, all the leaders of the anti-colonial movements in the region felt obliged to confront what they saw as the twin evils of European colonial rule and the imposition of the plural society. Not only did they have to fight to eject the Europeans, therefore, they also had to find a way to reclaim what they regarded as their birthright from generations of foreign immigrants.

These two struggles became intertwined from the very beginning, and remain so across South-East Asia, a region that experienced a fairly common history of colonial occupation. So, for instance, while Burma had experienced mass immigration from South Asia under colonialism, the Malays of Malaya and the Javanese or Sumatrans of what would become Indonesia witnessed the large-scale arrival of impoverished Chinese instead.

In the case of Malaya this immigration was on such a scale that by the time of independence from Britain in 1957 the city of Singapore, for instance, originally part of the Malay sultanate of Johor, was an overwhelmingly Chinese enclave (with a population that was about 85 per cent ethnic Chinese), while the old port of Penang was part of an eponymous Chinese-majority state. Overall, by independence immigrant Chinese in Malaya made up about 45 per cent of the overall population. As in Burma, many of these immigrants arrived to do back-breaking, poorly paid manual labour in the tin mines and rubber plantations, but a few of them also worked their way up to found businesses and become, eventually, extremely wealthy. Also, as in Burma, the Malay nationalist independence movement that gathered pace in Malaya during the 1940s and 1950s became inextricably linked with political antagonisms against the immigrants, and against the plural society in general.

The main political vehicle for these sentiments, the United Malays National Organisation, known as UMNO, was founded in 1946 expressly to campaign for Malay rights and privileges over other non-indigenous peoples (that is, the immigrant Chinese and Indians). UMNO was provoked into being by the threat of a decolonising British Labour government to give equal rights to all citizens of an independent Malaya, regardless of what at the time was called their "race" and religion. The united Malay opposition to this proposal scotched it, and so at independence in 1957, Article 153 was inserted into the constitution to guarantee the "special position of the Malays" in the country. And, by hook or by crook, that is exactly what UMNO has succeeded in doing over the course of the intervening seventy or so years. Through gerrymandering and other manipulations of the electoral system, UMNO has won every election it has fought and remained in power ever since independence, all in the name of Malay supremacy. UMNO's cause was helped by the expulsion of Singapore in 1965, which had been included in the newly federated nation of Malaysia only two years earlier. But as Singapore's large Chinese population was liable to tip the ethnic balance against the Malays within the new Malaysia, the island state was humiliatingly expelled to preserve the hegemony of the Malays.

At every election – including the most recent in 2013 – rural Malays, the backbone of UMNO's electoral dominance, are stoked up with warnings about the imminent threat to their ethnicity and religion from the unwashed hoards of immigrants and interlopers. Only UMNO, the message goes, stands between the Malays, Islam and oblivion. This is despite the fact that the non-Malay proportion of the population has actually been decreasing steadily since 1957. It is the politics of fear, post-plural-society style. Even as I write, one prominent ethnic-Malay Muslim leader, Abdullah Zaik Abdul Rahman, has been charged with sedition for accusing the minority ethnic Chinese of being "trespassers" in Malaysia. He has therefore questioned their right to

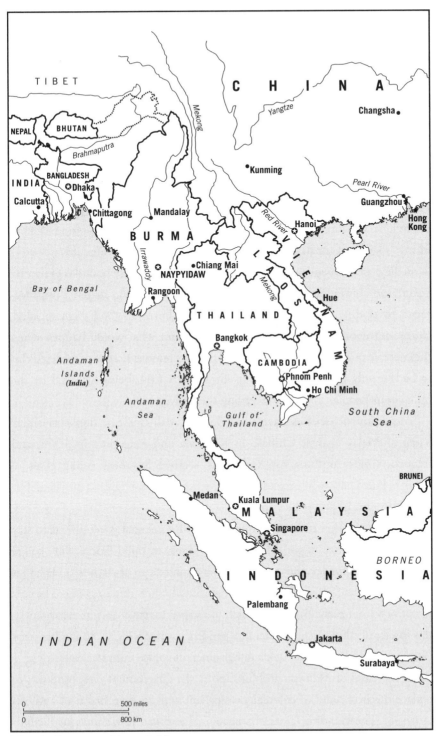

Map 3. Burma and its neighbours.

"citizenship and wealth". And who was responsible for inflicting the Chinese on the Malays? It was, he has written on his Facebook page, "all the doing of the British, who were in cahoots with the Chinese to oppress and bully the Malays". It may seem extraordinary that such feelings can still get an airing two or three generations after independence, but this only shows how deep these feelings run, just as they do in Burma.

As well as seeking to redress the loss of indigenous rights, power and wealth against the colonial-era immigrants, the regions' independence leaders were also concerned with another baleful consequence of the plural society, one that Furnivall was particularly worried about. By his account, the plural society might have produced wealth but it was essentially brittle and unstable, lacking in any "social will" or shared sense of community. This is because it was merely "a medley" of different races, rather than an organic society bound together by a common culture or religion. To share an interest only in material improve-ment, by trading in the market place, was, to Furnivall the Fabian socialist, clearly not enough. He worried, therefore, about what would happen when the coercive power of the colonial authority was removed, as he considered this to be the only barrier stopping the immigrants from being attacked by the indigenous peoples, or clashing among themselves.

Post-colonial societies have been dealing with this question ever since. Riots of Malay against Chinese in Malaysia and Singapore in 1969, and frequent similar outbursts in Indonesia, seemed for some ruling elites to confirm Furnivall's worst fears about "the whole society relapsing into anarchy" once the colonial power had gone.

Furnivall's answer to his own question was for colonial governments to stay on longer than they might otherwise have done, to build "social will" before handing over stronger and more resilient countries to their new indigenous rulers. But in the 1940s, the Burmese, Malays and others weren't going to be very receptive to that particular idea. In fact, the respective governments' responses to this spectre of ethnic anarchy after independence varied widely, and it is here that Burma under military rule took a rather different course from its neighbours.

In the cases of Malaysia and Singapore, the government's response was to replace the iron hand of colonial paternalism with its own brand of authori-tarianism. The founding father of Singapore, Lee Kwan Yew, always justified his particular brand of government, employing many of the same oppressive old laws from colonial days, as the surest way to keep in check the resentments and antagonisms consequent upon a plural society. Like in Malaysia, one party, Lee's People's Action Party (PAP), representing the interests principally of the majority ethnic-Chinese population, has been in power continuously since independence. As in Malaysia, the PAP has employed a similar blend of gerrymandering and other forms of electoral engineering, combined with the use of the courts to batter political opponents, to win every general election. Sometimes Singapore-style authoritarianism is more benign. Thus, for instance, Chinese, Malays and Indians have been forced to share all public housing in Singapore under a quota system in order to prevent the build-up of ethnic ghettos, which is probably all to the good. Equally, though, the state will bear down heavily on any journalist or critic judged to be "undermining the state" by questioning the idea that all races live in perfect harmony on the island. The media is tightly controlled and there is little freedom of expression.

In Malaysia, government has been only marginally less repressive. There is little that is genuinely "pluralist" (in the Western sense) about these societies. Political competition is kept to a bare minimum, despite a formal adherence to democracy, and both Singapore and Malaysia are ruled by parties dominated by one ethnic group.

In the case of Indonesia, the region's largest country has favoured a more tolerant approach, at least rhetorically; "unity in diversity" is the national motto. At independence in 1945, President Sukarno outlined the five principles of the country's new guiding philosophy, called Pancasila. The first was a "Belief in the one and only God", without any reference to Islam or any other particular religion, and the second was a "Just and civilised humanity". The fourth was democracy and the last social justice for all the people of Indonesia. This was notably progressive stuff for the time, and remains so to this day. Nonetheless, unscrupulous politicians and their henchmen know exactly how to exploit the bitterness against the immigrant Chinese, and smears (or worse) about ethnicity and religion usually surface at election time and on other occasions of national stress.

But the post-colonial military governments of Burma tried a radically different strategy. Rather than devising a way to cope with the reality of the society that they inherited, they tried to dismantle it and create a homogenous, Burman, society. Thus, the Burmese generals who took power after the early 1960s deliberately set about to destroy the plural society in the name of Burman nationalism. It was an agenda of "race and religion", directed against not only the colonial-era immigrants but also those ethnic groups on the fringes of the old Burman kingdom – the Kachin, Karen, Shan and others – who only joined the newly independent Burma on the understanding that it would certainly not be a homogenous society, but rather a confederated one. This was a fundamental clash of outlooks from the beginning, and one that has still not been resolved.[2]

War's opportunity

The near destruction of Burma's plural society was achieved in two phases, by the Japanese invasion in early 1942 and then by the imposition of military rule in 1962. The first phase was, at least in part, an expression of that brand of Burman nationalism that erupted out of Rangoon University in the late 1920s and 1930s. The second phase was a logical consequence of the first.

The fascistic, expansionist-minded governments that came to power in Japan in the 1930s eyed Burma with particular interest because of its vast reserves of oil, rice and other commodities vital for supplying a large army overseas. On top of this, the Japanese imperial army had its own vital strategic reasons to invade Burma in early 1942. The high command desperately wanted to cut the supply lines through the north of the country that were keeping Chiang Kai-shek's armies in the field against the Japanese forces attempting to complete the conquest of China. After invading the country from Manchuria in 1937, Japan had become increasingly frustrated at its inability to deliver a knockout blow to the retreating Chinese armies. After abandoning most of littoral China to the Japanese, Chiang Kai-shek's forces had withdrawn deep into the interior, to Chongqing, just as the rival communist forces under Mao Zedong operated a guerrilla campaign against the Japanese out of the north-west.

In fact, Chiang Kai-shek's armies had retreated so far west that they could only be reliably supplied by his Western supporters, primarily the Americans, through the rear, from Burma. The country thus assumed enormous strategic importance in the existential struggle over the world's most populous country. Chiang Kai-shek's government-in-internal-exile, the Kuomintang (KMT), was thus supplied through the famous "Burma Road", the arduous route that wound its way up the mountains of north Shan State and over the border via Lashio into south-west China. Heavily overweight trucks ply exactly the same route today. From the late 1930s onwards, tons of supplies would arrive at the docks at Rangoon to be loaded up for the long trip north.

For the Japanese, therefore, if they could capture Burma the even greater prize of China might come with it. Under intense military and diplomatic strain in Europe in the summer of 1940, Britain's new prime minister Winston Churchill acceded to Japanese requests to close the road for three months, in order to relieve the simultaneous Japanese threat against Britain's South-East Asian colonies. But once the road was open again about 20,000 tons of goods per month continued to reach the Kuomintang, much to Tokyo's anger and disgust. The decision to reopen the Burma Road undoubtedly made a Japanese invasion of Burma more likely.

However, quite apart from the broad strategic reasons for a Japanese invasion of Burma, there is no doubt that the Japanese were also encouraged to do so by Burmese pro-independence nationalists. They were eagerly seeking an ally – any ally, by some accounts – to help them throw off the British yoke.

By 1940, the diverse student groups that had struggled against the British in the previous decade, and between which there was a lot of overlap, namely the Dobama Asiayone movement, the Thakins and the Rangoon University Students' Union, had coalesced into a united front called the Freedom Bloc. The young student Aung San had become the Bloc's secretary. The term Thakin was used by Aung San and his peers ironically, as it was the Burmese word for "master" or "lord", commonly used to address the British. By appropriating the word for themselves, Aung San and his peers were asserting themselves as the masters of Burma.

Aung San, the leader of Burma's independence struggle, was born in 1915 in the small town of Natmauk in central Burma. Opposition to British rule ran in the family; his granduncle, Bo Min Yaung, had fought against the colonial annexation of the country. The young Aung San, so he said later, dreamed of playing his own part in Burma's liberation from an early age, but of more concern to his parents was the fact that he didn't speak until he was six years old; they had feared that he was mute. Once Aung San did start to speak, however, he quickly made up for his early reticence. He proved to be an outstanding high-school student, entered the prestigious Rangoon University in 1933 and graduated with a degree in English Literature, Modern History and Political Science in 1937.

Smallish, stocky and tough, he combined the attributes of a man of action with those of a political thinker, or at least a political strategist. Aung San was also a persuasive speaker. In sum, he was a naturally charismatic leader. Very shortly after enrolling at the university he became embroiled in student politics and the anti-colonial struggle, swiftly becoming acknowledged as the leader of his generation of Burmese nationalists. Later, in 1942, he married Khin Kyi. They had four children, the second of whom was Aung San Suu Kyi (the eldest son lives in America and has had nothing to do with Burmese politics, the second son drowned in an ornamental lake in their garden aged just eight and the youngest daughter died a few days after her birth).

Other student leaders during the 1930s included Thakin Nu, later U Nu, Burma's first prime minister after independence, and the later military dictator Ne Win. Another vital figure was Dr Ba Maw. He had been the country's first chief minister from 1937 to 1939 under a new devolved constitution that saw Burma administratively separated from British India in 1937, but he was jailed for sedition by the colonial authorities for opposing Burma's entry into the Second World War. This was a decision taken entirely by London with no consultation in Burma; the fait accompli caused enormous resentment in Burma, as it did in India. Ba Maw was older and of a very different political temperament from Aung San, but he also joined the Freedom Bloc.

It was Ba Maw who first contacted the Japanese consul in Rangoon, sounding him out for support for the independence struggle. The Japanese were receptive, eager to gain as much intelligence and as many allies as they could for a possible invasion. Ties between the Burmese nationalists and the Japanese were strengthened through the renowned Colonel Suzuki of the Japanese army, then posing as a newspaper correspondent in Rangoon. However, despite these existing ties to the Japanese, when Aung San slipped out of Burma in August 1940 to seek outside help for the independence struggle, he had "a blank cheque" from his comrades to make contact with whichever country or movement could be most useful.

According to his own account, Aung San first tried to make contact with the Chinese communists, whom he considered to be more ideologically compatible with the leftist Burmese nationalists than the fascist and militaristic Japanese. But he abjectly failed to reach the communists deep inside China, and instead had to be virtually rescued by the Japanese when he got to the island of Xiamen, across the straits from the Japanese colony of Taiwan. From there he was whisked off to Tokyo to be embraced by Colonel Suzuki. To Aung San, he now "had to make the best of a bad job".

If the initial coming together of the Japanese and the nationalists was somewhat haphazard, mutual self-interest quickly dispelled any further hesitations. Aung Sang and others from the Thakin Party – a group that became famous in Burma as the "Thirty Comrades" – were smuggled out of Burma to receive intense military training from the Japanese at a specially built facility on the Japanese-occupied Chinese island of Hainan. These men formed the core of the anti-colonial Burma Independence Army (BIA), established on 28 December 1941, which was assembled along the Siam/Burma border to march in with the Japanese when the invasion began on 20 January 1942. The Thirty Comrades took a blood oath together, which involved sipping their own blood, drawn from their arms, mixed with alcohol in a communal silver bowl, as a mutual pledge of loyalty and comradeship. As has often been noted, they were a very young bunch, with an average age of just twenty-four. The Burmese nationalists had got exactly what they wanted, military training and an active outside collaborator. Aung San seems to have imagined, fancifully, that while the Japanese and British fought it out, the BIA would seize power and declare independence.

The Japanese, for their part, had not only got a useful auxiliary force inside the country, who knew the terrain, but also, to some extent, an ideological justification for the invasion, to help their fellow Asians free themselves from British (and American) imperialism. These "ideals of Japan's war effort", as Japan's officially approved *New History Textbook* of 2001 puts it, were embodied in the concept of the "Greater East Asia Co-Prosperity Sphere", whereby Japan would lead the newly liberated peoples of Asia in their own freely determined, post-imperial union. The same textbook insists that "in order to satisfy the expectations of peoples in these territories, Japan granted independence to Burma and the Philippines in 1943."[3] Since the war, the victorious Western powers, mindful of the terrible atrocities committed by Japanese soldiers against both Western POWs and Asian labourers on, for instance, the Thai/Burma "Death Railway", have dismissed these Japanese "ideals". However, there is no doubt that some Japanese took them seriously at the time, as did many hopeful Burmese. Indeed, Burma was duly granted a notional independence by Japan in 1943, nearly two years after the Japanese invaded. Burma's new leader under Japanese tutelage, Ba Maw, subsequently attended the notorious Greater East Asia Conference of November 1943 in Tokyo, an occasion at which Prime Minister Tojo gathered together all of Japan's puppet rulers of its conquered territories to celebrate a new Asian spirit, an Asia free of Western colonialism.

This was, of course, mostly propaganda. But as the historian of Japanese-Burmese relations Donald Seekins has written, it still had "great appeal",[4] especially to those majority indigenous races that had been forced aside in their own countries by the plural society; not only the Burmans in Burma, but the Malays and the Javanese. Ba Maw announced theatrically at the Tokyo conference that "My Asiatic blood has always called to other Asiatic blood; in my dreams, both sleeping and walking, I have heard the voice of Asia calling to her children."

Yet, in practice his definition of "Asian" was strictly limited to Burmans. He certainly did not include Indians, for instance. The intermingling of Burman nationalism with Japanese-style nation building was to have a significant effect on post-independence Burma.

A terrible exodus

In 1942, as the Japanese and the Burma Independence Army swept into Burma, quickly driving the poorly equipped and badly led British forces before them, the BIA peeled off to deal with their own country's domestic issues. The BIA was, by most accounts, warmly received by the Burman majority, at least partly because they were intent on settling scores with the Indians and other groups whom they saw as usurpers. By contrast, to many Indians it was clear what was in store for them even before the Japanese invasion began. One such Indian, Nadir Tyabji, travelled extensively around Burma for the Indian-owned Tata Oil Mills, and recorded in October 1941:

> I got the feeling that the Burmese were just waiting for an opportunity to drive the Indians out and take their place in the scheme of things, however ill-equipped to do so . . . [The Indian population] has begun to get restive and from odd bits of gossip which I picked up, it became evident that any Japanese advance from the south would result in a massive movement of Indians towards Rangoon as a take-off point for the run to India, mainly by the sea route as the quickest and cheapest.[5]

Tyabji had foreseen what would become one of the most dreadful events of the entire war, a forced exodus in which half a million ethnic South Asians fled towards India, driven by the vengeful Burmese. As Seekins sums it up, "During the opening months of the war, Burman nationalists 'solved' the plural society problem in a Gordian knot manner. As the British began their retreat, Burman/Burmese mobs attacked Indians in urban and rural areas of Lower Burma, and hundreds of thousands of them left the country, often on foot."

These refugees were joined by thousands of others, including the Anglo-Burmese and the remnants of Britain's shattered army. At the time, with about one million people on the move, it was the biggest forced migration on record. It was to be the only time in British history that an army had to retreat together with all the soldiers' and officers' families in tow. It is estimated that as many as eighty thousand died en route as ragged lines of starving, sick and fearful people trudged hundreds of miles through terrible terrain to the mountain passes that led to Bengal, Manipur, Nagaland and the relative safety of British India. Entire families were almost wiped out. On a wall of the Armenian Church in Yangon remains a memorial tablet to the "beloved children and grandchildren of the late Arakiel Mackertich Minus and Woscoom Minus, who died on the trek to India in 1942." Below are listed thirteen names.

The wretched, humiliating retreat from Burma not only exposed the feebleness of Britain's imperial rule, but also spelt the end of a particular kind of colonial Burma. Many of those who survived the terrible retreat in March 1942 never returned to the country. British claims to moral leadership of the plural society were shattered by the inglorious scenes on the docks of Rangoon where white Europeans grabbed the last remaining berths ahead of the Indians and Burmese. Indian males were not allowed to travel as deck passengers at all, ostensibly to preserve Rangoon's workforce. This forced them to leave on foot. Similar scenes had been played out on the docks in Penang when the British evacuated Georgetown before the Japanese arrived. There, it was the local Chinese who felt abandoned by the fleeing British, and they had much more to fear from the fiercely anti-communist Japanese than did the Indians.

The BIA not only drove the Indians out, they also fell on other ethnic groups in the country, particularly those who had supported British rule and some of whom fought to protect the Indians. Even the Japanese were at times astonished and appalled by the ferocity of the BIA's attacks on other indigenous peoples such as the Karen and Karenni; in one incident, never to be forgotten by the Karen, four hundred of their villages in the Irrawaddy Delta were destroyed and about 1,800 of their kin killed. In Arakan, the BIA and local Rakhine got their opportunity to turn on the Muslim Rohingya, who, they claimed, had been armed by the retreating British. These bloody conflicts of 1942/3 reverberate down the decades. Frequent conversations I have had start, quite unprompted, with these massacres and revenge killings, or with the war years. In a country where time has stood still, such events remain fresh in the mind. [6]

Just before the end of the war, in March 1945, Aung San, recognising that the Japanese were going to lose, deftly switched allegiances, allying the BIA to a reinvigorated British army under the command of General William Slim, his country's best battlefield commander of the entire war. His 14th Army had stemmed the Japanese advance across Britain's Asian empire on the border of India, and then from the end of 1944 had begun to push the Japanese back down Burma. Thus, it seemed that the Burmese nationalists had emerged on the winning side of the war alongside the British. In truth, the BIA and Japanese had essentially destroyed the colonial regime and economy. An enfeebled Britain could not reimpose its rule over its former colony and thus granted independence to Burma on 4 January 1948. Unfortunately, however, Burma, bombed, looted and ransacked by successive waves of foreign armies, was economically prostrate by this time, and without a functioning plural society, the engine of growth in the pre-war years, it never really recovered.

The last hurrah for Burma's plural society was, appropriately enough, the reconquest of Burma itself, for General Slim's 700,000-strong 14th Army was as dazzlingly multi-ethnic as pre-war Burma had once been. One historian has speculated that the 14th Army must have "contained more diverse races than any other, perhaps in history", and at its core were the Indians: Rajputs, Dogras, Sikhs, Jats, Punjabis, Ahirs, Amirs, Chamars, Rawats, Minas, Mahars, Coorgs, Assamese, Adivasis, Kumaonis, Pathans, Brahuis, Mers, Tamils, Telegus, Paraiyahs, Brahmans, Hindustani, Mussulmans, Punjabi Mussulmans, Madrassi Mussulmans and Gurkhas, from Nepal. They were joined by a wide variety of soldiers from east and west Africa, including Hausas, Ibos and Yorubas from Nigeria, Mandis and Timinis from Sierra Leone, Baganda and Achole from Uganda, and Somalis from Somaliland – as well as white New Zealanders, Australians, Canadians and South Africans, to say nothing of the Scots, Welsh, Irish and English.[7]

The large and beautifully maintained Commonwealth War Graves cemetery at Taukkyan on the outskirts of today's Yangon bears silent witness to the sacrifice of the 14th Army in the reconquest of Burma. But the long lists of names from almost every part of the globe carved on plain white stone also testify to the pluralism of the army, even if the very society that those soldiers fought to preserve had all but disappeared by the time they reached Rangoon in August 1945. Even so, it was, quite appropriately, an Indian soldier, Mohammed Munsif Khan, who finally raised the Union Jack over the "liberated" city.[8]

The great lockdown

From independence in 1948 to 1962, a weakened nation, beset by civil war and a communist insurgency (of which more later), limped through several democratic elections under the relatively benign leadership of its first prime minister, U Nu. But in 1962, the military, led by General Ne Win, seized power in a coup, suspending the constitution and dissolving parliament. Ne Win declared that "parliamentary democracy was not suitable" for the country, and instead started to rule through a "revolutionary council". Burma had ruptured from the modern world. More than fifty years later, it is still struggling to return.

Ne Win, of part-Chinese descent, had been one of the Thirty Comrades, and was appointed head of the army in 1948. Soon after the coup, he and his military co-conspirators, known ubiquitously as "the generals", set up the Burmese Socialist Programme Party (BSPP). This was to be the new ruling party, and after 1964 the only one allowed under the new regime. It was the forerunner of all the other quasi-military "political parties" that have since ruled Burma.

The new ideology was to be the notorious "Burmese Way to Socialism". This has been described by those historians most sympathetic to the aims and aspirations of the new regime as "Marxist in inspiration, Leninist in implementation and Buddhist in its goals".[9] Most other commentators have been less generous about this incoherent mish-mash of undigested, out-of-date political and economic bunkum that had already proved disastrous everywhere else that it had been tried. So it was to prove in Burma.

At its core was an attempt to create a communist-style nationalised economy. In practice, the most obvious thrust of this policy was to drive all foreign, and thus privately owned, businesses out of the country, creating a Burman-run economy solely for the Burmans. Thus, the Burmese Way to Socialism took aim squarely at the plural society. Although it had been dealt a savage blow during the war, it was not really until now that deliberate steps were taken systematically to dismantle the colonial economy.

In 1963, the new regime passed the Enterprise Nationalisation Law, giving it the power to take over large businesses, including, most significantly, foreign-owned companies. In great haste, a wave of nationalisations began, often at gunpoint. All foreign-owned businesses were taken over by the regime, with the terms of compensation left vague. This effectively deprived all foreigners of their livelihood, forcing them to leave. One of the first businesses to go was the Irrawaddy Flotilla Corporation. All foreign banks, half of them Indian-owned, were nationalised and they were later merged into one entity known as the People's Bank of Burma. Big international banks like Standard Chartered could take the pain; the people who really suffered from the nationalisations were the hundreds of thousands of South Asian, Chinese and other small businessmen, largely in downtown Rangoon and the other colonial entrepôts.

Those who stayed on in Yangon still remember the day, 19 March 1964, when the soldiers came to take away whatever they could and shutter the rest. Residents who have lived through fifty or so years of military dictatorship are still reluctant to talk of these events, let alone give their names, but when pressed they can recall it all too well. One tall, stooping Gujarati with impeccable English on 26th Street tells me that he was twenty-five at the time, working in the family hardware store. At gunpoint he was ordered to close the shop and assured that he would get compensation. "I am still waiting", he says. Most of his family left, but he stayed on and later opened a paint-shop. He has a blunt message for today's would-be investors: "Don't trust these people. Don't open your factories here." He is very nostalgic for colonial rule: "The British built this city into the most beautiful in the world. They gave us laws, taught us and built the country." It is a common refrain in these streets.

Another Gujarati tells me that the army not only shut down his bicycle repair shop, but also took over his two godowns on the docks, with all their contents. They also stopped his bank account, and with subsequent demonetisation all his savings were wiped out. He stayed, he says, but all his children and nephews left, as there were clearly going to be fewer opportunities for them in the new Burma. His son, a doctor, lives in Britain; his daughter lives in Mumbai, also a doctor. Theirs are skills that Burma came to need desperately as the country sank deep into poverty and its healthcare systems collapsed. Nobody in power seemed to care about a brain drain.

Altogether about 400,000 ethnic Indians were forced to leave, people whose families had by this time often lived in Burma for several generations. About 100,000 or so Chinese left too, sped on their way by deadly anti-Chinese riots in Rangoon in 1967. Despite, or perhaps because of, his own Chinese roots, Ne Win was particularly harsh on the Chinese. He banned Chinese schools and language instruction. Many thought the anti-Chinese riots of 1967 and after were tacitly supported by the government; shops were looted and schools set on fire, forcing even more Chinese to leave. Thousands of Anglo-Burmese left too.

Ne Win gave each departing Indian businessmen a desultory sum in a parody of compensation. Disgusted by the new Burmese regime's racism and miserliness, Jawaharlal Nehru's Indian government sent over ferries and planes to bring their countrymen home. All the same, so favourable was life in Burma still considered to be by the Indians that two-thirds of them stayed on. Nonetheless, according to one estimate, by the early 1980s the non-Burmese population of Rangoon had been reduced from over 50 per cent to around 7 per cent.[10]

These actions clearly satisfied many Burmans – and Arakanese – at the time. Moreover, although the country might have differed in its approach to dealing with the plural society from regional neighbours such as Malaysia and Indonesia, it certainly wasn't alone in taking such draconian action. Another former British colony, Uganda, took even more severe measures against its own South Asian community, which had migrated there under colonial rule in the mid nineteenth century. The deranged and possibly cannibalistic president, Idi Amin, directly ordered approximately sixty thousand Indian immigrants (mostly Gujaratis, both Muslims and Hindus) to get out of the country at very short notice in 1972, claiming that he had had a dream in which God told him to expel them all. Long discriminated against and stigmatised in Uganda they were nonetheless very successful; they made up only 1 per cent of the population, but generated about one-fifth of the national income. As in Burma, the expulsion of the Asians was popular with most Ugandans, and helped to boost Amin's popularity. He had come to power only the year before, but then ruled (and ruined) the country for a further seven.

Indeed, in several other countries the rulers of post-colonial states discriminated against, or attempted to drive out, the Indians who had been invited in by the British to run their colonial economies, sometimes in place of slaves. South Asians in Sri Lanka, Tanzania, Kenya and South Africa all suffered varying degrees of oppression as their new rulers, like Burma's, tried to create more racially and culturally homogenous states. The Indian Tamils of Sri Lanka probably suffered the most; an almost twenty-year Tamil insurgency was only crushed by the Sinhalese-majority army in a bloody massacre on the island's north-eastern beaches in 2009.

In Uganda, the expulsion of the Asians had a disastrous effect on the country's economy. A good proportion of them were the entrepreneurial and internationally well-connected Indians who produced such a disproportionate share of the national wealth. Many of them had been traders and bankers, but after their Ugandan assets were seized by Amin and his cronies their businesses largely went to ruin. It was the same story with Burma. Along with the hundreds of thousands expelled by the generals went the skills, money and trading connections that had made Rangoon, and Burma, rich. Despite the ravages of the Second World War and the ethnic civil wars that broke out in the country on independence, Rangoon had remained a relatively wealthy city into the 1950s. It was, for example, becoming a regional commercial and transport hub again; its airport was regarded as the best in South-East Asia and served the region much as Singapore does today.

Only a decade later all this was gone. The silver threads of commerce that had bound the region's commercial communities together were frayed, if not completely broken. Rangoon came to resemble the equally dilapidated Ugandan town of Jinja, on the shores of Lake Victoria. This was where the Indian community had been concentrated, and much of the striking architecture is clearly Indian-influenced. Yet, after the Ugandan Asians were driven out there was no one left to maintain the buildings and clubs, and the once thriving town came to feel about as forlorn as Yangon did.

The plural society of Rangoon, which prompted Furnivall's reflections in the first place, was the precursor of today's globalised cities, with all the riches that accrue to them. It is no coincidence that Burma's precipitate economic decline occurred after the expulsion of the foreigners (including J. S. Furnivall himself) in the 1960s. The black market flourished, especially in the border areas, but the formal economy never recovered.

Old Burman society was agrarian and feudal, but never very commercial. All the empirical evidence in the business literature points to the benefits of diversity and immigration in terms of innovation and productivity. The vast majority of immigrants who came to Rangoon, Moulmein, Mandalay and the rest of Burma's colonial cities were destitute when they arrived, which provided them with every incentive to better themselves, and the country with it.

The imposition of military rule in 1962 thus led to the heartbreaking ruination of the country. As racism drove out diversity and creativity, so commerce dried up and Rangoon, in particular, began to fall into a state of miserable disrepair. With no attempt to maintain the buildings, much of the city has fallen prey to the invasive tropical climate. The generals' new policy of the Burmese Way to Socialism meant, in effect, an economic autarky. There was a change of heart in the mid 1990s, when the generals, recognising the failure of their socialist policies, adopted a version of crony capitalism instead, but by then most of the damage had been done.

Thus, all the fast-flowing currents of economic development that transformed every other big Asian city simply passed Yangon by. In Jakarta, Kuala Lumpur or Bangkok, frantic post-war industrialisation and globalisation have obliterated virtually any last features of Furnivall's "modern tropical economy" and replaced the rows of tiny family businesses with vast shopping malls filled with plasma TVs, designer labels and plastic surgeons. Most Asians wouldn't have it any other way.

The virtues, and profits, of tolerance

Of the proud, wealthy Eurasian communities of pre-war Rangoon there is little left today. Only twenty or so Jews remain, devotedly keeping up the synagogue with the help of funds from overseas. Like many such peoples they suffered a double blow, the Japanese occupation of the early 1940s followed by the generals' nationalisation programme. Those few who managed to flee the first returned only to escape the latter. The Armenians fared even worse. By 2013, there were precisely two families left, and the head of one of them, Basil Martin, a former electrical engineer, was eighty-seven and invalided. The head of the other family, Richard "Dicky" Minus, was a relatively sprightly fifty-eight and in charge of the upkeep of their church. "From my grandfather's time I was coming here", he told me, "and my father and grandfather were both trustees." Services were down to two a month, led by an Anglican priest. There were usually five or six worshippers, he told me, whose numbers were occasionally swelled by the family of the former Yugoslav ambassador and a lone Russian. Dicky used to have a business repairing old British and Japanese cars, but is now retired. He intends to stay until the end, he told me, even though everybody else has gone.

The new xenophobic environment cultivated by the generals was eventually translated into law with the passing of the Citizenship Act of 1982. This legislation sanctioned and codified the existing discriminatory arrangements; full citizenship would only be granted to the descendants of indigenous people, those who had lived in the country before 1823, and the rest would be granted some lesser category of citizenship, if any. The date was not picked at random; it was the year before the first Anglo-Burmese war broke out and the British started their relentless occupation of the country. Thus, the law attempted to wind the clock right back to a pre-colonial Burmese nirvana, denying the rights and opportunities of citizenship to all those whom the British brought along in their wake. To this day, therefore, the Indian (probably as many as two million of them) and Chinese descendants of the original immigrants often still cannot get passports or identity cards. Dr Binoda Kumar Mishra, an Indian academic in Kolkata, has called this "the largest number of stateless Indians in the world".

This discrimination applies to intermarried Indian-Burmese families too – anyone who is not of "pure" blood. As a consequence they cannot get degrees from public colleges or enter government service. They are, in a real sense, legally non-persons in a country where their families have often lived for at least four or five generations, often married into Burman families.

Even those few non-Burmans who did manage to get citizenship, often by paying enough money, could still suffer heavy discrimination. Take the Anglo-Burmese, the descendants of mixed marriages between the British colonialists and native Burmese. Almost all of the Anglo-Burmese left after 1962 when their businesses, mainly in the rubber plantations surrounding Moulmein, were nationalised. The majority went to Australia, New Zealand or back to Britain. Only a few, as we have seen, like Glenn Kyaw Nyunt in Moulmein, stayed on, but he and his family were rigorously excluded from mainstream Burmese life. His family lost its business after nationalisation, just as his mother's very good schools in Moulmein and Maymyo were closed down. Glenn and his wife stayed on initially to care for their ageing Burmese parents, and then simply forgot to leave. "We just 'fitted in'", Glenn says. They got a lesser form of citizenship, for the Anglo-flavour of their blood has effectively disbarred them from functioning as full citizens. In the immigration office in Moulmein, where they had to register, they are catalogued as English/Burmese – and after that is written "(suspicious)". Their daughter, on one side of her family a

Burman, a bright and well-educated young woman, tried to be a nursing cadet but was refused on the grounds of being an Anglo and a Christian.

Her skills have thus been lost to Burma. Indeed, this officially sanctioned Burman exceptionalism has deprived the country of an enormous amount of talent, finance and commercial drive. If Burma is to function and prosper again, it will have to rediscover a real pluralism. The Colonial-style plural society excluded the Burmese; a future, truly pluralist society will have to embrace all those who have been excluded from Burman ethno-nationalism.

It is also worth remembering that the values of the plural society that Furnivall recorded and dismissed so lightly in 1948 weigh much more impressively today than they did in Furnivall's era. His remark that "each group holds by its own religion, its own culture and language, its own ideas and ways" was written as a criticism. He felt it was detrimental to a wider social cohesion that the diverse people of a city like Rangoon did not integrate or intermarry. That might have been true at the time, but these myriad peoples did not persecute or harass each other either – and that, remarkably, remains true to this day.

Indeed, to the contemporary eye this is the greatest virtue of Rangoon's plural society; it might have shoved aside the indigenous peoples, but within its own bounds, within its own terms of reference, set by the immigrants themselves in conjunction with the colonial authorities, it was, and remains, an impressively amicable society. As we have seen, immigrants brought their religions and cultures with them to Rangoon, squeezing a multitude of churches, mosques, temples and synagogues into a few square miles. Yet, the bloody sectarian divisions and ethnic hatreds that have consumed much of the rest of the world seem to have passed these old streets by. Today's downtown Yangon, hidden away from the world, somehow survives as a remarkable exemplar of inter-faith harmony. Nowadays it is rivalled only, perhaps, by New York for its intoxicating variety of cultures and faiths, and is probably unequalled in its atmosphere of religious toleration and mutual respect.

You would barely guess at the blood shed elsewhere between Jews and Muslims since 1948. Take the Musmeah Yeshua synagogue. Flanking its entrance are the paint shops, all owned by Muslims. Sammy Samuels tells me that these shopowners will guard the synagogue if he or one of the other trustees has to pop out for a bit, and they also help him clear up after the

Hannukah festival. Even more remarkably, Sammy introduces me to the caretaker of the synagogue, Asslan, who is a Sunni Muslim. He has been cleaning and looking after the place for thirty years now, as his father did for many years before him. In part exchange he is given a tiny enclave on the site from where he runs a tea shop. Asslan's grandfather emigrated from north India, and he attends the Sunni mosque about two hundred yards down the road. I asked Asslan earnestly whether, as a Muslim, he has any problems working at the synagogue, but he merely looked perplexed. His family has always got on well with the Samuels, he replied, "There is no problem working here, all people are welcome." Sammy and I discussed whether there are any other synagogues in the world with a Muslim caretaker; he thought there might be one other in Mumbai, but he wasn't sure.

In fact, the Musmeah Yeshua synagogue is in the very heart of the Muslim quarter, called Pabedan Township, and is surrounded pretty well on every side by mosques and *madrassas*. Most people here emigrated from Gujarat, and still generally refer to themselves as Gujaratis. Directly behind the synagogue is the Ehlay Hadees Sunni Jamay mosque, dating from 1903. Here one Gujarati, happily indifferent to the divisions of India and Pakistan, tells me that he came to Burma with his parents in 1948; only ten people attend the mosque now, and they are all from the same family. He too looks faintly baffled when I ask him whether it is at all difficult being so close to a synagogue. Only a little farther down 26th Street from the synagogue is a Sunni Muslim *madrassa*, dating from 1884. The family here came from (then) Bombay; they welcome 250 students every evening. A few doors down is Asslan's Sunni mosque, dating originally from 1923.

Probably the biggest mosque in Yangon, at least according to those who proudly worship there, is a few blocks down on Shwe Bontha Street. The Surti Sunni Jamah mosque is over a century old, glorious in green and while tiles, with upper and lower prayer halls. With cool marble floors, washing pools and an abundance of fans, Yangon's mosques offer a welcome haven from the scorching heat outside. After prayers at 1 p.m., many worshippers stretch out for a refreshing snooze on the musty old carpets outside the prayer halls.

Of Yangon's seventy or so active mosques, just two are Shia.[11] There are nine Shia mosques in the whole of Burma as compared to 2,500 Sunni prayer halls. The minority Shias, who number about ten thousand in Yangon, don't report any problems with the Sunni Muslim community. While the ancient Shia/Sunni divide widens and sharpens in Syria, Iraq and the rest of the Middle East, as well as in nearby Malaysia and Indonesia, in Yangon Shia and Sunni institutions often share the same stretch of pavement quite peacefully. Standing on the corner of Mahabandoola and 30th Street, is Yangon's largest Shia mosque. The Moghul Shia *masjid* is probably the most architecturally impressive of all Yangon's mosques, with minarets that tower over the surrounding streets. The present structure was completed in 1918, replacing the original wooden Shia mosque that had lasted since 1854. I fail to interest any of the Sunni worshippers at the Surti Sunni Jamah mosque in a conversation about the rivalry, or even antagonism, between the Sunni and Shia. It seems that the strong influence of several traditions of Sufism within the Sunni community has helped to create a more tolerant strain of Islam in Burma. "We are all getting on well together here", says one. "It's all about the mind, we tolerate and understand each other."

And so the extraordinary variety of faiths and temples continues. As I stand outside the Shri Satyanarayan Hindu temple on 29th Street, with an eye-watering orange facade and colonnaded windows, a kindly man in a *pasoe* and white shirt who is passing stops and asks if I would like to visit. Yes, please. He introduces himself as Ardi Gupta. His grandfather moved to 29th Street from Lucknow, and Ardi lives in exactly the same place with his two daughters and three sons. He speaks English, Burmese and Hindi. The temple is clean and well looked after, the various deities brightly painted and clothed. The Lord Buddha has his own room.

The substantial Anglican, Catholic, Methodist and other Christian churches were mostly built just on the fringes of the downtown area. Holy Trinity, the Anglican cathedral, dating from 1886, has a side chapel devoted to the Allied dead of the Second World War, which has recently been spruced up. Being such a Scottish city, the Presbyterian church on Signal Pagoda Road (the present dull structure dates from 1931, opposite the Park Royal Hotel) became the de facto Scottish church and was nicknamed the Scots Kirk.

When the devastating Cyclone Nargis swept through Yangon in 2008, killing thousands, inter-faith prayers were held at the synagogue. Hindus,

Christians, Buddhists, Muslims and Jews attended together. "We all get along", says Sammy Samuels. He says that some of his American Jewish visitors on MyanmarShalom tours are initially "scared" by the location of the synagogue, surrounded as it is on all sides by Muslim shops, people, schools and mosques. They expect hostility, but instead are "shocked and amazed" at how everyone rubs along.

There are Salafists in Yangon too, says Aye Lwin, the head of the Islamic Centre of Myanmar. Elsewhere, he explains, this might be considered to be slightly sinister, but in Burma all it means is that Islam is very varied. The most distinctive feature of Burmese Islam, adds Aye Lwin, is that "it is very accepting and moderate". He himself is of mixed ancestry, like so many others in downtown Yangon; in this respect Furnivall's contention that the different "groups hold by their own" in the plural society is now out of date. Yet, the Burmese authorities certainly don't want to acknowledge this, as it would upset the carefully constructed categories of ethnicity that they inherited from the British. Aye Lwin is part Afghan on his grandfather's side, Mon and Burmese on his mother's side, and the Queen's English comes out of his mouth. He has one simple reason why all these people of widely varying faiths and ancestries get on so well: "All the different races here are still united by one thing – commerce."

CHAPTER THREE

Burmanisation

FOR THE CONTEMPORARY VISITOR, there is an easy way to understand what Burma's ruling generals' vision of a pure Burma was supposed to look like, unsullied by foreign or even ethnic-minority influence – just head up to the new capital, Naypyidaw. Whereas for many Burmese, Yangon remains a symbol of colonial humiliation, travel two hundred miles north of the old British capital and you will encounter a sort of fantasy retro-Burma. There are other strangely artificial capital cities in the world – Australia's Canberra and Nigeria's Abuja come to mind – but Naypyidaw must be the most peculiar of them all.

Here the military regimes have attempted to recreate the Burman kingdoms of old and to reimagine Burma as if much of the country's recent history had never happened. For in Naypyidaw (in their own minds at least), they have rebuilt the ancient royal capitals of Ava and Mandalay, presumably in the hope that the peoples' reverence for the old Burmese monarchy would rub off on them. The translation of the Burmese word *Naypyidaw* is "royal city of the sun". The new capital is also referred to as the "seat of kings", or "abode of kings".

No one is quite sure why the regime, and in particular the military dictator Senior General Than Shwe, picked this spot in the early 2000s. Naypyidaw lies on the fringes of the Burman central region called the dry zone, well away from the country's vulnerable coasts, and there has therefore been speculation that the move from Yangon was prompted by concerns about the former capital's exposure to seaborne invasion by America. At the time, such fears were not as half-baked as they might seem now. The administration of President George W. Bush had just categorised Burma an "outpost of tyranny", and the American army was busy rolling over such outposts wherever they could, in Iraq and Afghanistan. It was the era of the "axis of evil", and although Burma had not explicitly been included in that axis, President Bush and his political allies missed few opportunities to express their loathing for Burma's military rulers. The Burmese Freedom and Democracy Act, for example, passed by the United States Congress in 2003, formally gave the US president authority to "build democracy" in Burma and to prepare for the reconstruction of the country after the military government had gone. To Than Shwe and his ilk this must have sounded like a mandate for regime change; some of the more moralising and interventionist-minded American legislators did hope that it meant exactly that.

Naypyidaw was built in great secrecy and in great haste. One engineer who had been employed on the project told me that more than thirty thousand people worked on it, mainly under the direction of the Ministry of Construction and the ominous-sounding Department of Housing and Human Settlement, but the figure may have been as high as eighty thousand at one point. It was all done in such a rush, he says, that when the first government officials showed up for work the roads weren't finished, there was little running water and those buildings that were actually ready for occupation hadn't been connected up to the electric grid.

Several local villages were destroyed to make way for the sprawling new city – some got compensation, my engineer says, but many did not. In addition, a report from the International Labour Organisation of the United Nations alleges that at least 2,500 local villagers had been forcibly conscripted to construct army camps in the new capital. My engineer told me that the tight deadline and the customary corruption ensured that the "contractors were not good enough and there was little quality control". The result is a tawdry, gimcrack capital, a suitable testimony to the generals' way of doing business. Despite the impressive dimensions of most of the buildings, look closely and you will already see loose tiles, rattling windows and rusting ironwork. The Ministry of Foreign Affairs looks as if it might have been put up fifty years ago.

Despite the shoddy construction, Naypyidaw must still have cost several hundreds of millions of dollars, in an extremely poor country. Even the Chinese, the generals' most reliable friends, briefly complained about the folly of it all, not least because it involved the diversion of resources from repaying outstanding loans to China. Frequently exasperated by their erstwhile ally to the west, on this occasion the Chinese, according to one account, were so angry that in early 2006 they briefly posted a statement on their Yangon embassy website criticising the waste and expense of moving to the new capital.

Lucky stars

The key to understanding the enigma of Naypyidaw lies in the characters of the two generals who have dominated Burma since 1962, Ne Win and Than Shwe, the latter being the founder of Naypyidaw. Considering that they wielded so much power in Burma over such a long time, Ne Win ruling formally from 1962 to 1988, and then from behind the scenes for years afterwards, and Than Shwe from 1992 to 2011, remarkably little is known about either of them. At least the few portrait photographs of Than Shwe's squat, pudgy face actually suggest the brutality and callousness of his rule. What is certain is that both he and Ne Win worked assiduously to evoke Burma's royal and martial past in order to legitimise their own rule. There is plenty of evidence that despite their relatively humble beginnings both came to see themselves as descendants of the old Burmese kings. One of Ne Win's several marriages was to a descendant of the last Burmese king.[1]

Their military background was obviously important to both of them, but so too was astrology. Numerology and astrology permeate Burmese culture deeply, and have almost certainly accounted for some of the more surreal goings-on at Naypyidaw. The two generals' fascination is something they shared with Burma's old kings, and with much of the rest of the population. It was not unusual in men and women of their generation to keep astrological texts and charts at home to consult before taking even quite minor decisions; many young Burmese still do.

Some of the most reputable astrologers can be found today in slim booths flanking the steps of the northern entrance to the Shwedagon pagoda in Yangon. A young Burmese friend, who has a very handy astrology app on her mobile phone, took me to see one of them. She had consulted him at important moments in her own life and had found him very helpful. Indeed, her life seemed to be governed as much by the fortunes, good or otherwise, of the spirit world as by her admiration for Aung San Suu Kyi and the National League for Democracy (NLD). She admitted to me that she only ever washed her hair on certain lucky days of the week to avoid getting split ends.

I saw the astrologer Saya Khang Si Thu, an amiable, chatty man, in a little room filled with flowers, books, charts and, on the walls, a couple of enormous posters of waterfalls. I gave him my birth date, and with the aid of a few charts and some quick arithmetic he calculated that I was a writer and teacher – right on both accounts. This was the crucial test of an astrologer's powers, my Burmese friend told me; if he got this wrong, he was obviously a quack. Saya Khang Si Thu also calculated that my lucky numbers were one, four and seven. Thus, any combination of these numbers would be most auspicious for me. If, on the one hand, I was to be invited to dinner at numbers five, eleven or forty-seven Piccadilly, for example, I should go; dinners at numbers three, six and fifteen, on the other hand, were to be strictly avoided. My lucky colour was sky blue, apparently, and I ought to have a photograph taken of myself and my family in front of a (real) waterfall to increase my share of good fortune. For all this valuable information, I handed over $5. Saya Khang Si Thu had a long queue forming outside, so I was moved quickly through.

I was mildly intrigued by my own lucky numbers, but the Burmese generals could be obsessed by them – with ruinous consequences for the country. Ne Win was famously fixated on the number nine, so much so that it precipitated Burma's economic collapse under his rule (see Chapter Six). Almost as controversial was the list of 135 ethnic groups that the government inherited from the British, and which first surfaced as an official arbiter of ethnicity in 1989. Yet, there were so many glaring sins of omission and commission in this archaic inventory, used subsequently for the hotly contested national census of 2014, that people could only surmise that the generals wanted to keep the number because its digits (1+3+5) added up to nine.

It was Ne Win who is thought to have overseen the construction of a planetarium in 1987, conveniently close to the government quarter in Yangon. This was built courtesy of Japanese aid money in a corner of the People's Park, near to the Shwedagon pagoda. The official reason for constructing it was to promote science education, and Burmese of a certain age still remember being dragged there by their teachers. One well-informed journalist has alleged that its real purpose was to allow Burma's leaders to plot the stars and planets in the run-up to any important decisions that had to be made. Certainly, it was often closed to the public.[2]

But General Ne Win was only following in a long line of rulers who were deeply reliant on omens, numbers and stars. In 1948, the lauded founders of independent Burma felt spooked about the assassination of General Aung San the previous year. They intended to get the new nation off to as good a start as possible, so the departing British and other diplomats had to muster in full fig at 4 a.m. on the morning of 4 January 1948 to witness the proclamation of independence. This moment had been deemed by astrologers to be the most favourable hour and date.

General Than Shwe, the creator of Naypyidaw, was profoundly in thrall to the predictions of astrology and numerology, and this seems certain to have guided him in decisions about the planning and layout of his new capital. Thus, the civil servants began to decamp from Yangon to their new offices in Naypyidaw on 6 November 2005 at precisely 6.37 a.m. – indicating that Than Shwe's lucky number was probably six. A holy number for a new capital is eleven, so the first eleven ministries were subsequently opened at 11 a.m. on 11 November (the eleventh month). Likewise, according to some witnesses, the first move from Yangon to Naypyidaw was completed in 1,100 military trucks carrying eleven battalions of infantry, together with the civil servants for just the first eleven ministries. After years of construction the newly opened parliament finally began its first session at the oddly specific hour of 8.55 a.m., on 31 January 2011.

If astrology really has played such an important role in the evolution of Naypyidaw, it would only be in keeping with what we know of the astrological obsessions of the old Burmese royal courts and their kings. On the advice of royal astrologers, for instance, Burmese capitals were often moved due to bad omens. The transfer of the royal capital from Ava to Amarapura in 1783 was reversed in 1823 when a vulture inauspiciously landed on a palace spire – soon afterwards a large portion of the city was consumed by fire. In all, Burmese capitals have moved more than ten times, always due to a combination of strategic and astrological reasons. In this context, the move to Naypyidaw was hardly so remarkable.

Almost everything in Naypyidaw attempts to evoke the traditions and glories of Burma's royal past. In this vision, the plural society never happened and the ethnic groups who make up about 35 per cent of Burma's modern population, never existed. There are constant references throughout Naypyidaw to this singular interpretation of Burmese history, or what should be described, rather, as a chronicle of royal Burman history. Giant statues of three of Burma's most famous warrior kings, Anawrahta (ruled 1044–77), Bayinnaung (1551–81) and Alaungpaya (1752–60), tower over the enormous military parade ground in nearby Pyinmana. These monarchs conquered local kingdoms and extended Burman power well into territory that is now in Thailand and India.

According to his biographer, Benedict Rogers, one of Than Shwe's earliest appointments after the 1962 military coup was as instructor at the Central School of Political Science in Rangoon. Here he not only indoctrinated young cadets in the principles of Ne Win's ideology of the Burmese Way to Socialism, but also taught and lectured in Burmese history. This may explain, Rogers suggests, "Than Shwe's own fascination with Burma's ancient warrior kings and his construction of a new capital regarded as a royal seat."[3] Certainly, diplomats who met him were often treated to long lectures on his particular interpretation of Burmese history. Born in 1933, up to his appointment to the Central School Than Shwe was largely uneducated, so as an army man he might well have been attracted to a simplified vision of Burma's triumphant military past, when the court of Ava was one of the predominant imperial powers in the region.

Slightly out of the Naypyidaw city centre is the enormous Uppatasanti pagoda. This is a direct replica of the Shwedagon in Rangoon, only slightly shorter. Than Shwe and his family made offerings at the newly opened 99-metre pagoda on 9 March 2009. Standing in one corner of the precinct is a 108-foot-high "Great Sacred Flagmast", and an inscription on its base reads that this was erected "to pay homage to the splendid Uppatasanti pagoda glistening with invaluable gems and craftsmanship, on the sacred . . . hillock in the Royal city of Naypyidaw in the Union of Myanmar". Unlike the Shwedagon, this pagoda is hollow inside, and on the walls are a series of colossal murals depicting famous episodes from the life of the Buddha, as well as scenes from the life of the Burmese kings. Here, religion, royalty and the modern military rulers have become explicitly intertwined.

From the very start the generals were keen to capture the national religion for the benefit of the regime, to make it yet another organ of the all-controlling state. The community of monks, known as the *sangha* in Burma, had represented an important point of independent dissent to the colonial authorities, so the generals tried their best to prevent the same challenge to their own authority. Ne Win set up the *Mahanayaka*, or *mahana* for short, a committee of forty-seven monks all appointed by the government, to lay down policy for the *sangha*. The *mahana* was then replicated at division and township level, down through the governmental system.

The *mahana* was presented as being an instrument of harmonious co-operation between a benevolent Buddhist government and the *sangha*, but few monks were fooled. One of Mandalay's most prominent monastic heads, Ariyawuntha Bhiwunsa, told me that most monks did not accept the *mahanas* – "they are like a dictator . . . these monks have copied the dictators, who are trying to control the monks." The Saffron Revolution of 2007 finally exposed how badly the government had failed to take control of the *sangha* and mould Buddhism to its own ends.

As well as attempting to control the monks through the *Mahanayaka*, Ne Win, and later Than Shwe, were assiduous in trying to project themselves personally as good Buddhists, even if their cruelty and authoritarianism suggested otherwise. They, and other military officers, were responsible for the building of hundreds of pagodas around the country, to make merit and thus, according to some, atone for their earthly sins. Certainly, at many of the country's most prominent pagodas there are often photographs of Than Shwe and members of his family visiting and making offerings. Most famously, the military government was largely responsible for the construction of the present *hti* at the top of the Shwedagon pagoda, the holy of holies in Burmese Buddhism. There are photographs of the soldiers in their distinctive olive-green army fatigues hauling the *hti* to the top of the stupa in 1999; they are almost lost in a vast crowd of monks and onlookers, doubtless many of them cronies of the regime also trying to make merit.

The country's military rulers, like all Buddhists, also believed in *yadaya*, the practice of making merit, or doing a good deed, in order to stave off some misfortune that may have been predicted by a soothsayer or astrologer. It is plausible that the redenomination of the currency around the number nine might have been part of a *yadaya*. Like every Burmese boy, Than Shwe would almost certainly have served as a novice Buddhist monk over two periods in his young life; for a few days at aged three or four, and for a few weeks at aged seventeen or eighteen. There is also some evidence that after formally bowing out of the government in 2011 he may have spent substantial periods in a monastery. "The generals believed in Buddhism", says Dr Matt Walton, an expert on Burmese Buddhism, "and maybe they became more devout as they did more and more bad things."

Alongside the tradition of Theravada Buddhism is the mysterious world of the Burmese spirit cults, particularly of the *nats*. These are said to be the malevolent spirits of rebels and outlaws who had supernatural powers and met cruel and violent deaths resisting the rule of the Burman Kings. There is a pantheon of thirty-seven officially recognised *nats*, half of them women, called the Thirty-Seven Lords, as well as a host of lesser and more obscure *nats*. Most towns and villages have *nat* houses where Burmans can give offerings to appease these spirits, but the main centres for *nat* worship are Bago, Bagan, Mandalay and Mount Popa.

My Burmese friend who had introduced me to the astrologer was particularly fearful of two of the most powerful *nats*. She had visited the *nat* shrines in Bago to appease these two before her high-school exams in Yangon. As she explained to me: "You appease the *nat* by donating stuff to them, at the foot of their statues. It could be rice, whisky or cigarettes, whatever the individual *nat* liked. My *nats* liked whisky, fried chicken and smoked fish. I leave these by their statues, and the *nat*-soothers, who look after the *nat* shrines, will drink and eat it, or scatter it into the ground around the shrine." She passed her exams. Others looking for good luck employ these *nat*-soothers directly to appease the *nats*; the three-day *nat* festivals over which they preside are some of the most spectacular events in Burma.

Not every Burmese believes in the *nats*, and even if they do it is with different degrees of intensity. Those who are most fearful of the *nats*, for instance, do not eat pork. We will never know what role the *nats* played in the personal life of a man like Than Shwe, for instance. In general, though, the *nats* have, over time, been appropriated to support central royal power, and by extension contemporary central authority. The Burman kings, mainly Anawrahta, are considered to have subdued the evil spirits and turned them into benevolent *nats*, absorbing them into mainstream religion.[4]

White elephants

Royal symbolism abounds in Naypyidaw. Next to the Uppatasanti pagoda, tethered in their own separate pavilion, are five so-called "white elephants". These are albino elephants, more light pink, in fact, than white. They are extremely rare, and so have become near-magical symbols of power and good fortune in Burma, always associated with royalty and nobility. The more white elephants a king can accumulate, so it is believed, the greater his standing, and so Than Shwe made a great show of finding three of these elephants in the early 2000s. The naming of one elephant directly invoked this royal tradition; the poor beast was called "Royal Elephant that Bestows Grace upon the Nation".[5] The term "white elephant", meaning something expensive but useless, derives from this royal tradition. It was popularised following the circus impresario P. T. Barnum's experience with an elephant named Toung Taloung. He billed this beast as the "Sacred White Elephant of Burma". After paying a large amount of money to the king of Siam to purchase the elephant, and then going to great lengths to transport it to England, a disappointed Barnum discovered that his white elephant was actually "dirty grey in colour with a few pink spots".

The presidential palace in the new capital is obviously modelled on the old royal palace at Mandalay, home to the court of the last Burman kings, Mindon and Thibaw. The presidential palace, like that in Mandalay, is surrounded by a wide moat (although in this case not filled with water) and is accessible by two main bridges. In keeping with the generals' penchant for golf, the palace is also surrounded by a golf course and the vast empty road that stretches out at front is supposed to double up as an emergency runway. The public and waiting rooms are cavernous, allowing plenty of space for gargantuan chandeliers. "Is this as big as the White House?", asked an awe-struck Burmese journalist as we milled around the atrium during US Secretary of State Hillary Clinton's visit to President Thein Sein in November 2011. "Much bigger", I had to concede.

The president's reception room, where Thein Sein greeted Clinton, the first official high-level American guest to the country in thirty-odd years, is a barely disguised throne room. Everything is draped in gold and red; the president's high-backed chair looks, to all intents and purposes, like a coronation chair. By the second half of his rule, as Naypyidaw took shape, Than Shwe's own lifestyle matched that of a reigning monarch, a Burmese emperor. Occasionally, usually by accident, the world was allowed a glimpse into the obscenely lavish lifestyle of "King" Than Shwe. One such was the wedding of his daughter to her bridegroom Major Zaw Phyo Win in 2006. A leaked video of the wedding showed them sipping champagne and cutting a five-tier cake, apparently oblivious to the fact that their country was by now one of the poorest in the world. The wedding gifts that the couple received, including luxury cars and houses, were rumoured to be worth around $50 million, with sycophantic generals vying with each other to spend large amounts of money on gifts for the newly-weds, presumably to protect their own backs. There was public outrage when details of the wedding emerged, but Than Shwe and his immediate family floated above it all, buffered by priviledge and power.

As the original royal palace at Mandalay was bombed flat during the Second World War, first by the Japanese and then by the Allies, the military regime built a replica of it on the same spot in the 1990s. This was just one of many royal sites to be recreated by regimes anxious to physically recreate the royal past. The ancient city of Bagan, Burma's rival to Cambodia's Angkor Wat, was the victim of the most notorious restoration, having been so rebuilt in parts that it is still struggling to be listed as a UNESCO World Heritage site. Similary, there seem to be no architectural restrictions in Naypyidaw. The enormous, rambling parliament building is all mock-ancient Burmese style, with turrets and crenellations topping out the forbidding walls.

But tellingly, although there may be a parliament building, originally there was little accommodation for MPs, and certainly not for MPs from opposition parties (although that has now changed). The army's ruling proxy party, the Union Solidarity and Development Party (USDP), has a lavish headquarters, complete with pillars and a pediment. To complete the royal aura, the city, mainly comprised of the various government ministries and officials' housing, stretches out lavishly over hundreds of empty acres, creating an impression of space and power. Finally rid of the crowded, turbulent, alien streets of Rangoon, the generals generously built themselves vast sixteen-lane highways, all eerily empty of traffic. Indeed, the most striking difference between Naypyidaw and Mandalay or Yangon is that beyond the government compounds the place is almost entirely deserted. Many of the MPs and civil servants who were forced to move to Naypyidaw never brought their families with them, unwilling, perhaps, to inflict the loneliness on their wives and children.

On the fringes of the main government quarter of the city the regime's cronies and families built their own up-market hotels to cater for the anticipated influx of visiting diplomats and dignitaries. A large Chinese-built airport stands six miles outside the city, a dumb reproach to the spurious ambitions of Burma's generals. The monumental departures hall boasts thirty-two ticketing counters, supposedly destined for domestic and international flights, although as of 2014, only two were in operation, one for a privately-run shuttle service to Yangon and the other for the rather more infrequent and erratic "scheduled" flights laid on by the national airline, also to Yangon. Tellingly, like much of the rest of the city, the airport's gerry-built structure is already decaying. If Naypyidaw really is, as the Thai academic Dulyapak Preecharushh has charitably argued, "an important anti-colonialist project to recover Burmese national pride and maintain Burmese cultural identity in the context of globalisation"[5], then like the former capitals of Ava and Amarapura it may only serve its purpose for a brief moment before being reclaimed by the forests and fields from which it arose so abruptly.

The homogenous society

There is no doubt that the royal Burmese past that generals Ne Win and Than Shwe tried to appropriate for their own ends was, in its time, glorious.

The Burman monarchy used to be one of the most feared and respected in South-East Asia. Under the great warrior kings, the Burmans extended their sway over the Mon to the south, the Shan to the east and the Arakanese on the western coast. In the eighteenth century the Burmese army famously besieged and conquered the magnificent Siamese capital of Ayutthaya, at the time the most serious commercial and political rival to the Burmese court in the region. The razing of Ayutthaya forced the Siamese to relocate their capital to Bangkok, which was largely laid out according to the same plan as the old capital, now a UNESCO-designated city of ruins.

Thus, the experience of successive defeats by the British in the Anglo-Burman wars came as a devastating shock to the Burmese. It accounts, in many ways, for the generals' desperate, almost demented push to eradicate as much as they could of the colonial society that overwhelmed them, and to reclaim a purer, imperially dominant Burmese past. Aung San Suu Kyi, the daughter of General Aung San, has accurately contrasted the Indian experience of imperial conquest with that of the Burmese. It is a subject she knows about, as her mother was ambassador in New Delhi in the early 1960s.

"Conquest was an entirely new experience for the Burmese", writes Aung San Suu Kyi. "Unlike the people of India, who had been subjected to successive waves of foreign invaders from the north-west since their early history, the Burmese had not known any serious foreign intrusion other than a brief Mongol incursion which had destroyed Bagan in the thirteenth century." Indians have come to view the British occupation of their country not as a single devastating event, as the Burmese did, but as just one of a succession of foreign cultural and political intrusions that have shaped their country. One prominent Indian writer and historian, Raja Mohan, told me that for Indians, "colonialism is one minor, interesting encounter". Today thousands of Bengalis happily mill around Curzon's bombastic, white-stuccoed memorial to Queen Victoria in Kolkata. They enjoy it as a pleasant, cool escape from the city's stifling heat, whereas they could so easily have resented it, demolished it even, as a symbol of foreign occupation.

The Burmese, by contrast, viewed the British annexation of Burma as a one-off catastrophic event, an existential threat not only to their country but to their very identity. Aung San Suu Kyi continues:

The feeling that grew among the Burmese was . . . a more diffused xeno-phobia fed by a well-justified apprehension that their very existence as a distinct people would be jeopardised if the course of colonial rule was allowed to run unchecked. The threat to their racial survival came not so much from the British as from the Indians and Chinese who were the more immediate targets of twentieth-century nationalism. Not only did these immigrants acquire a stranglehold on the Burmese economy, they also set up homes with Burmese women, striking at the very roots of Burmese manhood and racial purity.[6]

Consequently, as early as 1939 a bill was passed in parliament (The Buddhist Women Special Marriage and Succession Bill) that attempted to discourage marriage between Indian males and Burmese females. Unfortunately, these sorts of bills have kept appearing through the decades. From 2013, no fewer than four bills started winding their way through the parliament, or one or other of its committees, attempting in various ways to regulate the private affair of marriage between men and women of different religions, to limit the number of children that Muslims can have and to prevent Buddhists from converting outside the faith. Some of these proposals originated with the monks, and all were designed, in one way or the other, to privilege the Burmese over other faiths, particularly Muslims.

Once the Burmese took power back from the colonialists, therefore, unlike the Indians they attempted to exorcise the demons of colonialism completely. The new post-independent state would therefore be a wholly Burman state, with Burman as the dominant culture. This political project started with the very first leader of "liberated" Burma, Ba Maw, leader of Japan's puppet government in 1943–5. He assumed the title of Naingandaw Adipadi, meaning Burmese head of state, borrowing a lot of the pomp and ceremony of the old kings to publicise and legitimise his rule. Ba Maw even dressed like the old kings. Furthermore, in line with the Japanese leadership principle, the new Burma was to be ruled very much from the centre and was to be a culturally homogenous state. Only one party, the Dobama Sinyetha Asiayone, or, later, the Greater Burma Party, would be in control, mobilising all Burmese; this party, as Ba Maw later explained, would be "a common melting pot for the native races of Burma from which will arise the Greater Burma nation. Our past tribal history has closed, tribal accounts are settled, a new nation and history now begins. In the past, parties overshadowed peoples. Now we are unifying from the right end, from the people."

In an important sense, all Burma's post-colonial governments, but especially those since the instigation of dictatorial military rule in 1962, have taken their cue from Ba Maw's political programme for the revitalisation of the Burmese people. There was no room, of course, for the colonial plural society, but more importantly for post-war Burma this also excluded the possibility of allowing any authentic expression of the culture and religion of the many other indigenous ethnic groups that were supposed to share the territory of Burma with the majority Burmans in the newly independent country. As one scholar has recently written, "Even before they gained political power, Burman leaders declared their superiority over the other ethnic groups and claimed that they were the rightful rulers of the country."[7]

Thus, when Ba Maw proclaimed that "tribal accounts are settled", what he meant was that the nation should be united under Burman hegemony. The Karen, Kachin, Chin, Mon, Shan and others of the so-called "hill tribes" were accepted as indigenous in the state's prescribed list of 135 ethnic groups, and so were supposed to have more rights than the immigrants of the plural society, even full citizenship. But in reality, from the 1960s onwards the military regime tried to construct a highly centralised, culturally homogenous Burman state, thus pitting them for decades against the Karen, Shan and more who saw themselves as having to refight older, pre-colonial wars against aggressive Burman revanchism – wars that are, essentially, still continuing.

These antagonisms had already been sharpened by the very different experiences of the Burmans, on the one hand, and of the hill peoples on the other, during the Second World War. Many of the minority ethnic groups, such as the Karen and the Kachin, were fighting on the side of the British and the Allies against the Burmans who, as we have seen, largely sided with the Japanese. Thus, the war in Burma came to be fought partly along racial lines, with the Japanese-trained BIA, composed mostly of Burmans, pitched against the Karen, Kachin and Chin, trained and supported by the British. This basic racial division fundamentally shaped Ba Maw's political convictions, as well as those of his Burman successors such as Ne Win and Than Shwe, most of whom had served with the BIA in the war. The two sides, the Burmans and the hill peoples, thus retain very different narratives of the war and its place in the development of an independent country.

At the very outset of building the new Burma there were, nonetheless, some attempts to accommodate a wider vision of Burma, principally to allay the quite justified suspicions of the minority ethnic groups that the freshly-minted country, led by Burmans, would quickly fall prey to a government of oppressive Burmese nationalism. The Panglong agreement of 1947, signed between General Aung San and the leaders of the Shan, Kachin and Chin peoples, just as the country was about to win freedom from Britain, promised full autonomy in internal administration for the frontier areas in principle, and envisioned the eventual creation of a Kachin State ruled by its own constituent assembly. Panglong also guaranteed that "Citizens of the Frontier Areas shall enjoy rights and privileges which are regarded as fundamental in democratic countries." This was the basis on which several ethnic groups reluctantly joined the new nation, and the Shan were even promised the right to secede altogether ten years after independence. But, as we shall see, the agreement was never fully implemented, something that has remained the main bone of contention between Burman and other ethnic-group leaders to this day.

The first post-war democratic Burmese government of the 1950s and early 1960s, largely under Prime Minister U Nu, also made some attempts to institutionalise this loose idea of a federal state. They spent federal money on projects for the country's many ethnic groups in a vague attempt to acknowledge and endorse the idea that the new state was not exclusively a Burman one. Broadcasts were started, for example, in twenty or so ethnic languages by the central Burmese Broadcasting Service, modelled on the BBC and based in Yangon. The Muslim Rohingya, whose existence is barely acknowledged today, remember being clearly identified in school textbooks.

Burmese brainwashing

Despite these gestures, however, the central thrust was always towards ethnic, cultural and religious homogeneity – to make Burman-ness a stand-in for an all-embracing national identity. It was U Nu, for instance, usually regarded as one of the more tolerant and democratic of the early independence leaders, who introduced Buddhism as the state religion in 1961, angering the largely Christian Kachin and Karen (although a separate bill, more of a fig leaf, was also enacted at the same time to guarantee freedom of worship). But it was really the military coup of 1962, which brought Ne Win to power, that marked the beginning of an all-out, state-sponsored drive towards Burmanisation. Whereas the Burman war against the plural society destroyed the engine room of the prosperous colonial economy, so the subsequent civil conflicts against the country's non-Burman ethnic groups drained the impoverished country of its slender reserves of money and lost it most of the international goodwill that had been its due at independence.

During the years of the military regime there were very few foreign books on sale in English, but one that could still be obtained was the novel *Burmese Days*. Presumably the generals allowed this to be sold because it offered a highly critical depiction of colonial power, written by an insider – Eric Blair, who later adopted the pen name George Orwell, a junior police officer serving in Burma from 1922 to 1927. But the Burmese like to joke that Orwell wrote not just one book about Burma, but three, so accurately did *Animal Farm* and *1984* predict what would happen to the country under the policy of Burmanisation. Naturally, these latter two were never for sale in Burma under the military regime. One sure sign of political change after Thein Sein became president was that the last two volumes of Orwell's "Burmese trilogy" finally hit the bookstands in Yangon, in 2013, and were eagerly devoured by a new generation.

As in Orwell's dystopian vision, the military came to encroach on virtually every aspect of life, no matter how obscure or unlikely, in order to shape people's views of the country as a one-party Burman society. Take language, for instance, a prime subject for Orwell and the basic denominator of communication and culture. It was only natural that the new authorities should start to replace all the old English names in the country; Rangoon's Phayre Street, named after a colonial historian, and Dalhousie Street, named after a British governor-general, for example, were traded in for the names of famous figures in Burmese history. The numbers on buses were changed into Burmese script.

This was commonplace for societies emerging from colonial rule, to reassert the indigenous culture. The same happened in Sudan, the first country to gain independence from Britain in Africa.

But the generals wanted to go much further. A new body called the National Language Commission ordered that the English language be dropped altogether from school curriculums as a language of instruction. It would only be taught as a second language. Much more importantly, the generals ordered that Burmese was to be the sole language used and taught throughout the entire country's school system, effectively denying all the ethnic groups in the union of Burma the right to use, teach or learn their own language.[8] This, more than anything, made language the central battleground of Burmanisation, the insistence that in this country of at least one hundred different languages, including at least three distinct language families (Tibeto-Burman, Mon-Khmer and Tai), everyone had to use only Burmese. It was a tongue that would have been as foreign to many of the Chin and Karen as Spanish or Russian.

In the words of an expert on the Burmese language, Dr Justin Watkins, a British academic from the School of Oriental and African Studies in London, millions of people who were not allowed to use their mother tongue were thus "linguistically disenfranchised", with devastating consequences. Alan Saw U, born in the late 1940s and one of the Karen's most articulate spokespeople, explains that this was the "main resentment of all the ethnic groups, that they could not teach or learn their own language", fuelling the armed conflict of the past fifty or so years. It was the tip of the spear of "forced assimilation", whereby all the non-Burman, non-Buddhist peoples of Burma would be thrust into accepting a Burman mono-culture. Minority ethnic languages were supposed to disappear down Orwell's "memory hole", and with it their distinct cultural and political identities.

The Kachin elders remember bitterly the time in the late 1960s when the orders arrived from Yangon that the Kachin language was no longer to be taught or used in their schools. Virtually all the centrally appointed teachers in the Kachin schools were Burmans, with no interest in learning or perpetuating the local ethnic language. Posters went up round the schools in Kachin State warning that "The speaking of a language that your teacher cannot understand is rude." Thus, the pupils were put off speaking Kachin even amongst themselves.

The Mon people felt the Burmese oppression of their language most keenly because they regarded themselves as being culturally superior to the Burmese; they were the founders, in part, of one of the region's language families, Mon-Khmer. The modern Burmese script is derived from Mon scholars. The Mon set up parallel working committees and support groups staffed by volunteers, often monks, to continue teaching their language, passing it down through the generations. This was dangerous work, and these efforts waxed and waned according to the severity of Burmese government repression at any given time. The official discrimination against non-Burman speakers also put the ethnic groups such as the Mon at a grave practical disadvantage, as those who could not become fluent in Burmese were then excluded from any official jobs in a country where the Burmese-speaking, Burman-dominated state was by some way the largest employer.

In 1989 the government went on the linguistic offensive again, passing the notorious Adaptation of Expressions Law. This claimed to be ridding the country of yet more old colonial names, but was in fact a further push for Burmanisation. The law was passed at a time when the regime felt particularly under pressure from the pro-democratic forces around the National League for Democracy, founded the year before. This law ordered the change of the English translation of Burmese place names, but only to reflect the translation of these place names from the language of the majority Burman group – Burmese – and not from the local language in which the places were geographically situated. These new names were thus far less inclusive as toponyms to the citizens of the whole of Burma than many of the spellings they replaced, as the British colonialists had usually taken great care to record the local names as they heard them, and then to render them as closely as possible in English. This had meant that the original English names were broadly reflective of the local ethnic ones, but these were now unceremoniously abandoned without any consultation with the local people who used them the most. Thus, the Burman ethnic group was renamed *Bamar*, and eight of the fourteen administrative state and division name spellings were altered as well, sowing confusion forevermore. Thus, Arakan became Rakhine; Karen was changed to Kayin; Magwe to Magway; Pego to Bago; Rangoon to Yangon, and so on.[9] As Watkins summarises, "It was a huge politicisation of place names, and a Burmese linguistic land-grab in somebody else's language." In general, linguistics as a subject was gradually dropped from Burma's universities. Even if a Burman had wanted to learn any one of the many minority ethnic languages that were used in his own country (rather than a Karen, say, having to learn Burman), it was now almost impossible to do so as there were so few competent teachers left.

The most notorious aspect of the 1989 law was the change in the country's official name, from Burma to Myanmar. This, again, was ostensibly done in the name of anti-colonialism. A seductive argument was advanced that as "Burma" was the name given to the country by the British, in order to throw off the colonial yoke completely the country now deserved a name that it had had before the British arrived – Myanmar. Moreover, so the argument went, as the name Burma reflected the existence only of the majority Burman ethnic group, so Myanmar better represented all the peoples of the country. In fact, as many have pointed out since, Myanmar and Burma were used pretty much interchangeably before the British arrived. Thus, "Burma" was never merely a colonial concoction, as Aung San Suu Kyi, for one, has argued: "No one should be allowed to change the name of the country without referring to the will of the people. They [the government] say that 'Myanmar' refers to all the Burmese ethnic groups, whereas 'Burma' only refers to the Burmese ethnic group, but that is not true. 'Myanmar' is a literary word for 'Burma' and it refers only to the Burmese ethnic group. Of course I prefer the word 'Burma'".

The name change further disenfranchised the non-Burman ethnic groups who had become used to forms of "Burma" to describe the whole country. To these groups, in the words of one expert body, "Myanma and its derivatives were totally alien words which were redolent only of the language of the dominant ethnic group." I use the word Burma throughout this book in recognition of their objections.

Just as language became an instrument of Burmanisation, so did education. What happened in the classroom increasingly became more about the maintenance of military control than equipping children with knowledge and skills. The result has been a disastrous decline in the country's educational standards over the past fifty years, starting with the forced closure of the excellent Christian missionary schools in the early 1960s and the expulsion of most of their overseas-born teachers. The solid Victorian red-brick buildings of the missionary schools were requisitioned by the state, and they remain, mostly, government-funded state schools.

The assault on the mission schools was understandable, inevitable even, to end or reduce the predominant position that these foreign schools occupied in the country's education system. But the missionary schools were never replaced by anything remotely as good or, often, by anything at all. It soon became clear that the generals' ambitions for education in Burma extended far beyond the eradication of a fading colonial influence.

The pedagogy of the oppressed

The process of forced acculturation, or Burmanisation, was to begin in school, and specifically with the textbooks. I sat down on one occasion with some schoolchildren in Yangon to discuss what they learned from their Grade 6 to Grade 9 history books – painfully thin, string-bound volumes – and the results were very illuminating. The Grade 6 book began with a longish account of the Burmese kings, and particularly of their military victories over the Thais and the sacking of their royal city of Ayutthaya. The pupils had learned a lot about Bagan, and the customs of the Burmans were explained in some detail. But there was almost nothing about the other ethnic groups in Burma. When they were referred to at all, the Mon, Shan and Karen were described as "colourful insurgents". The textbooks told of how their rebellions were dealt with easily by the mighty Burman army.

There was an explanation of Indian immigration to Burma on the coat-tails of the British, but only the evils of the *chettyars* were referred to in any detail. There was no mention of Islam or Muslim immigration, or of other religions. History ended with Ne Win and the imposition of army rule to care for the country. Presumably, to judge by the official silence on the course of Burmese history since then, that's what the munificent Burmese army is still doing.

The young girls I spoke to had only learned about the old kings to pass their exams, and they clearly couldn't remember much about them. To them, the names of the Burmese kings were just boring old facts that they needed to retain in their minds for a few weeks in order to move up a class or two. But then they were mostly Burman girls in the Burmese capital of Yangon. This same, partial history of modern Burma, however, was taught in all the government schools all over the country, and in the lands of the Karen, Chin or Kachin, this same royal Burmese narrative was much more politically charged. All the more so as it was taught only in the Burmese language, and to the almost total exclusion of the local history of the country's other ethnic groups.

I met up with one of the brightest of the younger generation of Chin, human-rights activist Cheery Zahau, in Yangon, and she remembered using many of these same textbooks during her schools days in Sagaing Division, west of Mandalay, in the 1990s. To her, it had been one long propaganda exercise in Burman nationalism. She remembers being taught (in Burmese) all about the heroic Burmese kings of old, whereas the various minority ethnic groups mostly had "negative connotations", according to the teachers' accounts. Thus, the Shan "used a lot of drugs"; the Karen were just "separatists"; and the Chin, her own group, were "backward and uncivilised". Many young Kachin swear that in the old Burmese geography textbooks, which their fathers were obliged to use in the late 1950s, the Kachin were described as "savages living in a mountainous area in the north". None of my Kachin friends were able to produce this book for me, but it's still what many Kachin firmly believe.

In general terms, these negative images of non-Burmans, cultivated by the official textbooks and in the schoolroom, were also equated with disloyalty and opposition to the state. A sound Burmese, a good citizen of Burma, could, by this account, only truly become so by renouncing his or her own minority ethnic identity – and thus by implication his or her naturally subversive tendencies. As the scholar Matthew Walton has written, "by equating non-Burman ethnicity with disloyalty, [the military government] views those ethnic identities as something that non-Burmans must overcome in order to become part of the nation." I have been told many stories of Muslims and Christians being asked to convert to Buddhism, for instance, or change their Karen or Kachin name to a Burmese one, in order to be considered for even quite lowly jobs in the Burmese government bureaucracy. However, if people did make the effort to disguise their own ethnicity and religion in this way to join the one and true Burmese nation, they found that they still remained slightly apart, and suspect. It was, in other words, an impossible task.

In Grade 8 at school, Cheery, a Baptist, learned a great deal about the life cycle of the Buddha, but there was nothing about other religions such as Islam or her own Christianity, which were treated as "alien creeds". In sum, she felt "brainwashed". Cheery finished high school in 1999 and, like many Chin, escaped over the border to India where she joined a Chin women's group in Mizoram. Here, she confesses that it took a year "to de-learn everything that I had learned in school . . . my dad had to work on me very hard to get the idea that the *Tatmadaw* [Burmese army] is the protector of the nation and the Burmese is the ruling class out of my mind."

By her own account, though, a lot of her friends "remained brainwashed". Mostly, this was because she and her peers in the isolated, sanctioned Burma of the 1990s and early 2000s had "no access to any other sources of information, TV, papers, the Internet or anything". Thus, what they read in school textbooks, which were by some accounts sanctioned at the very top of the military leadership, and what they heard from the government-appointed teachers, almost all of whom were Burmese, assumed canonical importance. Independent enquiry or questioning of the teacher, a traditional authority figure in Burmese society, were strongly discouraged.

Indeed, the authority of the teacher was reinforced by painfully boring rote learning. It is a system that still prevails throughout the Burmese education system, even in the universities. One rather more free-thinking teacher, a 40-year-old Hindu in Yangon, still today fearful of being quoted by name, told me more about how this pedagogical method worked, and the effect that it has had on Burma's children. The system of "parrot-learning or spoon-feeding totally blocked students from having critical or creative thinking", he told me. Academic performance was judged merely on how accurately a pupil managed to repeat everything the teacher said, and students had to stick only to what was prescribed in the texts for information. As a pedagogical system, of course, rote learning had been very common in schools all over the world, especially in Britain up to the 1950s, but it was maintained in Burma decades after it had passed out of fashion elsewhere (although not in other totalitarian countries like China). It was clear to most victims of this system that the main purpose of rote learning in Burma was to ensure that young boys and girls would never learn to question any authority, and by extension that of their military rulers.

This was truly the *Pedagogy of the Oppressed*, except not quite how Paulo Freire, the celebrated anti-colonialist Brazilian educator, had imagined it. My friendly teacher told me that if his pupils had been equipped with some faculties of critical thought and independent enquiry, then "the student could sort out right from wrong for himself, and wouldn't be easily persuaded by others – essential ingredients to develop a democratic system in the country." He himself always tried discreetly to import some alternative sources of information into the classroom – copies of *Reader's Digest*, *National Geographic* and *Discovery Channel Magazine* were his favourites – to compete with the government textbooks, to show that these could not be relied upon to give the whole truth about the world.

In any case, regardless of how good or well intentioned the teacher, it was usually impossible for children to learn much at the government schools anyway. The number of pupils in a class, even at the best high school, could be seventy or more. I know Burmese children today who are being taught in classes of eighty – and in the hill areas that number can rise to one hundred. At that point, a Burmese woman told me, it was mainly a question of crowd control. Neither do the children attend school for very long. Most schools operate a two-shift system: the first welcomes pupils at 7 or 7.30 in the morning, but ends as early as 11 or 11.30, the second shift starts at midday and ends at 4 p.m. These four-hour days include a half-hour break.

Despite some attempts at reform in 2013 by the new government of President Thein Sein, in this respect little has changed. To compensate for the shortness of the official school day, as well as the fact that they learn so little, most children whose families can afford it have private tuition (in class sizes of about twenty-five) for at least a couple of hours a day. Thus, a child's education, ostensibly free at the government school, can in fact become quite costly. Such is the expense that many families often choose just one child, the eldest or the brightest, to receive a full education. Most families that can manage it send these children to private school for the entire main four-month holiday (March to June), costing them about $20 for thirty-two hours of teaching. Here the children will often be taught by those exact same teachers who teach them at the government schools.

Thus, in effect, many children in Burma are being taught twice. They attend the government school principally to get the officially recognised leaving certificate, which any future employer will ask for, or to go on to university, and then go to private classes in order to actually learn something. This can be taken to almost absurd extremes, especially in the hill areas. In 2014, I visited a Baptist Christian leadership-training centre in Wai Maw Township, in the middle of Kachin State. At the time, the centre was also doubling up as a student refugee camp, taking in the children of those Kachin who had been forced to flee their homes by the Burmese army. The 110 Kachin children, of all ages, were obliged to attend the two nearby government high schools – but on top of this they were also putting in two extra shifts of classes each day at the centre. Thus, their day began at 4.30 a.m., in order to be ready for two hours of classes at the Baptist centre starting at 6 a.m. They went off to government school at 9 a.m., and on returning they did another two hours of classes starting at 4 p.m. It was lights out at 10 p.m., and no rest at the weekend. There were afternoon classes at the centre on Saturdays and Sundays, and the odd improving lecture in the evening. Even twelve-year-olds were doing this long, long day.

Missionary schools are still banned in Burma, so these boys and girls could claim no official credit, or qualification, for the hours of extra work they were putting in at the Baptist centre. The best the Baptists could hope for was that they were giving their charges a good unofficial education to make up for the flimsy official education. Some of the Kachin pupils I spoke to admitted to being tired at the end of a schoolday, but none of them were complaining. They got nothing out of the government school, they said, except the leaving certificate. History, as usual, was all about the Burmese kings; almost all the teachers were Burmese and all the teaching was in Burmese. The Kachin boys and girls struggled with Burmese, and complained that they learned nothing about the Kachin people, culture or geography; they were extremely bored, as all they were allowed to do was listen to the teacher drone on. They would memorise stuff for an exam, and then forget it.

More vexing still, for Chemistry, Physics, Biology and Maths the textbooks were in English, in order to allow the Burmese authorities to claim that they were meeting international standards, yet these subjects were still taught in Burmese, by teachers who knew almost no English. The art of passing an exam, therefore, was to memorise the passages of English in the book and try to apply them to a question when it came up. Hence, the popular joke in Burmese schools that if a pupil hides a small piece of revision paper up their sleeve to copy off during an exam, that's called cheating, but if he or she copies out whole sentences and paragraphs from memory to answer an exam question, that's called a thesis, and you get a degree for it.

The United Nations Development Programme estimated that public spending on education in Burma constituted less than 2 per cent of the country's GDP in 2009, a tiny amount by international standards.[10] Spending on health was also miniscule, only about 0.5 per cent of GDP. In 2000, the World Health Report said that Burma had the world's worst health system bar only the desperately poor and war-ravaged west African state of Sierra Leone.[11] By way of contrast, spending on the military amounted to about 40 per cent of the national budget, although in very recent years this figure has come down significantly. But this budget also provided the military with the money to run its own schools for the sons and daughters of the military within the army cantonments. They are much better than the ordinary government high schools. These all count as government schools, of course, but as Orwell reflected, some are more equal than others.

One of the most serious consequences of the gross shortage of qualified teachers, vast class sizes, chronic lack of textbooks and crumbling old school buildings (frequently unusable in the rainy season) has been, by many accounts, a steep decline in literacy and numeracy rates. As usual, in the rural areas, especially among the Kachin, Karen and other minority ethnic groups, the situation is usually much worse than in the Burman-dominated cities. The UN-sponsored census of 2014, for instance, found that whereas an average of about 90 per cent of adults were literate in the country as a whole, this figure sank to 74 per cent in Kayin state and 65 per cent in Shan state, reflecting the inequity of spending throughout the country. Even when there was so little money to go around as in education, the Burmans still received the lion's share.

If anything, higher education fared even worse than the schools under military rule. The authorities were well aware that the student body of Yangon University, sitting in plush, extensive grounds on the outskirts of the city, had been the epicentre of resistance to colonial rule (after all, Aung San and many of the generals had been there). From the very beginning, therefore, the generals were determined to prevent students from undermining their own rule. One of their very first acts after grabbing power was to blow up the famous Student Union building where Aung San and others had plotted in the 1930s. Troops stormed the campus in 1974 after a wave of demonstrations, but it was the large and widespread anti-government protests of 1988 that finally sealed the fate of the universities. Those protests were again mainly led by students, so afterwards the military regime set about hollowing out not only Yangon but the country's other colleges and universities, to prevent them from ever again becoming loci of resistance to the government. Thus, what had previously been one of the region's best tertiary education systems was largely destroyed solely for political purposes.

Khin Lay, once a prominent NLD figure and close aide to Aung San Suu Kyi, remembers the assault on Yangon University well. She was studying physics there in 1988 (her future husband was studying economics), when they were caught up in that year's pro-democracy protests. Up to that point, the course and teachers had been very good. After 1988, however, classes were suspended for months at a time, and most other non-academic activities were halted altogether. Eventually, all regular lectures were stopped as well. Then in the 1990s Yangon, like other urban universities, was entirely gutted of its 60,000 or so students, to be redistributed around a collection of new, smaller universities on the fringes of the capital: Dagon University, East Yangon University, Yangon Technological University and the University of Computer Studies. The sole purpose of this dispersal was to ensure that there would never again be a critical mass of young, educated, relatively freethinking people to challenge the government's authority on its doorstep. As these new universities were so remote it often took the students hours to get to them, wasting much of the day.

By universal consent, these new universities were, and remain, terrible. They operate with tiny budgets, few lecturers and little teaching. Students could pick up the requisite degree at the end of a course, but as employers well knew such pieces of papers were practically worthless as a guide to a student's real ability and intelligence. Hence, it is common for job adverts in the Burmese papers to ask applicants to provide evidence of a particular skill as well as a university degree – so at least they will have some vaguely useful qualification.

If the standard of higher education slumped badly in the Burman heartlands, among other ethnic groups and in the hill areas it positively plummeted.

An intelligent, amiable Kachin, now an English teacher, told me of his experiences at Myitkyina University, the most important in Kachin State, during the early 2000s. He studied English language for three years, but the student/teacher ratio was so bad, about one hundred to one, that he actually never met his lecturer – not once – to discuss his work. Like at the schools, all teaching was by rote learning: "I just sat in class, listened to my teacher and copied out all the bits in English that we had to recite." He stayed the three years necessary to pick up his own piece of paper, but acknowledges that he only really learned his English outside the university. His contemporaries told me very similar stories. Sometimes these institutions were also used as instruments of ethnic filtering. In Sittwe, for instance, I was told that the university that had been built on the edge of the city had mostly admitted only Buddhist Rakhine students – very few Muslim Rohingya had ever been allowed in and certainly not in proportion to their numbers.

Those few who could afford it went abroad for their further education, often to America or Australia. For the sons of the elite, and for those who wanted to move up in the regime, there was another well-established option, the Defence Services Academy (DSA) at Pyin Oo Lwin, just outside Mandalay, the former British hill-station previously known as Maymyo. Set up in 1954, the DSA was modelled on Sandhurst and West Point, respectively the British and American military colleges, to train the officer corps of the army, air force and navy. Aged about sixteen, candidates to enter the DSA sat two separate tests after the matriculation exams, one physical, the other psychological. Courses lasted three or four years, but only the last year was concerned strictly with military training. The first two years were largely devoted to those subjects – maths, science, basic literacy – that the aspiring officers had never been given the chance to learn adequately at school. In short, the DSA course was designed in large part to make up for the educational shortcomings that the military inflicted on everyone else.

The literary *Kempeitai*

Strict censorship was the means by which the government ensured that school children and everyone else had as little alternative information as possible. This was handled by the Press Scrutiny Division, set up after the 1962 coup, later called the Press Scrutiny and Registration Division (PSRD). Appropriately enough, the office was housed in the former headquarters of the *Kempeitai*, wartime Japan's dreaded secret police, the equivalent of Germany's Gestapo. One prominent journalist, Pe Myint of the *People's Age*, told me that in the old days the director of the PSRD seemed to be very proud of the connection and used to boast to him that he and his staff were the "*Kempeitains* of literature". Unfortunately, this was all too true.

Pe Myint described to me how the system worked. All editors of privately owned newspapers, magazines and journals had to submit their articles to the PSRD for pre-publication censorship, and then return with the galley proofs so that the censors could double check that all the offending words, passages or even whole articles had been taken out. The system was as cumbersome and long-winded as it could possibly be, with the result that all the independent publications could only be weeklies or monthlies. Government publications, on the other hand, like the perennial *New Light of Myanmar*, were churned out daily. The *New Light of Myanmar* continues its work of reporting the good news about all the wonderful things that the government does to this day.

Most of the censors, about one hundred of them, were from the army. Many would have trained in intelligence, propaganda and psychology, giving them an educated eye for spotting anything that journalists might try to sneak through. They were organised into teams with a strict hierarchy of supervision. Armed with red marker pens they were rotated frequently, to ensure that they did not become too friendly with the journalists. Nonetheless, some of them clearly did, and Pe Myint recounts how some censors were inspired to be writers themselves: "They thought they had learned their trade from the stuff they had censored. They then had their own stories published in the independent magazines – and they had to be published, or else!"

Beyond such fraternising, censorship was a deadly serious business. If the censors' amendments were not followed to the letter, literally, then editors and journalists could go to jail immediately. Unsurprisingly, several prominent journalists became founding members of the NLD, compounding their sins in the eyes of the government. One prominent journalist, Soe Thein, better known in Burma by his pen name Maung Wuntha, was jailed three times for his involvement with the NLD. He was only released for the last time in 2001. A charming and inspiring man, he became a powerful advocate for a free press after the military regime started to change in 2011, before his untimely death from cancer in 2013. He was also one of the best at playing cat and mouse with the censors, to smuggle real news past them. He learned, so he told me, to "write between the lines". He used metaphors, literary allusions and historical comparisons to disguise his commentaries on political events, trusting that his readers would understand references where the censors did not.

Others did the same. Soe Thein remembered one example of the genre particularly well; no mention of Aung San Suu Kyi was ever allowed, so the dilemma then arose as to how to report her release from house arrest in November 2010. One sports paper cannily employed some seemingly innocuous headlines from English premiership football. The list "Sunderland Freeze Chelsea", "United Stunned by Villa" and "Arsenal Advance to Grab Their Hope" was highlighted in varying colours to give readers the real news: "Su Free Unite and Advance to Grab the Hope."

The great unmentionables

The government was particularly antagonistic towards Muslims. As far as possible, they were excluded from the mainstream of national life. In Rakhine State, the local Muslim Rohingya, numbering up to one million or so, out of a total population of about five million, were not even recognised. The Emergency Immigration Act of 1974 was passed specifically to ensure that this was so. Since they were therefore considered to be little better than illegal immigrants the Rohingya enjoyed no constitutional rights, and so were completely defenceless against the waves of attacks upon them in the following decades, often led directly by the Burmese army. Some of their mosques were demolished, to make way for a variety of sports stadia, police accommodation, roads and even pagodas. Cemeteries were also built over. In 1978 and 1991, following serious bouts of such destruction, and harassment, more than 200,000 Muslims fled across the border into what had by then become Bangladesh.[12]

But such acts of violent agression against Muslims were not restricted to Rakhine State; there were many similar stories from all over Burma. In Myitkyina, capital of Kachin State, for instance, the central Muslim cemetery was destroyed to allow for new buildings to house police families. In Lashio, in northern Shan State, the central Muslim cemetery was moved well outside the city because apparently it did not comply with sanitary regulations. In its place the authorities put up yet more police accommodation, and parking space for trucks. And just as the Rohingya were not even counted as citizens of the country, so the government did as much as it could to downplay the significance of the Muslim community as a whole both numerically and spiritually.

Thus, in the census of 1983, for instance, the number of Muslims in the country was very likely deliberately under-reported. Out of a population said to be just 34 million, itself an improbably low figure, only 3.9 per cent were identified as Muslims. But this census certainly did not count the Rohingya. In fact, many agree that the real figure is more like 10 per cent of the population, making Muslims the largest religious minority in the country, ahead of Christians, and second only to Buddhists. And whereas individual government members and generals have been active patrons of many Buddhist monasteries, pagodas, schools and the like, the Islamic component of Burma's heritage and culture has barely been acknowledged, let alone supported or protected.

As a final insult towards Burma's many different ethnicities, all round the country the government built cultural museums in the capitals of the ethnic minority states, mainly designed for tourists. But these museums were built without any consultation with local people, whose culture they were supposed to represent. They seemed primarily designed to portray Kachin or Shan culture as quaint relics of the pre-colonial past rather than as vital, contemporary ways of life. The dank, underfunded and rarely visited state museums are much resented by local people, but particularly by the Mon. Indeed, the Mon State Cultural Museum in Moulmein is singularly gloomy and depressing. Its dusty collection of musical instruments, texts and ceramics is so poorly illuminated that even on a sunny day I was issued with a flashlight at the reception desk to navigate my way around.

It's much the same story with the National Museum in Yangon, put up in the mid 1990s. The big, airy ground floor is devoted to the Burmese kings; the centrepiece is the enormously impressive golden Lion Throne of King Thibaw. In 1902, the British shipped the throne out to India where the Burmese court was living in exile, but it was returned to the newly independent country in 1948. There are expansive maquettes of the royal palace at Mandalay, as well as several elaborate golden betel receptacles salvaged from the old court. Upper levels deal with the natural history of the country, music and the visual arts – but it's only on the very top floor that there is finally a very dimly lit "Showroom for the Culture of the National Races". Instead of maquettes there are mannequins dressed in local ethnic costumes, and lots of bows and arrows, spears and drums. The general impression is of picturesque, backward people living on the fringes of a more civilised Burman society.

Soldiers and spooks

The most important institution for the military regime, of course, was the army itself, known by its Burmese name *Tatmadaw*. To this day, it remains the most powerful organisation in the country. It has usually taken the lion's share of the national budget, contains virtually the entirety of the national leadership, occupies a crucial role in the economy through the existence of various holding companies, and above all else provides the very *raison d'être* for the military regime to hold on to power. For according to the mantra of the generals, repeated at length every 27 March on Armed Forces Day, the *Tatmadaw* is the only Burmese institution that can stop the "disintegration" of the Union of Myanmar and safeguard the constitution. This is shorthand for arguing that only the army can coerce all the ethnic groups into accepting central Burman authority. Thus, only the army has the right to rule a united Burma.

A great deal of this fervent, self-righteous belief in the central, guiding role of the military stems from the army's traumatic experiences in the very first years of the newly independent republic of Burma. The *Tatmadaw* was founded by General Aung San in September 1945. Aung San Suu Kyi is revered by many Burmese not only for her attachment to democracy, but more simply as the daughter of the country's independence hero and founder of the Burmese army.

In agreement with the retreating British authorities the new Burmese army incorporated the Patriotic Burmese Force and the British Burma Army into one supposedly "united" force. It was to be an amalgam, therefore, of those Burmese who had fought on either side of the wartime divide, often against each other. The Patriotic Burmese Force (PBF) was Aung San's successor to his Burma Independence Army, which had fought largely for the Japanese, while the British Burma Army was composed of those who had stayed loyal to the British, including all those now well-trained ethnic militias. There were thus a total of fifteen rifle battalions at the time of independence, all organised along ethnic lines, including, for instance, the Karen and Kachin Rifles. Only four battalions were drawn from the PBF. The head of the new army was a famous Karen fighter, General Smith Dun.

Not surprisingly, perhaps, this flimsy alliance of historical antagonists fell apart almost as soon as the new nation declared independence. The Karen rebelled against the new Burmese-dominated government and so the Karen Levies soon went over to the rebel side. Three Burmese battalions deserted to join a powerful communist insurgency. All in all, the army lost nine of its fifteen battalions within a year of independence. The remainder, down to only about two thousand men at one point, fought desperate battles on the outskirts of Rangoon itself against the Karen and the communists. It was remarkable that U Nu's weak and uncertain first post-independence government survived at all. But even if the *Tatmadaw* just managed to turn back its various opponents from taking the capital, from the very beginning the army failed to exert any authority over vast swathes of the country beyond Rangoon. To a lesser extent, that remains true even today, sixty years later.

As a Karen himself, General Smith Dun was obviously suspect as a commander of the army fighting Karen rebels, so he was sacked in 1949. He was replaced by Ne Win, the man who, more than anyone, remodelled the *Tatmadaw* into what it is today. He had been one of Aung San's Thirty Comrades trained by the Japanese during the war, and some have remarked on how the *Tatmadaw* came to take on a very Japanese hue in its tactics and training during the 1950s.[13] Much more importantly, however, advancement up the military came to depend almost entirely on how close you were to the golf-loving Ne Win. His old regiment was the 4th Burma Rifles, which eventually supplied most of the military's top hierarchy as well as the members of the junta, or Revolutionary Council, that took over after 1962.

Ne Win's mission was to ensure that the army would never again be threatened with the sort of humiliation that it had faced in 1948. He turned a small, underequipped, multi-ethnic army into a vast, sprawling, largely Burman military-economic complex that came to dominate every aspect of national life. The numbers alone tell a large part of the story. From just a couple of thousand in 1948, by the 1980s the *Tatmadaw* was 186,000 strong. By 1999, it had reached 370,000, and by 2010 it might well have topped 400,000.[14] By way of contrast, Britain, a wealthy country with a population roughly the size of Burma's, has about 90,000 troops.

The main task of this huge army was not to defend the country from foreign invasion, but to fight the government's internal enemies. The Burmese armed forces, therefore, focused almost entirely on counter-insurgency, against both the communists, mainly in the east of the country, and the various ethnic rebel militias, such as the Kachin Independence Army (KIA), the Karen National Liberation Army (KNLA) and the Shan State Army. To fight its civil wars the Burmese army got increasingly sophisticated weapons from an unlikely selection of overseas partners, including, in the early days, Britain and West Germany. Cold-war America, keen, as ever, to help anyone who was fighting communists, gave weapons to the *Tatmadaw*, before China probably became the main supplier from the 1990s onwards.

Under Ne Win, from the 1960s onwards, the army developed its main counter-insurgency strategy, called the "four cuts". The aim was to cut off armed opposition groups from their support in their rural, or jungle, heartlands by depriving them of food, funding, information and new recruits. In practice, this often amounted to a ruthless scorched-earth policy of simply forcing people out of their villages to new sites chosen by the military, burning their crops and killing suspected insurgent sympathisers. The army also closed access to large areas of Karen or Kachin land by blocking roads and rivers. In effect, every village community had to make a stark choice, in the words of one commentator, to "fight, flee or join the *Tatmadaw*".[15] The four cuts strategy was applied first in the Naga and Kachin hills, and then most devastatingly in the Shan and Karen States. The latter was particularly ravaged by the

Tatmadaw's campaign. Hundreds of thousands were forced to flee over the nearby border to Thailand where many of them still live in long-established refugee camps hugging the hills that separate the two countries.

The cuts "strategy" involved gross human-rights abuses, including the well-documented rape of women, torture, summary executions and more. Many witnesses have also testified to the use of conscripted labour and the employment of civilians and prisoners as human minesweepers. According to a member of the Free Burma Rangers, a group that infiltrates the eastern Burmese borders to help the persecuted villagers, "If the Burmese army is trying to move something they don't want the resistance [ethnic militia groups] to destroy, for example a bulldozer to build roads, they often put people in front of it, usually about thirty or so, to clear the area of landmines and to step on them if there are any."

This practice continues, it seems, right up to the present. During fighting against the Kachin in northern Shan State in 2014, soldiers were still arresting local villagers and using them either as porters or as human minesweepers. One such conscripted porter told the Democratic Voice of Burma: "They do not deliberately enter into villages and arrest villagers but they arrest those who are working at their fields near the villages located along their way . . . Burmese soldiers force us to walk in front of them in a group of ten to twenty to clear mines, sometimes they don't even ask us to carry a thing, just ask us to walk in front of them."[16]

Some have suggested that it was the very implementation of the four cuts strategy that drove the *Tatmadaw* to the depths of barbarity and callousness for which it has become notorious. Others argue that such was the feeling of racial animosity against the Karen, Kachin and other ethnic groups among the Burmese that the *Tatmadaw*'s soldiers were perfectly happy to prosecute the dreadful strategy from the start. A senior officer in the Kachin Independence Army, Lieutenant Colonel Myangyng Naw Li, has been fighting the Burmese army in the Kachin hills since 1968, and when I spoke to him in Myitkyina in 2014 he was able to shed some light on the motives of his lifelong opponents.

He joined when he was just twelve years old and has thus seen the four cuts strategy up close for many years. These were his views of the Burmese army:

I was very young when I started fighting against the Burmese troops. I heard they were looting, raping children etc. At first I did not believe these stories, but when I started fighting, I realised that they did do this. They wanted to clear the [Kachin] areas completely. They tried to destroy everything, pigs, cows, livestock, and burn the houses. They had clearly had systematic training to do this. They targeted children as well. When Burmese troops came to villages, usually the villagers ran away. Burmese troops stayed, and when the villagers came back from their hiding places, they shot them. I heard a lot about this, then they would loot the village, and torture and rape women. Why would they do this? It was attractive for Burmese foot-soldiers; they were told by their officers that if they fought the KIA they could take anything from the villages, including the women, alcohol, goods etc.

Clearly, this has been going on for so many decades now that Burmese soldiers feel that it is virtually their natural right to rape Kachin women. And, at best, their officers don't seem particularly perturbed by what they do. This is an edited account of a victim's testimony of a rape by a Burmese soldier of a mixed-raced Kachin/Shan girl just a few years ago, collected by a Kachin NGO:

On November 7, 2011, about 12 (noon) a Burmese soldier got drunk and came into the village. My name is Htwe Htwe, 10 years old and was attending Grade-1 in Basic Education High School . . . At lunch break, I went home and while I was eating my lunch, a man came into my home. I had never seen that man in the village, but I knew the clothes he was wearing. The clothes he was wearing were the clothes of the neighbouring old man.

The man spoke to me in Burmese, but I did not understand and did not know the Burmese language. As I did not understand what he said the man got angry and threw away the rice plate that I was eating. And he dragged me to my bedroom, later to my parents' room. In the room, he took off all my clothes, I attempted to run away, but he grabbed me very tightly. He also put some cloths in my mouth and I could not shout for help . . . and he raped me. After he raped me, I bite [*sic*] his hand and ran away to my grandmother's home.

We complained to a Burmese military officer and the officer let my teacher and my grandmother look for the soldier who raped me. After the rape, I was not able to walk for four days, as it was very painful.[17]

The victim's grandmother continued:

We looked for the soldier, but he ran away and we could not catch him. In the evening, two officers . . . came to the house of Htwe Htwe's parents and asked their forgiveness paying 30,000 kyat ($30). Those two officers requested to let the case end here. I said that I would call the headman of the village, but they did not let me call the headman. We took the money, but it was not that we were satisfied and happy, it was because we were afraid of their guns. [Even if] they give us 1 million kyat we could not be satisfied.

Unfortunately, the *Tatmadaw* operates in such tightly sealed official secrecy that we shall probably never be able to make such judgements as to whether the soldiers are encouraged to do this sort of action by officers, whether they do it voluntarily, or whether the whole army had just become so warped that rape is now a collective reflex action. Certainly, no Burmese general has ever apologised for the army's actions, even among the reformers around Thein Sein. Equally, every Armed Forces Day the head of the army continues to offer up exactly the same justification for the army's role in the state, as the sole guarantor of national unity, solidarity etc.

As well as developing the army's counter-insurgency arm, the military regimes also paid special attention to the black arts of intelligence gathering, psychological warfare and electronic warfare, including eavesdropping and signals intelligence. Ne Win's special creation, writes one expert, was the army's notorious Military Intelligence Service (MIS). This was founded by Tin U, who had been trained in Britain and America. MIS was regularly purged, a testimony to its success as one of Asia's most effective secret police forces. It gathered information not only on obvious opponents of Burma's military governments, but also on members of the government as well. Tin U was thus eventually arrested and imprisoned in 1983 for being too good at his job, having collected so much incriminating information on his superiors that he had become a threat rather than an asset. His successor, Khin Nyunt, who also took control of the Directorate of Defence Services Intelligence, was similarly purged by Than Shwe in 2004. Khin Nyunt was only released from jail in a general amnesty in 2012. But twenty-one of those military intelligence officers who were arrested with him remained behind bars, long after most political prisoners had been released.[18]

A high priority was given to psychological warfare, or "psy-war". The Directorate of Psychological Warfare was set up in the mid 1950s at a time when army officers were flying around the world cherry-picking the best ideas for such activities from countries as diverse as Yugoslavia, Israel, America, Pakistan and Britain. One retired Burmese officer described to me through an interlocutor how psy-war worked, as he was given a lecture on it by a major in psy-war while stationed in Lower Burma in the early 1990s. The visiting major was training his audience in how propaganda should be conducted, and he divided the field into three types. The first, "white propaganda", was concerned with giving real, "correct" information to people. The second, "black propaganda", was concerned with giving out misinformation, or straight lies (for this to work successfully, he said, "you just repeat it endlessly"). The third, more intriguingly, was called "brown propaganda". The major said that this was what the regime used to "change the mindset of the people."

Brown propaganda was, and remains, the murkiest activity of psy-war, for it entailed the military getting deeply involved in propaganda work masquerading as ordinary books, magazines and even entertainment. One Western researcher, Mary Callahan, was given access to the archives of the *Tatmadaw* of the 1950s, and she has written that "over the next decade, psy-war initiatives included . . . sponsoring *pwe* (traditional variety show) performances, radio shows and pamphlet publication and distribution." They moved into commercial magazine publication. One popular magazine they started successfully undercut a rival leftist publication that was very critical of the *Tatmadaw*, forcing it to close. Naturally, the psy-war magazine bore no trace of its origins within the military.[19]

Another example that the psy-war major boasted about in his lecture to my military officer was a notorious book that circulated in the early 2000s propagating lies and myths about Islam and Muslims. Called *Myò pyauk hma sò yauk teh* (roughly, *Fear of Losing Our Race*) in Burmese, this had been produced anonymously, but was allegedly the work of the psy-ops division. It was full of spurious references and footnotes, to give it an air of authenticity, and was made widely available. It was intended as a sort of Buddhist Burmese version of *The Protocols of the Elders of Zion*, an earlier hoax purporting to expose the world conspiracy for Jewish domination. From its very beginnings in the mid 1950s, psy-war work was explicitly political, designed to buttress the legitimacy of the Burman-dominated *Tatmadaw* by any means.

After 1988, with most of the ethnic militias and the communists no longer posing a real threat to the integrity of the nation, much of this intelligence, black propaganda and surveillance apparatus could be applied to the pro-democracy movement that emerged under Aung San Suu Kyi. Thereafter, Burma became very much a classic Orwellian police state, with an intricate variety of human and electronic eavesdropping. Many channels of communication were banned altogether, such as the Internet, smartphones and international SIM cards. When they were allowed, the secret police were sure to be involved.

Unsurprisingly, the choice by successive military regimes to expand the *Tatmadaw* to such an extent, and to build up its related intelligence agencies, introduced massive financial distortions into the economy, with crucial consequences for the political economy of the country as a whole. Devoting as much as 40 per cent of the budget to the military had catastrophic consequences. Furthermore, as this was a proportion of a fast-shrinking national income anyway, even this 40 per cent was never enough to fund the totality of the state's counter-insurgency, secret police and intelligence operations. Consequently, the army was encouraged to boost its own revenues by fending off the land. So, battalions stationed in the hill areas have been obliged to become their own farmers and businessmen to feed themselves and pay wages. After 1962, the army also grabbed for itself a very privileged position in the national economy. It was able to dictate the terms on which it got involved in every sort of money-making business in Burma, from hotels to logging, from bottling to selling cars, from domestic banking to the airline industry, and even pig farming. Often the military was awarded monopolies on imported goods, such as edible oils, cigarettes and used cars. By Burmese standards, these were very profitable businesses. Thus, the interests of the higher echelons of the army merged inextricably with the country's business and finance sectors.

. . . and kleptocrats

Officers originally got involved in some of these businesses with the nationalisation of foreign-owned enterprises in 1964. These were often simply confiscated by Ne Win and his cronies, particularly the most lucrative ones such as those dealing in gems. The gemstone trade subsequently generated much of the senior generals' vast wealth. Partly to justify this the generals contrived to elevate the country's famous gems into a source of national pride, building large, pompous museums to show off the country's best in Yangon and then Naypyidaw.

The country's distinctive deep green jade is highly prized, especially by the Chinese, who buy it in vast quantities (see Chapter Four). Burma also produces about 90 per cent of the world's rubies, considered to be so fine that they have become the most expensive gems, per carat, in the world. Burma's "pigeon's blood" rubies and sapphires are also famous. But the jade and rubies are mined in near slave-labour conditions overseen by companies owned by, or intimately connected to, the Burmese military.

In 1964, the junta presided over the first annual Myanmar Gems Emporium, which has been held in recent years in the cavernous Maniyadana Jade Hall and the Myanmar Gems Museum in Naypyidaw. This is the showcase of the Burmese jade and gems trade, attracting thousands of dealers. The 2013 edition of the event attracted about 4,000 foreign gem dealers and raised $2.4 billion – a record. This sum gives an idea of the untold amounts of money that flowed through the generals' hands, especially as after the mid 1990s military-linked companies displaced the local or private businesses that owned most of the mines, especially in Kachin State. Direct control of the gems and jade business has dramatically boosted production. Output from the jadeite mines, for example, soared to about 45,000 tons in 2011 compared to just 10,000 tons in the early 2000s.[20] One emporium a year is no longer enough to cope with this vast flow of gems. Now there are mid-year fairs and "specials", rotating between Yangon and Naypyidaw.

The Burmese ruby and jade trades were heavily sanctioned by America and Europe from the late 1990s onwards because of the military's involvement in this sector. It is still considered so corrupt, and so riddled with labour abuses, that America has kept these particular sanctions in place to this day, even while almost all others have been lifted. Nonetheless, the insatiable Chinese appetite for jade, rubies, teak and all of Burma's other precious resources has effectively negated the effect of these Western sanctions.

The army's involvement at every level of business has deeply skewed the Burmese economy. Its main holding company, the Union of Myanmar Economic Holdings Limited (UMEHL), has become one of the biggest players in the Burmese economy. Founded in 1990 to take advantage of the economic reforms that were then being ushered in after the palpable failure of Ne Win's Marxist economics, the UMEHL's share capital is held jointly by the Directory of Procurement of the Ministry of Defence and by several armed forces co-operatives, regimental associations and veterans' organisations.[21] Its operations are totally opaque, its finances and personnel obscure. The same goes for the other of the army's two holding companies, the Myanmar Economic Corporation, also owned by serving and retired military officers.

A road trip from Mandalay north-east to Lashio, a distance of about 120 miles, and then beyond to the Chinese border, affords a few glimpses into the army's grip on the local economy. Lashio is the main city of northern Shan State. It has a strongly ethnic-Chinese presence, as it is the last major stop-off point before the border town of Muse, which gives onto the south-west Chinese province of Yunnan. This is the base area of North-Eastern Command, which in tactical terms has been mainly involved in counter-insurgency operations against the local Shan and Kachin militias. Beyond this purely military role, however, the command's commercial activities are much in evidence.

Signs outside Lashio proudly announce the entrances to the North-Eastern Command's enormous farms, and all along the road up to Muse lie more of the army's various forests and plantations. Commanders use their troops here to extract higher prices from customers. As an illustration, Ye Tun, a member of the federal parliament for the local Shan Nationalities Democratic Party, points to the army's battery-chicken farming business at Lashio. For years, soldiers manning checkpoints into Shan State turned back all vehicles carrying chickens, so as to keep the prices of the army's birds artificially high. Ye Tun claims that he exposed this particular scam in parliament so it has now come to an end, but these sorts of stories abound in Burma.

More egregiously, the army remains heavily involved in the large-scale cultivation and sale of opium poppies in the region. After pressure from the United States, Thailand and China to eradicate poppy fields in the early 2000s, the army has since been working with armed gangs known as People's Militia Forces (PMF) to grow yet more poppies, farther away from prying eyes. These PMFs, also known as Border Force Guards, were originally allowed to form by the first post-independence governments as they were considered to be helpful in fighting separatist movements. Nevertheless, many of them have become little more than private armies to protect the drugs trade. The army can use its checkpoint soldiers to wave PMF drug shipments through, while choking off supplies from competitors among the local ethnic groups. One Shan lobby group based in Thailand says that the links between the army and PMF have become so close that in 2010 seven PMF barons were elected to Burma's new parliaments (federal and state) under the banner of the army's proxy party, the Union Solidarity and Development Party. Their big pitch for votes to local farmers was that they would let them grow poppies without fear of persecution.

Devastatingly, much of the area's teak has been cut down and smuggled over the border to China, often with the help of the army. In the hills near the Chinese border it looks as though someone has taken a giant electric shaver to the landscape, so thorough has been the deforestation. In theory, all private logging was made illegal as far back as 1993. Yet, one British NGO, Global Witness, estimates that from 1990 to 2005 Burma lost 18 per cent of its forests – and this in a country that once had four-fifths of the world's teak.[22] The situation has improved slightly, although in 2008 the Chinese authorities still recorded imports of 270,000 cubic metres of logs and 170,000 cubic metres of sawn timber into Yunnan province just over the border from Muse. Nine-tenths of this timber, from Burma, was felled illegally, and army officers are assumed to have helped smuggle the timber over the border.

As pay was, and remains, so low in Burma all government officials, whether it be from the army, the civilian bureaucracy in Naypyidaw, policemen, censors or customs men, are expected to supplement their meagre pay by leveraging their official positions to make more money. Thus, poor official pay has encouraged, even necessitated, graft and corruption, and this has become ingrained in the system. This doesn't mean that every official has to be knee-deep in the murderous drugs trade, but even the relatively well-meaning and honest bureaucrats assume that they must exploit their positions to make enough money on the side to allow them the privilege of continuing in their official jobs.

One senior bureaucrat, a deputy director of a government department in 2014, talked me through his finances. He would not allow me to use his name. With all benefits, at this very august level he was taking home $380 a month; his basic salary was $220 a month. He made most of his money over and above his official income, however, by importing manufactured goods and running a family business in Naypyidaw. He acknowledged that his official position "helped and protected" his companies, enabling him to win more business, for instance, especially in the capital, and also giving him some security of contract with the government, a luxury rarely enjoyed by most non-government-linked contractors. An unusually dedicated and intelligent administrator, he told me that he did his government work "only for the dignity, not for the money".

Everyone's illegal

The trump card for the military regime, though, was that the system made everyone, in effect, illegal, and so everybody was vulnerable. A member of the NLD, Nay Chi Win, who spent much of the 2000s living and working for the party underground, explained this to me: "Everyone needed a licence for everything – like having a TV, or opening a restaurant, or having a laptop. There were so many licences to obtain that nobody bothered with it. So everyone was illegal. But if somebody did something political, or spoke out, then they [the secret police] would threaten to sentence you for being illegal, or they would demand that you sneak on friends." Thus, the government built up an army of spies and informers, who would infest political opposition parties as well as foreign NGOs, embassies and the like.

"There were thousands of informers in the NLD", recalls the young activist. "So many real NLD people had to flee and were out of the country that many of the remaining NLD people must have been informers." In the late 2000s, the NLD held youth meetings every Wednesday evening, and it was part of Nay Chi Win and his friends' job to vet those who came. One evening, a young man who attended the Wednesday meetings was spotted handing over papers to police special branch at a café – clearly an informer. Nay Chi Win describes what happened next: "So, at the next meeting, we generally mentioned the fact that there was an informer in front of everyone, and we politely requested that he not attend the next meeting. But at the next meeting he was the first one to take his seat, and he still works in a senior level at the NLD . . . The number of informers is less now as a proportion of the overall membership of the NLD, but they are still there."

Other, more brutish elements of the military regimes are still much in evidence too. "Many criminals", continues Nay Chi Win, "were also put on the payroll, in exchange for getting a reduced sentence. So it was very easy to get people on the payroll. Everyone could be an informer, or acting for the *Swan Arr Shin*." These were the regime's hired thugs and bully-boys; Aung San Suu Kyi has called them the regime's Brown Shirts, a reference to Hitler's murderous enforcers. The Burmese phrase means "the people with strength". They would be deployed to intimidate and beat up political opponents, and particularly to harass the NLD.

It was probably men from the shadowy *Swan Arr Shin* who nearly killed Aung San Suu Kyi in 2003, attacking her motorcade while she was on a speaking tour of the country during a rare break from house arrest. As it is, about seventy of her supporters were hacked or beaten to death on this single occasion. The *Swan Arr Shin* has been linked by many to Aung Thaung, a notorious hardliner and close friend of Than Shwe. He was a military-appointed MP and industry minister. The *Swan Arr Shin* is still active; many Muslims blame them for inciting and carrying out much of the anti-Muslim violence of the last few years. Their Muslim victims note how well trained and well organised their assailants often are, and how they will be brought in from out of town in cars and small buses. These hired hands often use the same weapons – clubs, blades and torches – against Muslims that they had previously employed against the NLD, and also against the monks during the Saffron Revolution in 2007.

Less violently, but more insidiously, other branches of government, mainly in the police and the various labyrinthine units of the domestic intelligence agencies, were expected, like the army, to profit from the very people whom they were ordered to investigate and prosecute. One victim of police special branch, who wanted to remain anonymous, told me her own family's experience of the bureaucracy's parasitical methods by way of illustration.

Her husband, caught in the middle of a bout of political infighting within the regime, was arrested on fabricated charges of corruption in the early 2000s. Two plain-clothes officers from one of the police special branch directorates were assigned to the case, mainly to follow him around during the investigation period. From the start, they expected to be fed by him; if he was having lunch at home, they expected to have lunch as well.

She and her husband had a car each, so the officers took one of the cars. They had a condo and another family apartment, so the officers took the apartment for a year before giving it back. She felt obliged to give a small gold chain to one of the officers for his daughter. To the other she had to give the kyat equivalent of $2,500, delivered to him in a bag by an intermediary. She and her husband were strongly advised by the authorities not to get a lawyer; if they did, they were told, her husband would only get a harsher punishment. In the end, he got sixty years (as well as another life sentence on top of that) for currency violation. He was eventually released after just eight years.

Given these deep, exploitative and parasitical links with Burma's economy, will the army ever extricate itself, or be forced to do so? That is one of the crucial questions hanging over attempts by the government of Thein Sein and his successors to reform the country. In order to create a more balanced, investor-friendly economy, where free competition is allowed, the old monopolies and economic privileges of the army will have to be broken up. But so far the army has shown little sign of accepting this logic. Bending to the release of Aung San Suu Kyi and a little bit of democracy in exchange for an influx of foreign money and the lifting of sanctions is one thing. But foregoing the economic privileges and rents of a lifetime in exchange for any further reforms is quite another.

Laudably, President Thein Sein has been prodding the army into extricating itself a bit from the economy by forcing it to give up some of its import monopolies, on beer for instance. But according to one firm of western financial investigators who briefed me, the two big military holding companies have not changed at all, and are still "very toxic", just as most of the quasi-military businessmen are "clearly not reforming". Given how much they have enjoyed the benefits of the status quo, why would they?

CHAPTER FOUR

Under enemy occupation: The test of the Kachin

If the old capital of Yangon and the new one at Naypyidaw speak of, successively, the oppression of the Burmans by foreigners and their subsequent search for a new national identity, on the fringes of the country a very different dynamic prevails. Here, the many other indigenous ethnic groups are continuing to struggle for the right to express their own cultural and political identities against the Burmans. This is the final part of the shattered mosaic.

Unlike the immigrants to Burma during colonial rule who constituted the plural society, at least the Karen, Chin, Mon, Kachin, Shan and others (but not the Rohingya) have always been formally accepted as indigenous peoples by the majority Burmans, as defined in the 1982 Citizenship Act. In many cases their struggles against the Burmans pre-date the colonial era, just as their armed confrontation with the Burmans since independence has run parallel to the regime's distinct quarrel with the plural society. In general, living in the more remote and inaccessible parts of the country, the minority indigenous peoples were never as affected by the plural society as much as the city- and coast-dwelling Burmans were, save in one very important respect. Christian, principally Baptist, missionaries began to evangelise among the then-animist hill peoples, mainly the Karen, Kachin and Chin, from the mid nineteenth century. The result was that these minorities developed a very distinctive religious and cultural identity of their own, marking a profound cleavage between them and the Buddhist Burman majority of the country's central plains.

Officially, as indigenous peoples the Kachin, for instance, should be equal citizens with the Burmans, enjoying all the same rights and opportunities. But the real story has been, and continues to be, very different. Religion has come to be just one of many markers by which the Buddhist Burmans discriminate against them. They are treated as second-class citizens, or worse, in their own country and this has been both a cause and a consequence of the bloody civil wars that most of these peoples have fought with the central Burman authorities since independence.

Thus, the division between the ethnic Burmans, who mainly occupy the low-lying central plain of the country, and the ethnic groups along the country's extensive, winding borders, remains the most serious fault line in the country. Geography counts for much here. The horseshoe-shaped ethnic minority region surrounding the Burman core is the distinctive politico-geographic feature of Burma. The life of the country runs north to south, following the course of the great rivers, principally the Irrawaddy, that drain down from the Himalayan mountains through the relatively flat and placid lands of middle and lower Burma to the coast (see map, page 111). There is relatively little movement east to west across the country. Just as the Burman army has never prospered militarily in the hills, so the ethnic armies have never been able to link up across this vast country, at 420,000 square miles about three times the size of Britain.

Probably about one-third of the people in the country are non-Burmans. If the conflicts that this horseshoe fault line has produced are not resolved, then Burma will never have peace or prosperity, for the first is a prerequisite for the second. And it is in Kachin State, in the far north of the country, stretching from the central plains to the foothills of the Himalayas, that the differences between the ethnic minority groups and the ruling Burmans are at their most stark. Thus, the real test as to whether the Burmese government really wants to reform, and whether Burma can genuinely look forward to a peaceful, democratic future will be here, in the lands of the Kachin.

Captive Myitkyina

Today, visiting a city like Myitkyina, the capital of Kachin State, feels like venturing into a city under enemy occupation. Indeed, this is very much how

1 The Shwedagon pagoda, Yangon: the most famous symbol of Burmese Buddhism during one of its periodic regildings.

2 The former headquarters of Standard Chartered bank on Pansodan Street, Yangon. One of the most modern buildings in Asia when it opened in 1941.

3 Colonial-era Yangon today.

4 General Aung San, Burma's first liberation hero. The famous outzise greatcoat was a gift from India's first prime minister Jawaharlal Nehru.

5 Burma's second liberation hero; Aung San Suu Kyi, the general's daughter.

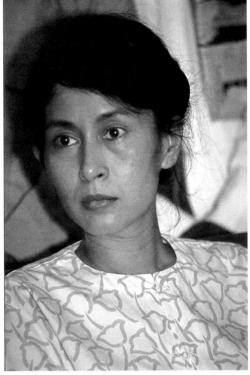

6 Hoping for something better? President Thein Sein, the leader of the reformers.

7 Naypyidaw, the new capital of Burma; General Than Shwe's "abode of kings".

8 Than Shwe, Burma's most ruthless, and perhaps most surprising, military ruler.

9 General Ne Win, freedom fighter turned dictator. Ruler of Burma from 1962 to 1988.

10 Two *nats*, the malevolent spirits of rebels and outlaws.

11 The *sangha*, the monks of Burma, protesting against the government during the Saffron Revolution, 2007.

12 The Chin; amongst the poorest people in Asia.

13 The Kachin dance in front of the *manau* posts at a *manau* festival, honouring their ancestors.

14 Where Burma's famous teak goes; a gargantuan lion for sale in Ruili, over the border in China.

15 Fantasyland – a plastic pastiche of Burma in the theme park at Ruili, China.

16 Tin Oo, general turned freedom fighter, stalwart of the National League for Democracy.

17 Win Tin, the conscience of Burma's political opposition.

18 The dark side of reform. Muslim Rohingya fleeing their homes as Sittwe burns, 2012.

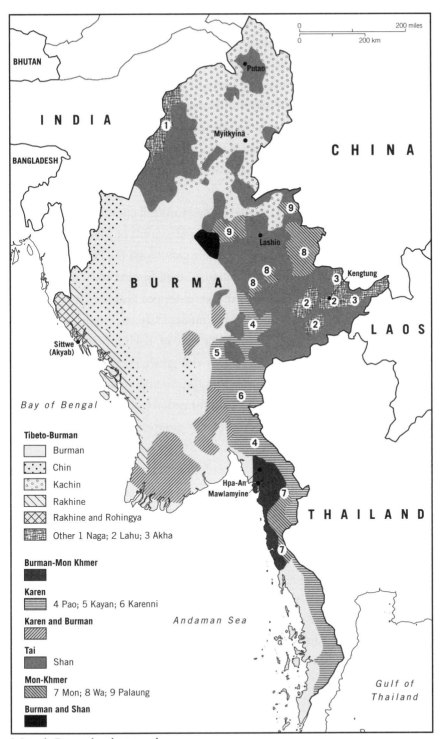

Map 4. Burma's ethnic make-up.

the Kachin have experienced modern Burman rule. In early 2015, the KIA, the armed wing of the main Kachin political grouping, the Kachin Independence Organisation (KIO), was the last main ethnic militia to sign a formal ceasefire with the reforming government of Thein Sein, part of a putative nationwide ceasefire agreement. But the rivers of hatred run deep in Kachin State, and even if such a ceasefire holds it is not yet clear whether it will lead to any meaningful political talks. The Kachin, as we shall see, have been down that road before, with little to show for it. For now, Burman rule over Kachin State is still imposed largely by brute force.

Although Kachin State is usually referred to as hill country, the capital lies in the lowlands of central Burma. It is fifty miles north of Myitkyina that the hills start. The hill peoples, therefore, really come from the far northern part of the state, from the areas around Putao, a small frontier town nestling in a valley surrounded in the distance by the white-topped peaks of the Himalayas. More Kachin live pressed up against the modern Chinese border to the east, particularly around Pajau. The lowlying part of Kachin State around and south of Myitkyina, all rich and verdant rice-growing agricultural land irrigated by the waters that drain down from the mountains, was added onto the frontier area only by the British. This formed the modern administrative entity of Kachin State. Various Kachin sub-groups then migrated south to settle in and around Myitkyina.

Central Burmese government rule in Myitkyina is confined primarily to a large compound occupying one of the best sites on the banks of the Irrawaddy River. It is sealed off from the rest of the city by roadblocks, armed guards and barbed wire. Here lives the centrally appointed governor of the state, called the chief minister. Like all such heads of a state or region, he is directly appointed by the central Burman authorities in Naypyidaw. He is answerable only to them, rather than to the people that he actually governs. In Myitkyina, every governor (and subsequently chief minister) from 1988 to 2011 was an ethnic Burman. Only the latest one has been an ethnic Kachin, and he is regarded as a Burman stooge by most Kachin. Such stooges are the norm in the other states.

In any case, as experts have noted, chief ministers and their cabinet members "have very limited authority to make decisions".[1] In reality it is the secretary of the state, the principal adviser to the chief minister, who really wields the power, and he is usually a former *Tatmadaw* officer. District officers, those at the next administrative tier down from the chief minister, also wield considerable power over their own fiefdoms – and they are usually all Burmans too. They also report up to the chief minister rather than down to the people they rule. My Chin friend Cheery Zahau once asked the authorities why district officers in Chin State were Burmans. The answer came that there were "no ethnic Chin qualified to do this". There are about one million Chin in Burma, and about the same number of Kachin.

Through this administrative structure the Burmese government has control of all the schools in the state, tax revenues, hospitals, the judiciary and, of course, the police. Burmese rule is backed up by an intimidating display of force in Kachin State, as it is in the rest of the hill areas. Next to Myitkyina airport is a large military base; overall, the KIA estimates there are about 25,000 Burmese soldiers stationed throughout the state.

Most of the official jobs in Myitkyina go to imported Burmans, an enormous cause of resentment in a place where steady, regular employment is extremely scarce. As we have seen, the central government also sets education policy. All the teachers are employed by the ministry of education in Naypyidaw, and from what I was told by the students, almost all these teachers were Burmans too. As in every other state capital the Burmese government has helpfully constructed a museum, damp and barely visited, as a guide to the ethnic peoples of the state. There are the usual displays of local costumes and maquettes of ancient bamboo-built houses – but nothing on the Burmans.

The central Burmese government also lays claim to the natural resources of every state or region, be it jade, gold, nickel or teakwood. It has become, by any standards, an extremely centralised system, vesting almost all power in the ethnic-Burman government in Naypyidaw. The authorities rigorously control all movement in the state as well. A large sign in my hotel advised me, as a foreigner, exactly which townships I could visit and which were out of bounds. Naturally, those out of bounds vastly outnumbered the ones I could visit. Burman immigration officials carefully record everyone who arrives and departs from Myitkyina airport. It is strictly prohibited to visit the jade-mining areas, or to venture much off a straight north-south axis that follows, roughly, the course of the Irrawaddy. Burmese army patrols in shallow boats set off from the government compound on their way up the Irrawaddy. All the roads are peppered with roadblocks.

Even battered old Yangon can feel positively futuristic compared to rundown, impoverished, blacked-out Myitkyina. When I visited the Kachin capital for the first time in 2012 it was clear it had remained exactly as it had been for decades: dirt poor and virtually cut off from the rest of the country, let alone the rest of the world. What seemed like the oldest train in the country occasionally crawled along the rails on the lengthy journey up from Mandalay. At night even the main streets were so dimly lit that it was difficult to pick your way between the potholes. Unlike in Mandalay and Yangon, the Internet service was so sluggish as to be unusable. The phone service barely functioned. There were only three places in the city thought to provide international calls, but all were closed when we found them. My guide brightened up when he remembered that my seedy old hotel had "a phone for international calls". Take me back there, I demanded. On the front desk were several dusty old devices, and I was directed to the red one. I tried six or seven times with no success, which seemed to surprise my guide. "But it worked three years ago when I tried it", he exclaimed.

The centuries of resistance

There has not always been such tension between the ethnicities. As with everything else in Burma there are specific reasons for the animosities and conflicts between the Burmans and the Kachin. As Mandy Sadan, the most recent chronicler of the Kachin, has shown, before the mid nineteenth century there was little friction between the Burmans and the Singpho (or Jinghpaw) peoples, who, together with others, would later be grouped as Kachin. The Singpho and Jinghpaw were successful traders, largely in the raw materials that lay on, or more often under, their lands, which then extended west into Assam and east into Yunnan in China. Jadeite was their main source of income, extracted from the area of the Hukawng Valley, to the north-west of Myitkyina.

The Singpho-Jinghpaw communities had already established intricate connections with Chinese merchants from Yunnan province by the seventeenth century. Jade would be stockpiled by the Yunnan merchants at Yunnanfu (modern Kunming), where Cantonese merchants would travel in order to purchase what they needed. Rubies and other precious stones were also being traded. Theirs was an extensive and sophisticated trading culture, instilling an outlook that remains very pan-Asian to this day. About 130,000 Kachin still live in Yunnan province, just over the border from Burma. They retain the name Jinghpaw, as they are called by the Chinese, and are officially recognised as one of fifty-six ethnic groups by the Chinese government. Equally, thousands of Kachin still live in the north-east Indian state of Arunachal Pradesh, which also shares a border with Kachin State.

The extensive, relatively prosperous and borderless realm of the Singpho-Jinghpaw world began to change rapidly, however, as a consequence of the British colonial wars against the Burmans. After defeat by the British in the second Anglo-Burmese war, King Mindon determined to extend his control northwards in order to compensate for what his country had gradually lost to the British in the south. In 1869, Mindon therefore declared a monopoly over the jade mines, insisting that he alone would now purchase all of their production. This effectively cut off the Singpho-Jinghpaw traders from their high-paying Chinese customers; similar monopolies were extended to other goods. Never mind that the Singpho-Jinghpaw traders got around the new orders by only bringing in their lesser-quality stones for sale to the Burmans. More importantly, as Mandy Sadan writes, "The Singpho/Jinghpaw traders in this area saw Burmese kingship operating with a new, assertive force that was apparently set on squeezing their economic opportunities."[2] Much the same could be said today.

But after the toppling of the Burmese monarchy in 1885, the Singpho-Jinghpaw quickly came to experience colonial rule more directly, but in vitally different ways from the Burmese – with consequences that continue to divide the two peoples to this day.

The Kachin, like the Burmese, at first resisted British rule. The British encountered significant resistance to their conquest of the Kachin hills, and their officially designated policy of pacification was, again, at times a bloody affair. The last Kachin resistance was only squashed as late as 1915.

In other respects, though, colonial rule went very differently for the Kachin than it did for the Burmans. For a start, the Kachin and the other hill areas were to be administered separately. Just as the newly-conquered territories of Burma were to be ruled from Kolkata, so the Indian Scheduled Districts Act of 1874 would provide the model for the separate administration of the Kachin, Shan and Chin regions after 1885. In the process, for ease of understanding, the British now began to lump all the Singpho-Jinghpaw who were in Burma together as "Kachin", in order to distinguish them from the Singpho-Jinghpaw who lived on the Yunnan side of a new border delineated with the Chinese. The Kachin and other hill peoples thus began to develop politically in a different sphere from the Burmans. In 1922, a new Frontiers Areas administration was set up by the British to oversee the hill areas, with its own elite class of officers, further entrenching the differences.

Moreover, the hill peoples, unlike the Burmans, were as likely to be co-opted into British rule as they were to resist it, principally through soldiering and spirituality. The modern identity of the Kachin is bound up with a very Victorian brand of martial Christianity, and the most important difference between the Kachin and Burmans to this day is still religious. As we have seen, American Baptist missions started coming to the Kachin hills in 1877, followed by those from other Christian denominations. Now, almost every Kachin is Christian; about half are Baptists, the rest are mostly Anglican, Catholic or from the Assembly of God, an American church. In recent times well-heeled South Korean evangelists have also been making inroads. There are fifteen Baptist churches in Myitkyina alone, and over 300 throughout the country, most of them in Kachin State. Here, the Christian faith is not just a matter of religious observance; it has become a vital, living expression of Kachin culture, identity and autonomy.

As well as encouraging the missionaries, the British also decided, as they had done in Nepal, another frontier "province" of the Indian empire, that the people of the hills must be a martial race like the Gurkhas. Quite apart from their undoubted military prowess, this had a lot to do with the fact that the Nepalese and Kachin hills were now on the frontier of an empire that had to be defended against a potentially hostile China. Thus, the Kachin began to be recruited into the imperial army. Apart from anything else, for young Kachin men the pay was extremely good by local standards. Such a career was also considered to be prestigious and opened up new opportunities on the world stage.

The recruitment of the Kachin was slow going at first, but accelerated with the outbreak of the First World War in Europe. In 1916, hundreds of Kachin started joining up, and appropriately enough the Kachin military police were sent for training with the Gurkhas. Kachin joined up from the Chinese side of the border as well. Together with some Burmese they formed the 85th Burma Rifles and were sent off to fight in Mesopotamia – or *Ma Sawp Amya Ga*, as they jokingly referred to it, translated as "the great unknown". And here, in the sands of Mesopotamia, was born the legend of the modern Kachin soldier. They so impressed their British officers with their bravery, technical prowess and discipline that they won an almost unprecedented number of medals for such a small force. One, Jemadar Sau Tu, became particularly famous and was consequently made a King's Orderly Officer, standing guard in the throne room at Buckingham Palace in London. He was also awarded one of France's highest military medals.

These men were lionised by the Kachin when they returned from Europe, replete with thumping good stories, their soldiers' pay and great ambitions for their people. The gloriously named Major Colin Metcalf Enriquez was the Kachin recruits' commander in Burma and Mesopotamia, and he recorded meeting the legendary Sau Tu on his return from his adventures:

> "Well", I said, "and what have you seen in England?" . . . "Ah, *Duwa* [which roughly translates as "chieftain"]! I saw everything. I saw the King, and Glasgow, and your father. And *Duwa* all the Indians got their own *ghi* and became jealous of me because I asked for an ordinary British ration and ate like an elephant. I had electric lights and four blankets at Hampton Court, and I shall die of dirt and dullness in this village of mine. Look at the paths! Look at this bamboo floor! Only fit to spit through. I and Jemadar Kumje are going to build a timber house together."[3]

Having proved their worth during the war, upon the arrival of peace most Kachin recruits stayed on as regular soldiers in the new Burmese army, which was composed by now mostly of Kachin, Karen and Chin – the official martial races. Their inter-war service further exacerbated the Kachin alienation from the Burmans, for as a regular part of their imperial soldiering they were involved in snuffing out little rebellions not only in other parts of the British Empire, such as Malaya, but also in Burma itself. In 1930–1, the Kachin were among those brought in to suppress the Saya San uprising against the British, one of the earliest Burman anti-colonial struggles, while in 1935 Kachin soldiers were also involved in stifling a rebellion in the Wa States in the far east of the country. These military forays further established the fighting credentials of the Kachin, but also helped to identify them even more firmly as being on the side of the colonial power against the Burmans. This antagonism was then carried, fatally, into the Second World War, to be fought out in the jungles of Burma itself rather than the deserts of Mesopotamia.

The great betrayals

Who better to take up the story of the Kachin than a quintessential Christian soldier, Ho Wa Zan Gam. I met him in his spruce, tidy wooden bungalow in the centre of Myitkyina in 2014. Short, stocky and clearly extremely tough, the 86-year-old could recollect the formative years of the modern Kachin experience as if it were yesterday. He was born among the Kachin in northern Shan State but moved to Kachin State when he was young. When the Japanese conquered Burma, his family melted into the Kachin hills. But when the British and Americans started to reconquer Burma in late 1944, the 17-year-old Ho Wa Zan Gam, like tens of thousands of other young Kachin, joined up with the Allies to push the Japanese out of their country.

The newly recruited private soldier joined the 5th Battalion of the Kachin Rangers and was assigned to a specially formed American unit called Detachment 101, part of the Office of Strategic Services, the wartime forerunner of the CIA. Detachment 101 was tasked with gathering intelligence and harassing the Japanese often deep behind their own lines. As Ho Wa Zan Gam already spoke five languages – English, Chinese, Kachin, Shan and Burmese – he was assigned to intelligence duties under an American officer. He described his missions to me:

> We used to go behind the frontlines of the Japanese, and visit the Kachin
> and Shan and Palong people. We carried two or three kilograms of dry

opium, and we gave them opium for information on where the Japanese were, and they told us the Japanese strength and location. Then my officer would send messages back to headquarters, and they would shell the Japanese. We used to go around the frontlines, three or four of us together, all on foot. Before the Americans came we did not use shoes – but they issued us with boots. We used to take the boots off while walking, and only put them on again when we entered a village.

We were issued with small carbines and some British-made Sten guns. But we never confronted the Japanese; we used to try to avoid them, because we were very lightly armed. We had k-rations, tinned provisions, and something to cook with, so we could sustain ourselves for three or four days like this. We did many such missions; we would rest for two days after a mission and then would do it again.

The opium was just to get information from opium-smokers. They looked very old and stupid, so the Japanese would not think they were spies. The Japanese called the Kachin Rangers the "ghost army" because when they tried to confront the Kachin Rangers, within minutes they had disappeared, because we were the natives and we knew our country, where there was a river, a ravine or a valley. So we knew where to hide to surprise them.

So useful were men like Ho Wa Zan Gam to the Allies that up to 11,000 Kachin were eventually deployed in Detachment 101. They were credited with, among other successes, gathering about 90 per cent of the intelligence collected in the region. They were also estimated to have killed up to 10,000 Japanese. Ho Wa Zan Gam fought at the liberation of Mandalay, and also in the particularly brutal fight for Myitkyina. Here, 10,000 Japanese fought almost to the last man to defend the city's strategically vital airfield. For a few weeks in 1945, this became the busiest airfield in the world. There is a Japanese memorial to the thousands of Japanese soldiers who were killed in the battle for Myitkyina, a huge reclining Buddha just behind the Burmese government compound. It was erected in 1990 by some private Japanese citizens, a moving reminder of what was, even by the standards of the Burma campaign, an intensely bloody battle.

General "Vinegar Joe" Stilwell, the irascible and only nominal commander of Chiang Kai-shek's forces in the region, was once unwise enough to question a Kachin commander's account of how many Japanese he had killed in one particular encounter. In response, the Kachin opened a bamboo tube and tipped a pile of dried human ears onto the table. "Divide by two", he told Stilwell tersely.[4]

The Karen Rangers' most famous moment came just before the end of the fight for Myitkyina, when four hundred of them attacked seven hundred retreating Japanese. After an all-night battle, 281 Japanese were killed at a cost of just seven Kachin casualties. As Ho Wa Zan Gam told me about this, he stood up and pointed to a framed citation on the wall. Dating from January 1946, it commends the Kachin Rangers for the encounter and is signed by General Eisenhower himself.

Men like Ho Wa Zan Gam were happy to fight with the Allies to evict the Japanese from their lands, but the Kachin were also fighting with the British and the Americans in the expectation that they would give the Kachin independence at the war's end. As the old soldier recalled for me: "We wanted freedom from the British government, and we looked to the Atlantic Charter [signed between Churchill and President Roosevelt in early 1942] that the British would release their colonies. We knew after the war that Burma would have independence . . . so the Kachin from Myitkyina quickly wanted independence from Britain. We were confident about that." In fact, this was considered to be merely a logical development of the pre-existing constitutional arrangement whereby the frontier areas had been governed separately from the plains. One historian has written that "whether deliberately or not, this had fostered a sense of difference between Kachin, Shan, Karen and Chin peoples and 'ethnic' Burmese. The war had made the difference starker."

It was a shock, then, to find that the British had no plans to grant the Kachin independence – rather they supported General Aung San's attempts to win independence for the whole of Burma as one united country. For the Kachin, this was the first betrayal. It is a recurring theme for the Kachin, and Karen leaders. Indeed, betrayal became the main theme of the hill peoples from 1945 to the present day.

With no support from the British and Americans for their own state, the Kachin had no option but to negotiate with the Burman leader Aung San as to the terms on which they would join the newly independent nation – terms that came to be enshrined in the famous Panglong agreement. This was signed between General Aung San, as we have seen, and the leaders of the Shan, Kachin and Chin in 1947, just as the country was about to win independence from Britain. The Panglong agreement promised "Full autonomy in internal administration for the Frontier Areas" in principle, and envisioned the eventual creation of a Kachin State ruled by its own parliament.

The Kachin argue that it was only on those conditions that they integrated into the new independent Burma after 1947. Famously, the Kachin Rifles stayed loyal to the Burmese army in the horrendous weeks of early 1948 when the new government of U Nu was nearly toppled by the communist and Karen insurgencies. In return, the Kachin expected that their rights to a new state, though vaguely defined, would be honoured. The fact that this never happened constitutes the second great betrayal for the Kachin, this time by the Burmans.

For the Kachin, the Burman failure to honour Panglong, or what they call the "spirit of Panglong", is the original sin of modern Burma. The head of the Kachin Baptists, Hkalam Samson, another embodiment of muscular Christianity, explained to me why. The minister greeted me in his ample office inside the main compound of the Kachin Baptist Convention (KBC) in central Myitkyina, and within minutes of pouring the Chinese tea, Samson had plunged into a well-rehearsed lesson about the heroic contribution of the Kachin people to the defeat of the Japanese, and their subsequent betrayal by the Allies. His father had also fought in the Kachin Rangers, at the battles for Myitkyina and Mandalay, and Samson lamented the fact that the British, from what his father called the "Never Sun Set Country", afterwards failed to help the Kachin.

Then he turned to Panglong. If the Burmans had honoured this agreement, maintained Samson, everything might have been very different. Instead, he described the way in which, even during the democracy period from 1948 to 1962, the Kachin came to be persistently "discriminated" against by the Burmans. "Religious persecution in Burma was not as obvious as in Sudan", argued Samson, referring to the north's jihadist wars waged against the Christian south, "there is no torture etcetera." More subtly, however, permission to build churches would be denied by the Burman authorities and the Kachin were not able to get government jobs. They had been promised equality of rights, but none of that seemed to be forthcoming. "We are viewed as very low class", he reflected.

Even the renowned Kachin Rifles, the embodiment of Kachin valour, were dropped from the new Burmanised army – yet this was one of the regiments that had saved the nascent republic in 1948. This was the last straw for fighting men like Ho Wa Zan Gam. For others, it was the declaration in 1961 by Buddhist prime minister U Nu that Buddhism would now be the national religion. This pitched the Buddhist Burman state into direct confrontation with the Christian Kachin. Although the Kachin were not by any means majority Christian at this time, Christianity was already deeply rooted enough to be a significant marker of Kachin self-identity, as was the English language – the language of the worldwide Baptist community.

Samson, for instance, is fluent and gregarious in three languages, Burmese, Kachin and English. Yet, due to the banning of English as a medium of instruction from schools and colleges after 1964, most Burmans of Samson's age barely speak any English. The Kachin, by contrast, have always tried to maintain English as their link to the wider and very cosmopolitan community of Baptists, Anglicans, Catholics and Seventh-Day Adventists. Samson himself polished up his English during a two-year stint as a mature student at a theological college in Canada. Ironically, therefore, despite being boxed up in the remote northernmost part of Burma, the Kachin are far worldlier than many Burmans in Yangon or Naypyidaw.

Onward Christian soldiers

To end the Burman onslaught on their culture, religion and people, in early 1961 the Kachin finally took up arms against the Burman state, founding the KIA. Given his wartime experience, Ho Wa Zan Gam was called on by the younger Kachin who started the KIA to organise the new army. Most, but not all, of the commanders of the new KIA had wartime experience with the Allies, so many observers have seen the new struggle as merely a continuation of the wartime fighting against the Japanese and their Burman allies. "We organised the youngsters to join the KIA", recalls Ho Wa Zan Gam, "and set up village defence forces. I trained them, and other retired soldiers, some captains and some sergeants. We did not have good arms. Only old British and Japanese rifles and some old rounds. We did not base ourselves on any particular army; we organised ourselves, with our own ideas."

He was eventually caught by the Burmese army and imprisoned for over four years in a concentration camp for Kachin combatants and families on the outskirts of Myitkyina. Young Kachin, however, flocked to the cause. One such was Myangyung Naw Li, now Lieutenant Colonel in the KIA. He joined up in 1968, aged twelve, rather than going to school. It wasn't really a choice. His grandfather was a Kachin Levy and had fought against the Japanese. His father had joined the Kachin Rifles after the war in the belief that he was contributing to a new country in which all the ethnic races would be equal, as pledged at Panglong. They were both Baptists, as is Myangyung Naw Li. He has teenage sons, he told me, and he hoped that they too will one day fight for the KIA. "Generation by generation we will fight for freedom", he said quietly.

He initially joined one of the Village Defence Forces. He remembers that when he joined "propaganda was very strong then . . . the spirit of independence was booming. All wanted to take basic military training with the KIA. We had no uniform then, and food was from the villages. Only the section commander had a rifle. We had a home-made gun called a *htung hpah*. We put the gunpowder in the muzzle, primitive but very effective."

Contrary to legend the hills were not awash with second-hand World War Two ordnance. Myangyung Naw Li remembers the KIA as, from the start, a very do-it-yourself outfit. They captured the weapons of the Burmese army: "the enemy's weapon is our weapon". Otherwise, they improvised. They deployed football bombs, for instance, "We put lots of explosives in a football, fused it, and then threw it, like a big grenade". Eventually, they came to make their own guns and rifles with precision machines.

Revulsion against the relentless savagery of the Burmese army's four cuts campaign ensured that there was a steady stream of recruits to the KIA willing to protect the villages. It was true that the Burmese army could always deploy better weapons, including jet aircraft, and more men, but the KIA guerrilla fighters enjoyed the crucial advantage of knowing the land better. The KIA was also supplied over the Chinese border by their kith and kin from the Kachin villages there. The result was that neither side could gain a decisive advantage, and in 1994 they declared a ceasefire. The headquarters of the KIO and KIA were re-established at the town of Laiza right on the border with China. The slither of land around Laiza was declared to be free Kachin territory, with the Burmese army based menacingly around it on the Burmese side of the border. All the KIA brigades were kept intact, so Kachin State became a patchwork of armed camps in a stand-off between the two sides.

The Kachin were hoping that the ceasefire would lead to political talks to address their numerous grievances. In Laiza, the Kachin established a lively and authentic Kachin cultural identity, producing school textbooks in Jinghpaw, for instance, and teaching people their own history. But in Kachin State itself it was more of the same, merely a further deterioration in the rights, status and culture of the Kachin. The war had only exacerbated the differences between the Kachin and the Burmans, and this continued. With mass conversions to Christianity, the churches, and in particular the Baptists, became the principal havens of Kachin language and culture. They remain the only working alternatives to the hated official Burmese institutions, their schools and hospitals.

As Mandy Sadan writes, the Christian theological colleges in cities like Myitkyina became "hothouses for a further generation of new Kachin elites, who were raised with the combined rhetoric of Christianity and ethno-nationalism as if they were bloodlines."[5] The pace of conversion speeded up. In 1977, on the fiftieth celebration of the translation of the Bible into Jinghpaw by the Swedish-American missionary Ola Hanson, it was estimated that 6,213 were converted and baptised on one day – more than the total number of Baptist communicants in the whole of Kachin State in 1931. For the Kachin, conversion and baptism now marked a decisive rejection of the Burmese state.

The continuing marginalisation of Jinghpaw in the government-run schools was keenly felt. Some Kachin worried that the language might disappear altogether, as the young had little opportunity to write in it. The Burman authorities seemed to relish any opportunity to crush Kachin culture. The censors, for instance, demanded that the only local Kachin newspaper be translated into Burmese for them; as this was so laborious and costly, it contributed to the closure of the paper. The primary manifestation of Kachin culture, the traditional *manau* festival, a ritualised dance in honour of the Kachin ancestors, could not be held during these years due to the fighting. There were also fears that the Burmese state authorities were trying to buy the piece of land in the middle of Myitkyina on which the *manau* dance had always been held. In a deeply symbolic defence of their culture the Kachin resolved to construct six giant *manau* posts on the sacred site, all paid for by local Kachin businessmen, to reoccupy their own space in the heart of the capital (see plate 000). They were to be built in concrete, to make sure they stayed there; in other parts of the state wooden posts would be taken down by the Burmese authorities.

They stand there today, the towering *manau* posts, in dumb reproach of the Burmese authorities. The annual *manau* festivals, held in January, are still not guaranteed, though. The festival in 2012 was cancelled as fighting had again broken out between the KIA and the Burmese army the previous year, at about the same time as the new, supposedly reforming, president Thein Sein came to power. The KIO and KIA had judged that they had gained nothing from the seventeen-year ceasefire, and that if they did not fight back again the Kachin way of life was in danger of being extinguished altogether. If anything, the military confrontations during 2011 and early 2012 were fiercer than ever, with the Burmese armed forces deploying fast jets over Laiza. At one point Laiza came close to being captured by the *Tatmadaw*.

When I visited Myitkyina for the first time in October 2012 there were about 20,000 refugees living in makeshift camps on the edge of the city, all Kachin displaced by the new round of fighting. In all, about 100,000 people had been made homeless. That same week four Kachin civilians had lost their lives in an army artillery attack in the west of the state. When I returned to Myitkyina two years later it was obvious that no one was going home soon. There were still eighteen camps organised by the Christian churches around Myitkyina, and more by other faiths on the east bank of the Irrawaddy. I visited one, simply called "Baptist Rescue", that had originally been set up in July 2011. About 450 people lived in the camp, supported by international donors such the World Food Programme and World Concern. Already, thirty-four babies had been born in the camp, and this bleak home was probably the only one they would know for a long time to come. The government made a few concessions to the refugees; they waived the tiny amount that parents had to pay to schools, for instance. But otherwise, as usual, these people were largely on their own, supported just by the church.

It is little wonder, perhaps, that after the two great betrayals and the decades of fighting, the Kachin appear to be such a sturdy and independent-minded people. They have had to learn repeatedly the virtues of standing on their own feet. Consequently, the KIO and KIA have, at times, been almost as predatory as the Burmese army in order to sustain the struggle, using child soldiers themselves and exhorting money out of local businesses. One now perfectly respectable Kachin activist told me about his early years as a KIA hoodlum:

> I was recruited when I was seventeen, and given a pistol. My job was to collect tax. I went round every shop and business in Myitkyina, and they had to pay a tax to the KIA. If they did not, they got three warnings and then the business would be blown up. I did not have to do that, but this was extortion . . . no one wanted to pay the tax, which depended on the size of the business. I did not like what I was doing, but it was a duty. It was necessary for us to survive.

Decades of civil warfare have inevitably corroded what little trust and goodwill had previously existed between the Kachin and the Burmans, and this extends even to Aung San Suu Kyi and the NLD. To the outside world Aung San Suu Kyi might be a beacon of democracy, a doughty advocate of human rights, but in Myitkyina she is regarded as, first and foremost, a Burman. "I regard the NLD as just another Burman nationalist party", says my activist. Whereas the Burmans of the NLD might have framed the country's problems in terms of democracy, to Baptist minister Hkalam Samson, for example, "Burma is an ethnic issue". Therein lies a world of difference. Samson told me that Aung San Suu Kyi does not care "deeply enough" about the ethnic issues, and does not refer to the Panglong agreement enough. "She is more concerned about foreign investment", he added.

It is a view often repeated by leaders of the Kachin, Karen and Shan, and points to the ongoing rift between the minority ethnic groups, their political parties and the NLD. Ultimately, they do not see their interests as being naturally aligned with the Burman-dominated NLD, and Aung San Suu Kyi, by the time of writing, had not done enough to make up for that in her hopes to form a broad, nationwide coalition to replace the military-dominated governments.

The Chinese dams

The Kachin know all too much about foreign investment, and particularly the rapacious and destructive side of it. For the Kachin, more than any other of the ethnic groups in Burma, can see perfectly well that if they were allowed a fair share of the fabulous mineral riches that have been extracted by outsiders from beneath their feet they would now be relatively wealthy, rather than crushingly poor. This compounds their sense of grievance. For Kachin State contains many of the country's biggest and most valuable mines, mostly of jade and amber, but also of gold. Many of the largest mines are clustered around Hpakant, said to be home to the highest concentration of bulldozers in the world – 12,000 or so of them. Here, entire hills and mountains regularly disappear in the mechanised quest for jade. Such is the demand for the famously dark-green stone from the Kachin hills that a jade bracelet sold just over the border in China can fetch up to several thousand dollars.

Yet, the Kachin see almost none of this money, which ends up mostly in the pockets of the Burman generals, their cronies and the Chinese. Inevitably, most of the trading is done off the books. Officially, Burma produced 43 million kilograms of jade in 2011/12, which, even at a conservative estimate, is worth about $4 billion. Yet, official exports of jade stood at only $34 million. Likewise, an independent Harvard University study estimated that jade exports in 2011 might have been worth as much as $8 billion, most of it from Kachin State, yet the official tax take on this was negligible. Worse, from the Kachin point of view, despite the fact that their mines might be producing jade revenues of about $6 billion a year, the state government has a budget of only $37 million to dispose of, which is supposed to cover schools, medical care and everything else. No wonder that the Karen see the Burman state as little more than a parasitical, corrupt monstrosity.

Foreign companies are not officially allowed to extract jade, but in fact most of the twenty or so mining concessions in Kachin State were given away in the 1990s to firms owned by Chinese businessmen or their proxies. A few companies are also directly owned by Burmese cronies of the military regime, and a couple by Kachin. "Of course, some [profit] goes to the government", Yup Zaw Hkawng, chairman of Jadeland Myanmar – the most prominent Kachin mining company in Hpakant – has been quoted as saying, "but mostly it goes into the pockets of Chinese families and the families of the former [Burmese] government."

The Kachin work for relatively small wages in the mines. Crucially, they are mostly not involved in the value-added processes of cutting the raw jade and shipping it out to China via Mandalay. The ethnic-Burman mine-owners also have the Burmese army at their disposal to protect their concessions against the KIA and other armed local militias who contest the ownership of these mines. It is no coincidence that the civil war in Kachin has lasted as long as it has. Here, the economic stakes are higher than in the rest of the country as all sides fight over the spoils of Burma's single biggest source of export earnings (more so even than gas or oil).

But the unequal terms of trade between the Kachin and Burman cronies linked to Chinese interests do not stop with the mines. Kachin State is also the site of several of the country's biggest development projects – for which the Kachin were forced to give up their land and from which they derive virtually no benefit. These are projects, mostly dams, agreed on by the central Burman authorities with their main economic backers, the Chinese. Kachin leaders are barely consulted, and the local people, who bear the brunt of the subsequent environmental destruction, not at all.

The biggest and most costly such project (at $3.6 billion), the Myitsone dam, was slated to be built twenty-seven miles north of Myitkyina, just below the confluence of two rivers that carry the icy waters from the Himalayas down into the Irrawaddy. The project, agreed between the Burmese government and the China Power Investment Corporation in 2006, came to symbolise all that was rotten about the Burmese central government's relations with the Kachin, and Burma's relations with China more generally. By any measure the dam was going to have an overwhelming impact on local lives and landscape. An area roughly the size of New York City was due to be flooded and thousands of Kachin from about forty villages would have to be relocated, yet the people most affected were never even invited to offer their views on the subject. The dam was also being built on a sacred site, the head of the Irrawaddy, and the dam's reservoir basin was due to submerge not only villages but scores of churches, temples and pagodas as well. To add insult to injury the Burmese government had agreed that the Chinese should get 90 per cent of the electricity from this dam for the first fifty years of its life. The Kachin, for their part, would remain in semi-darkness.

Unsurprisingly, the dam provoked militant opposition from the Kachin. At the vanguard of the struggle against the dam were, perforce, priests, pastors and monks, the traditional leaders of the Kachin. And the most heroically stubborn of them all was Father Thomas Gum Rai Aung, the Catholic priest at the village of Tang Hpre, just by Myitsone itself. I talked to him in October 2012 at his church house atop a sandbank on a narrow spit of land in between the rivers flowing into the Irrawaddy. They merged in a gentle froth just below our feet, after which the Irrawaddy carried on majestically into the distance.

Apart from being sacred to the local Kachin, the place is exceptionally beautiful. Still, most of the villagers had already been evicted from here to make way for the dam. On the opposite side of the river, at the top of a steep bank, we could clearly see the prefabricated huts thrown up for the two hundred or so Chinese engineers who had been working on the project. All around, the high banks of the Irrawaddy and its tributaries had been walled over, in preparation for the reservoir. If the dam were to go ahead, the water level here would rise by about two hundred feet, submerging everything in sight, including most of Father Thomas's parish. Despite countless requests and blandishments, he refused to budge. Father Thomas had been keeping up an increasingly lonely vigil. Wracked by diabetes and occasionally invalided out to Bangkok, stooped and looking old beyond his years, he was born in these hills, he said, and this is where his home was. He told me he would only leave "when the water level is coming up to my nose. At which point I will make a bamboo raft and float down the river to the mountains where I came from."

Remarkably, unprecedentedly, Father Thomas's courage was eventually rewarded. In October 2011, the new president, Thein Sein, unilaterally suspended work on the dam. The announcement came as just as much of a surprise to the Chinese as it did to the Kachin. It was a momentous decision, indicating that the government of Thein Sein was willing to listen to the views of its own people, as there had been widespread protests against the dam among civil society in Yangon as well as among the Kachin. Thein Sein, on this occasion, prioritised their objections over the economic interests of the Chinese, the government's paymasters. The decision was a milestone in the nascent reform programme, showing that Thein Sein's quasi-civilian government was different from its military predecessors.

Nonetheless, the episode also illustrates how far Burma still has to go until it works out a peaceful, working relationship between the Burman-dominated governments and the ethnic minorities on the periphery. After all, Thein Sein was careful to emphasise that the Myitsone project had merely been "suspended" – for the length of his five-year presidency – and not cancelled altogether. Although the government might have recognised the obvious injustices in this specific case, at the time of writing it is by no means clear that the government has conceded any wider principle, that the Burman central government might always be obliged to consult local people on economic development.

Sadly, the courageous Father Thomas was never to discover whether this particular dilemma will ever be resolved. He succumbed to his illnesses the year after I met him.

CHAPTER FIVE

The catastrophe of drugs: The Karen and Shan

IF THE KACHIN HAVE suffered the most at the hands of the Burmans in recent years, it is the Karen who have fought them for the longest. They might well be the largest ethnic group in Burma after the Burmans themselves. Estimates vary widely, but the Karen could number anything from five to nine million people, or about 7 per cent of the population. If this is correct, they are slightly more numerous than the Shan, often considered the second biggest group, who populate the most extensive geographic region of the country, abutting the Chinese and Thai borders to the east.

The Karen are also the only ethnic group who live largely outside their own state of Kayin, as it has come to be called, which nestles up against the Thai border in the south-east of the country. In fact, most live in villages spread out across the Irrawaddy Delta, and hundreds of thousands live over the border in Thailand as refugees fleeing from the relentless assaults of the Burmese army. Unusually, also, the Karen are a relatively diverse people in terms of ethnicity and religion. Originally from the lands that now comprise southern China, there are three main groups, the Pwo, Sgaw and Pa'O. The Karenni (Red Karen) are a sub-group of the Sgaw, and a sub-group of the Karenni are the Padaung, known chiefly for their women with necks artificially elongated by rings; most of them live in southern Shan State. The majority of Karen are Buddhist, but an important minority, about one-quarter, are Christian, mainly Baptists. Animism was, and remains, an important aspect of Karen belief, easily intertwined with the more formal religions.

The longest-running civil war in history

Nonetheless, despite these apparently profound differences, Karen leaders argue that what unites them is more important than what divides them. One of those leaders is San Dar Wara, the head monk of one of the biggest Buddhist monasteries in Hpa-An, the capital of Kayin State. I had a long talk with him one early morning as the sun came up over the hills in front of the monastery, and he described to me how the distinctive and coherent Karen culture always trumps what he referred to as "little differences" over religion.

He told me that there are five main components of that culture: literacy; language and oral traditions; poems and songs; ceremonies; and clothes and costumes. Since the transmission of this culture from generation to generation has been done largely through the churches and the Buddhist temples, "religious institutions became essential for the survival of Karen culture". Thus, as with the Kachin, keeping their language alive in the face of relentless Burmanisation has become a major act of Karen resistance against Burman oppression. To most Karen, it is "Burmese chauvinism", cultural as well as political, that has always been the country's major problem. As one Baptist Karen told me, "there is a lot of disunity in the Karen community, and we are only united to fight the Burmese."

Before the British arrived the Karen were frequently threatened by the expansionist ambitions of the Burman kings at Ava. Consequently, they were also the most welcoming of all the country's peoples to the arrival of an outside power – Britain – that would help to redress the balance of forces in their favour. An American Baptist missionary, Harry Ignatius Marshall, wrote one of the first anthropological studies of the Karen at the beginning of the twentieth century, and recorded how the inevitable result of the constant conflict with the Burmans had been "mutual hatred of the races, which was intensified on the side of the Burmese by their feelings of contempt for the subject race ... There was nothing in the religion or life of the Burmese that appealed to the Karen, even if it had been offered to them – certainly nothing from which they could expect any amelioration of their condition."

Helpfully for the Baptist missionaries, at least as they recorded it, Karen folklore had apparently foretold of a "white brother" who would deliver them from the oppression of the Burmese and other enemies. This white brother duly appeared in the saintly form of Marshall, as well as the soldiers of the invading British armies.[1] Thus, from the very beginning of the first Anglo-Burmese war in the 1820s the Karen sided with the British to help them defeat the Burman armies. The British quickly found a use for the skill and knowledge of the Karen scouts; in the second Anglo-Burmese war they were deployed in the storming of the Burmese defensive positions around the Shwedagon pagoda.

Thus, as the British conquered Burma, Karen fortunes changed, very much for the better. Like the Kachin, the Karen therefore experienced colonial rule very differently from the Burmans, for to this day the Karen often describe this period as their "glory days". As they were considered by the British to be more politically reliable than the Burmans, the Karen were enrolled by the British into helping them run the colonial state. The Karen thus rose up through the ranks of the colonial civil service to positions of considerable power and importance, and were duly rewarded for their efforts by the colonialists.

The Karen Baptists, closest to the British in religion and education, did particularly well. Many went on to university for the first time. At one point the Karen numbered 22 per cent of the student body at the University of Rangoon, although they made up only about 2 per cent of the national population.[2] Some even won scholarships to American Baptist colleges. Modern schools and hospitals were built in their villages. The missionaries were clearly gratified by the success of their charges and tended to romanticise and exaggerate the changes that they undoubtedly witnessed. Marshall wrote of the Karen in the early years of the twentieth century: "Where only a few years ago were tribal wars, child-stealing, house-burning and savagery, now are quiet, orderly villages, each with its preacher and teacher, chapel and school."[3]

Less gratifying to the colonial authorities, Karen success also raised expectations that they would finally be rewarded with, at the very least, their own semi-autonomous state. In 1881, the Karen National Association was founded to advance their political aspirations. As they became used to being administered separately from the Burmans, more and more of their people lobbied for complete independence. Fatally, the British prevaricated. They made nice noises about it, but were careful never to give any firm commitments.

Following on from the deployment of the Karen scouts during the Anglo-Burmese wars, above all else the British came particularly to value their fighting skills. Like the Kachin, they were thought of as another martial people. Thus, the Karen swelled the ranks of the British-led Burmese colonial army, later known as the Burma Defence Force (BDF). By contrast, Burmans were largely disarmed and ignored, to such an extent that on the eve of the Second World War the BDF counted amongst its ranks only 472 Burmans (a figure which also included Mon and Shan), compared to 3,197 Karen, Kachin and Chin, with the first taking the largest percentage of those three. The Karen rose to the top ranks of the army, and the most conspicuously successful of them was the legendary Smith Dun. He was appointed the first head of the army (and police force) in 1948. The achievements of the "four-foot general", as he was generally called due to his small stature, remain a source of great pride to the Karen.

Vitally, however, for the future of inter-ethnic relations in post-independence Burma, the BDF was used for internal control, to hunt down Burman insurgents. Like the Kachin, the Karen were thus used as soldiers by the Anglo-Indian army against Burmans protesting against colonial rule. Accustomed to being the hegemonic imperial ethnic group in the country, the Burmans now found themselves being hunted down, even killed, by Indians, who made up most of the police, and by the Karen whom they had once vanquished. As San Dar Wara put it to me, already by the time of the Japanese invasion in 1942 "the Burmans hated us", and were more than ready for revenge.

Thus, when Aung San's BIA swept in with the invading Japanese, they took a terrible toll on the Karen. They destroyed Karen villages in the delta and in the hills, killing hundreds, if not thousands. These events are seared into the collective memory of the Karen to this day. As many Karen see it, any remaining trust or empathy between the two peoples was shattered during the war, and has never been regained. Like the Kachin, the Karen stayed largely loyal to the British during the war, contributing far more to the eventual Allied victory than Aung San and his BIA ever did. The Karen proved to be indispensable to guerrilla operations behind Japanese lines. Their value to the Allied cause may be judged by the fact that the British and Americans supplied

12,000 weapons to them by air-drop. It has been estimated that the well-armed Karen and Karenni guerrillas killed over 12,500 Japanese in the last months of the war as they retreated towards the Thai border. To put that in perspective, the Japanese lost only 2,000 troops during the whole of the invasion in 1942.[4]

The bonds between the British officers of Force 136, the unit set up to organise resistance to the Japanese behind the frontline, and the Karen Levies who fought with them, were very close. One such officer, Major Hugh Seagrim, is still revered. After conducting several successful guerrilla operations against the Japanese, he gave himself up in a vain attempt to stop them exacting increasingly bloody reprisals on Karen civilians in revenge for his attacks. Seagrim was taken to a prison under the High Court building in Rangoon, where he was held with other Karen, before being executed. He pleaded for the lives of his Karen fellow-prisoners to be spared, but they were shot as well. Seagrim, like the Karen, was by all accounts a deeply religious man, as was one of his successors, Colonel John Cromarty-Tulloch. Aged fifty when parachuted into the Karen hills, according to legend the colonel landed with his monocle still in place. He was an expert in jungle warfare, and under his command Force 136, composed almost entirely of Karen, was able to pin down about 30,000 Japanese troops in eastern Burma.[5]

Not surprisingly, given their strong support for the British in the war and their considerable contribution to the liberation of Burma, the Karen were thus expecting a major say in the post-war political settlement, if not outright independence. Even as it became clear that their British allies were going to grant the country independence quickly after the war the Karen believed that they still had a "gentleman's agreement" with the colonial power for a separate state within the new Burma. Yet, as it turned out, the departing British would not even discuss a semi-autonomous Karen State, let alone independence. The many Karen petitions that poured into London were simply ignored.

Like the Kachin, the Karen felt betrayed – a feeling that remains to this day. Alan Saw U, the Karen Baptist who later served with the Anglican Archbishop, told me over tea in the Strand Hotel in Yangon in 2013, over sixty-five years after these events: "It's been handed down generation to generation that we were deceived by the British. We were very loyal to the British, but naïve."

Also to this day, the Karen believe that they could have made a great success of their own state, and that Burma would have consequently been at peace. San Dar Wara, for one, argues that "At the time Karen [State] did have the capacity and quality to govern itself. We had army chiefs and politicians etc . . . it could have governed itself." But the Karen got little out of the new Burmese authorities negotiating for the country's independence in 1946–7. The Karen were only invited to the Panglong conference as observers, not as signatories, like the Kachin. They thus felt completely cut out of the constitutional arrangements for independent Burma made by Aung San and the Burmans. Alan Saw U points out that National Independence Day, 4 January 1948, was therefore not celebrated by the Karen. Instead, an angry and disillusioned Karen were preparing to take up arms against the new Burmese state to win independence by force – essentially continuing the war that had begun in 1942, except that now they were much more heavily armed. The Karen National Union (KNU), an amalgam of all the main Karen political parties, was formed in 1947 to push for outright independence, and its armed wing commenced hostilities in late 1948. By January of the following year their well-drilled forces had come perilously close to taking Rangoon. More Karen took control of Mandalay for a while, as well as large tracts of the rest of Upper Burma.

Of course, the cruelty of some of the fighting only exacerbated the bitterness between the two sides. The Burmese army retaliated against the Karen by surrounding their communities in Rangoon and driving them out; they attacked more villages in the Irrawaddy Delta, killing the men and raping the women. The dates of individual massacres by Burmese forces are still fresh in the minds of survivors. Alan Saw U tells how his own family was caught up in the fighting. His mother was pregnant with him when her village was burned down by the Burmese army, so she took refuge with a Chinese family who owned a restaurant in Rangoon. The head of the family was a close friend of her husband's. To blend in, she had to cut her hair and curl it in order to look more like a Chinese woman. After living over the restaurant for a while, she moved in with a neighbouring Indian family. The Indians and Chinese, he remembers her mother saying, "were much more hospitable than the Burmese", and for some time after that she rented a place to live within the

Indian community. It was only much later that she felt confident enough to return to the Rangoon Karen community, in what he calls their "Baptist ghetto".

In the end the Karen assault on Rangoon in 1949 was just turned back, and after that the Karen were eventually pushed into their core territories. Nonetheless, a civil war had commenced that would eventually become the world's longest-running such conflict – a final ceasefire was not signed until 2011. But even at the time of writing, no political settlement has yet been signed.

The consequences of the civil war for the newly independent Burma were severe. It drained both sides of scarce financial resources and manpower to fight it. The war destabilised the country politically, and also turned the Burman state into a predominantly military affair, focused on counter-insurgency. For decades the war ebbed and flowed in the Karen hills, where the Burmese army committed dreadful atrocities under its four cuts strategy in order to try and defeat their opponents once and for all.[6]

The ghost town of Hpa-An – and the catastrophe of drugs

If the Karen civil war fatally wounded the early post-independence Burmese state, it eventually did far more damage to the Karen themselves. Kayin State was turned into a war zone, with the seven-brigade-strong KNLA, the armed wing of the KNU, at times exerting military control over much of the south of the state, especially in the more remote hills pressed up against the Thai border. From bases in Thailand, principally around Three Pagodas Pass, they received supplies and support from their fellow Karen, and were joined by well-wishers and soldiers of fortune, motivated by religion, anti-communism or just a simple love of adventure.

The war ravaged the once-thriving Karen hill economy, as the Burmese army clearly intended. There was massive depopulation as hundreds of thousands fled the fighting, many of them braving the arduous journey through the jungle to scores of refugee camps around Mae Sot in Thailand. These camps contained about 145,000 people by 2010. Many who fled were the young and better educated, as there were no more jobs available in Kayin

State. Much of the land became off limits due to landmines, laid by both sides, rendering it impossible to cultivate.

As normal administration broke down completely in the state, so over the decades it became one of the poorest in Burma, itself the second-poorest country in Asia. Increasing malnutrition, disease, displacement and the stress of war contributed to a steady and marked decline in the Karen peoples' health, so much so that they now have some of the worst such statistics in the world. Dr Cynthia Maung and the remarkable Backpack Health Worker Team in Mae Sot have been tracking this deterioration. By 2010, they and other such groups had found that 41.2 per cent of children under five were acutely malnourished in the hills of eastern Burma, and that 60 per cent of deaths in children under five were from preventable and treatable diseases. Child mortality rates were nearly twice as high as in the rest of Burma, and the maternal mortality figure three times the national average.[7]

The terrible consequences of all these decades of conflict, military, political and cultural, are all much in evidence in the city of Hpa-An. Road access to it is rigorously controlled by Burmese army checkpoints. And like in Myitkyina, the central Burman authorities are confined to a small enclave, where they occupy the choicest buildings leading down to a lake that gives on to some memorable views of the local limestone outcrops. It is the only part of town that could vaguely be described as picturesque. For the rest, Hpa-An is mainly a depressing collection of shabby concrete and corrugated iron houses, sagging electricity wires and crumbling masonry.

Everyone agrees that the main social problem here and throughout the hill areas, is drugs. The monk San Dar Wara was too pained to talk about it much with me, but he reckoned that 60 per cent of young people are either taking drugs, or pushing them. A very intelligent, articulate thirty-something Karen doctor who showed me around Hpa-An, thought that the percentage would be nearer 80 per cent. "Among my friends and community", he said bluntly, "nobody is not taking drugs." My doctor was born and educated in the refugee camps around Mae Sot, but did not want to be named for this book. By far the most common drug of choice, he told me, is methamphetamine, known locally by its Thai nickname of *yaba*, which means, literally, "crazy" (ya) "drug" (ba). Sometimes it's also referred to as *yama*, or "horse medicine", a tribute to its first use as a stimulant dissolved in water to make horses work harder. *Yaba* can be injected intravenously, inhaled after burning it on foil, or, most commonly, ingested in the form of a pill. It is the curse of modern Burma.

Most of the sweetened, brightly coloured little pills are produced in the eastern Shan region and over the border in Thailand, but there are also three manufacturers in the Hpa-An region. "There are lots of dealers in town", said my doctor, "so one can buy it easily around the township . . . It's all quite cheap. Children at school even use drugs." It can cost little more than $1 for a pill, and at the most $3. This doesn't sound much, but some children will be taking five or more pills a day, and as there is little chance of earning money via licit employment, many start stealing to fund their drug habit. The doctor himself had one friend who had turned to stealing money from his family to pay for drugs. Once that source of funds runs out they start taking furniture and other possessions from home to sell, and then they start robbing the neighbours.

The doctor said that everyone, the police, the armed groups, local militias, professional drug dealers, made money out of selling *yaba*, "so they all have a vested interest in keeping the drugs going." The police knew all about it, but take no meaningful action. "Some of the dealers are occasionally arrested, but it's just for show", said the doctor. "In the villages even more people will take drugs. The army when it goes to fight, they take methamphetamine too." And the reason why so many boys and girls turn to *yaba*, or even heroin? "The young have no future, no jobs, and so nothing else to do." The effect of *yaba* is to repress feelings and emotions, enough, at least, for frustrated, bored and disconsolate Karen youth to get through the day. *Yaba* has become very popular in Cambodia, Thailand, Laos and elsewhere in South-East Asia, but nowhere near as high a proportion of people consume it as they do in Kayin, Mon, Shan and Kachin States.

In Kachin the problem of drugs is still more insidious. Here, again, all the local leaders I spoke to in 2014 estimated that at least 60 per cent of people were addicts. Probably every household has an addict; the elders call it a catastrophe. Little opium is grown in Kachin State itself, so most of the stuff is imported – within one of the most restricted and heavily militarised regions in the world. Little wonder, then, that the Kachin find evidence of collusion between the authorities and the dealers, for that is the only way drugs can get in. In the absence of any official government initiative to combat drug dealers, the churches have stepped in. A deacon at the Mauhkring Baptist Church in Myitkyina leads a local Drug Eradication Committee, a volunteer group. He told me about his own run-ins with the police:

> We arrested two men who were taking drugs with another deacon's son, and maybe selling them. They were not wearing uniform, but were wearing sports shirts with the police logo on the breast and a number on the back. They were certainly police, so we told the police station and they sent some officers to collect them and took them back to the station. We were promised that the two officers would be charged and taken to court, but nothing has happened since.
>
> Our Committee is not sure whether the police are dealing for certain, but obviously the police are co-operating with the dealers. The Committee informs the police, for instance, that there is a dealer in a certain house, expecting the police to arrest him. We wait, but when the Committee goes to see what happened the dealer has usually gone . . . Now we go and lurk near the dealers' houses immediately after phoning the police, to make sure he can't get away.

I quizzed a 24-year-old Kachin recovering heroin addict about his experiences with drugs and the police. I will let his testimony speak for everyone, as it's now a sadly common tale:

> I started taking drugs aged sixteen. My friends used them and I had no job. I was addicted to heroin and *yaba* for seven years. I was an only child; I stole money from my parents, maybe 30,000–40,000 kyat each time ($30–40). Sometimes they knew. We had lots of quarrels over this. I got hold of drugs so easily, there were so many dealers selling it. The police are the guards for the drug dealers . . . every day the police, two or three of them, would stand by the drug dealer to protect them, and the dealer gave money to the police in turn. Sometimes they wore uniforms, sometimes

they were just in ordinary clothes. I had five or six friends who have died of drug overdoses . . . they were twenty or twenty-one when they died.

Drugs and dirty needles also bring HIV/AIDS. The Baptist deacon on the Drug Eradication Committee estimated that "not less than fifty out of the 1,800 people in his part of Myitkyina are infected", a rate of about 3 per cent.

The Shan and the narco-economy

San Dar Wara argued that drug abuse may be a serious problem, but it is merely a symptom of "bigger political and economic dilemmas". Poverty and lack of opportunity are common incentives for people to turn to drugs, but the Burmese assault on the Karen political and cultural identity has left many with little self-respect or ambition. The drugs, the monk argued, "mainly come from the armed militias, but the government helps them, and they are tools in keeping the youth inactive, preventing them from thinking about politics and the future."

Many Karen and Kachin argue the same, that the Burmese government has positively encouraged the production and use of drugs in order to destroy their sense of self-worth and dignity, thereby sapping political resistance to the authorities. Having observed the explosion of drugs from close-up in Kachin State for many years, for example, my Baptist deacon in Myitkyina is certainly convinced. "It is a conspiracy", he says. "This is government policy. It is a coherent, planned policy."

If that's true, there is no better evidence for it than what has happened to the peoples of Shan State over the past fifty years. They have seen their old kingdom culturally and politically obliterated, only to be divided up into so many narco-statelets pushed up against the Chinese border. The eastern Shan region is now the epicentre of the booming regional production of heroin and *yaba*. Much of this is smuggled out of the country, mostly to China, but the main victims of the drugs trade are increasingly the Shan themselves. Khun Htun Oo, the most respected of contemporary Shan leaders, is in no doubt of the consequences: "The government has deliberately flooded Shan State with drug production to keep the Shan down."

The Shan are a Tai ethnic group, speaking a language closely related to Tai, and originally came from the area that is now Yunnan province in south-west China. There are probably about six million Shan, consisting of several subdivisions. Unlike the Karen, who are spread out among several Burmese states, the Shan are mainly confined to their own very large state, the biggest in the country, occupying about one-quarter of Burma's land mass. It is dominated by the high Shan plateau, although the capital at Taunggyi is close to the lower, and picturesque, Inle Lake, deservedly one of the country's most renowned tourist attractions.

Another very important distinction between the Shan and Karen is between their traditional forms of government. Whereas the Karen have had very little overall government structure, with each village exercising a large degree of autonomy, the Shan have traditionally been divided into principalities, ruled over by *saophas*, or princes (*sawba* in Burmese). There used to be about thirty of them. These principalities were largely left alone by the British during the colonial period, when the area was known as the Federated Shan States. Today's Shan State is the successor to these old principalities.

Hkun Htun Oo, born in 1943, is the nephew of one of the most revered of the *saophas*, Sao Kya Seng, the prince of Hsipaw. He is also the chairman of the Shan Nationalities League for Democracy (SNLD), the Shan's most important political movement. He thus straddles both the feudal and the democratic strains of his people, and as such he has had to bear personally the full weight of the Burmese government's oppression. Having helped to found the SNLD for the 1990 elections that were annulled by the military, in 2005 he was arrested for allegedly plotting against the authorities. After a summary trial he was sentenced to ninety-three years in prison.

Like most such prisoners he was first taken to Insein, the large, grim, British-built prison just to the north of Yangon. This was the principal locus of incarceration for most of Burma's political prisoners. But then he was taken off to a jail in Putao. The main problem here was the opposite of that facing prisoners in hot, dusty Insein, namely the extreme cold. With temperatures normally just above zero, he was issued only with a short-sleeved prison shirt and a *longyi*. He could sometimes get hold of a blanket and jumper, but nonetheless four fellow inmates died of exposure while he was there. Due to the remoteness of Putao his family could only come to see him every three months, when they left money with the jail superintendent so the inmates could buy rice, onions and other staples to cook. "If you had just the jail food", he says, "you would die." All this took a severe physical toll. When I visited him at his home in Yangon, amongst a little Shan enclave just beyond the centre of the former capital, he seemed frail and weakened beyond his years. Eventually, he was released as part of a general amnesty by Thein Sein's new government in early 2012.

But Hkun Htun Oo's family had always lived with the spectre of imprisonment, or worse, hanging over them. His father was jailed in 1962 when the military took power, and remained in prison until 1968. His uncle, the prince of Hsipaw, was stopped by soldiers at a roadblock in Taunggyi on the day of the 1962 coup and was last seen being taken off in a military truck. There followed years of contradictory reports as to his fate, but he was never seen again. He is presumed to have been executed shortly after his detention.

The prince had married a young Austrian woman, Inge Sargent, who later wrote an account of their idyllic life together at the prince's hereditary residence at Hsipaw, in the north-east of Shan State on the road between Mandalay and Lashio. The book is called *Twilight over Burma: My Life as a Shan Princess* (University of Hawaii Press, 1994). She now lives in America. A visitor to Hsipaw, a popular base for hiking around the Shan hills, can see something of their large house behind a now rather overgrown metal gate, but still no visitors are allowed in by the Burmese military.

The reason that the Shan leaders were particularly targeted in 1962 is because one of the justifications for Ne Win's coup was to forestall Shan attempts to break off and form their own autonomous state – "to prevent the disintegration of the union", as the military put it. The Shan had won the right to a referendum to secede under the Panglong agreement ten years after independence, by 1958. Thus, Burma's leaders saw the Shan, above all, as an existential threat to the union of Burma, as they not only had the theoretical right to split off but also a distinct and widely supported structure of extant royal government to lead them if they chose to do so. Indeed, it was a convention in Rangoon in February 1962 to discuss further such loosening of the federal constitution that immediately prompted the coup on 2 March of that year. But even for most of the preceding years, the Burmese military had tried to intimidate the Shan into political acquiescence. Sargent chronicles how her husband Sao's life as leader of his people had become little more than a battle of attrition against the Burmese army:

> Hardly a day passed without someone from the state coming to see Sao with a complaint against the Burmese army; villagers were intimidated and forced to provide free labour, women were harassed and sometimes raped, and elders who tried to protect their people were arrested and taken away. The army behaved as if it were the enemy and not the protector of this land. Strong protests to . . . the central government of the Union of Burma went unheeded. Whether the leadership was not in control of its troops or whether these excesses were part of a greater plan against the minorities was not clear. Sao, among other Shan leaders, raised these questions in Shan State Council and parliament, but did not get a satisfactory reply.[8]

Having pre-empted, in their own minds, a Shan breakaway, and arrested or killed the main Shan leaders, after 1963 the generals of Burma's new military regime forced the remaining Shan *saophas* to give up their power; some had already been obliged to resign. And this was accompanied, as Hkun Htun Oo relates, by a concerted Burmese attempt to "eradicate Shan culture". Thus, as elsewhere, the Shan were no longer allowed to use their own language in schools and in official business. Their place names were changed by the government. Due to the 1989 law on place names the capital of eastern Shan, Kengtung, for instance, was unilaterally changed to Kyaing Tong.

The campaign against Shan culture also took a more physical form. Take Kengtung itself, situated around a small lake among rolling hills. It is a beautiful setting, and the town remains one of the most striking in Burma, at least from a distance. But one of its proudest sights has gone. On the north side of the lake there is now an incongruously large, ugly, black plate-glass hotel, the New Kyaing Tong. It was put up by the Burmese government on the site of the palace of the former Shan *saopha*. This latter had been built in 1905, an extraordinary confection to judge from old photos, but was demolished in 1991 by the Burmese government, determined to destroy the most obvious symbol of the old local authority. Opposite the New Kyaing Tong hotel remains the crumbling, shuttered house that was once used by the *saopha*'s staff. Farther up the hill are the mausoleums of the Shan princes, now firmly padlocked off from public access. The only building that still evokes something of the splendour of the Shan princes is the monastery that used to be in the grounds of the palace, Wat Jong Kham, tucked in behind the hotel.

Despite its strategic geographical location on many of the main trading routes north from neighbouring Thailand and east to China, Kengtung is a shadow of its former self. With barely any electricity, cut off by checkpoints after curfew time from much of the rest of the country, the only entertainments for the young are the few desultory bars and nightclubs by the lake. The decline of the town from its former status as a prosperous, mercantile Shan capital has mirrored the political decline of the Shan more generally.

Nang Voe Phart, a straight-talking, well-dressed middle-aged woman, is the head of one of the few local NGOs trying to help the Shan, and she told me more about the problems and conditions in the region. There are few full-time jobs, she said, so most of the young emigrate to nearby Thailand or the border town of Mongla (of which more later) to get a job. For fourteen- to eighteen-year-old girls in particular the options are painfully bleak – "they can go to work as sex workers, or housemaids, or karaoke singers in restaurants, or masseurs." The boys have little choice either; they can become construction workers, or endure appalling conditions on Thai shrimp boats, where they will often work as bonded labour – slaves, effectively. The lucky ones pick fruit and vegetables in the fields of Thailand.

Yaba, again, is the great palliative, together with glue sniffing. The NGO head estimates that almost two-thirds of young people do one or the other regularly, but mostly *yaba*. The consequences, Nang Voe Phart says, can be terrible. In Kengtung the "crazy drug" lives up to its name, with many reports of boys committing suicide or physically attacking their friends and families after taking the drug. My Shan guide in Kengtung, called John, told me of his own family's experience with *yaba*. One of his brothers and two of his friends had once spent three days hiding in a cemetery consuming two hundred pills, after which his brother went completely berserk and nearly stabbed his wife in the neck. He would always feel "very active and strong after *yaba*", so wouldn't feel the need to eat anything for five days or more. He also drank, and eventually developed gastric problems. He was only fifty-five when he died. John's other brother also took a lot of *yaba*, and died at fifty-seven.

Just getting worse

For the victims of *yaba* and heroin, and those families that have to pick up the pieces, Kengtung's geographical location is nowadays more of a curse than a blessing. For the trade routes that were once the source of the town's prosperity now mean one thing only, drugs. Kengtung is in the heart of the area known as the Golden Triangle, where the three South-East Asian countries of Burma, Thailand and Laos adjoin their giant northern neighbour China. It is an area that has long been synonymous with the drugs trade, and on the Burmese side of the border it is unfortunately Shan State that has been most particularly ravaged by the drug economy. This is where the majority of Burma's opium poppies are grown, where many of the region's heroin factories are located, and where *yaba* is produced in enormous quantities. The Burmese government, Shan militias, drug lords and impoverished farmers, have all become inextricably linked to each other in this very lucrative business.

The Burmese government has always tried to persuade the international community, especially the Chinese and Americans, that it is serious about cracking down on drugs. Even when the country's diplomatic and economic isolation was at its height after the imposition of sanctions in the mid 1990s and early 2000s, the UN, America's Drug Enforcement Administration and other sundry agencies were co-operating with the Burmese military on trying to clear the poppy fields of Shan State.

The Burmese government periodically received substantial amounts of money and kit to help them do this, so they have been correspondingly keen to advertise their alleged successes. Thus, standing sentinel over one of Burma's main border crossings to China, in the town of Mongla, is a lurid pink building, the Drug Eradication Museum. In this sleazy frontier post the authorities have chosen to portray how the cultivation of opium poppies and the production of heroin and other drugs apparently shrivelled in the face of a determined eradication programme from the 1990s onwards. In 1985, Burma produced more opium than any other country in the world, but according to this account the trend in production thereafter was relentlessly downwards. Afghanistan replaced Burma as the biggest supplier in the early 1990s. Dog-eared black-and-white photos in the museum record all the diplomats and foreign journalists coming to witness the triumphant destruction of thousands of hectares of poppy fields. Here and there among the exhibits Than Shwe descends by helicopter to survey the good work.

But the chronicle of relentless success ends in 2006. Beyond the museum walls since then, and particularly recently, it has been a very different story. According to the latest report from the UN Office on Drugs and Crime (UNODC), drug cultivation, production and use is now rising at the steepest rate in years.[9] In 2013, poppy cultivation in Burma rose by 13 per cent on the previous year, to 57,800 hectares (143,000 acres). This is well over double the total acreage in 2006, the year with the lowest level of cultivation. The combination of more cultivation and higher yields has resulted in a rise of over one-quarter in opium production in Burma since 2012, to some 870 tons. This quantity is worth about $500 million – a lot for such a poor country. Cultivation has also increased, albeit more modestly and from a much lower base, across the border in Laos. Overall, whereas in 2005 the two countries produced 326 tons of opium, or 7 per cent of that year's world total, in 2013 they produced 893 tons, or 18 per cent of the total. Afghanistan continues to produce the lion's share, but Burma is catching up.

Most of the opium poppy is produced by small farmers in the Shan hills. Despite decades of trying to lure them away from cultivating these flowers, the region still accounts for more than nine-tenths of Burma's poppy harvest. An estimated 200,000 or more households have resisted the temptation to switch to rubber, maize or other crops. Many farmers here are so poor that, given the chance, growing poppies remains by far their best economic option. Demand has been soaring in recent years, especially from China, so the price of heroin in local markets has doubled or tripled. That is one of the blessings, or curses, of having one of the fastest-growing countries in the world on Burma's doorstep. As the Chinese become exponentially richer, so the demand for heroin rises at a commensurate rate. Officially, there are already two million heroin addicts in China, but many put the real number at five times that, and rising. The Chinese demand for *yaba* and other meth-based products is also growing, as teenagers latch onto it as an easy stimulant, akin to smoking tobacco or drinking. Meth, in theory at least, is less harmful than heroin. Either way, China's rapidly growing wealth must mean that the demand for Burmese heroin and *yaba* will continue to move in only one direction.

UNODC estimates that poppies provide typically half of a Shan household's annual income, or $920. There are risks attached to the illegal cultivation of opium poppy, but the farmers know that they are protected by the well-armed People's Militia Forces (see page 104), which take a cut of the price. Almost always led by commanders of ethnic minority origin, these militias were allowed by the *Tatmadaw* to finance themselves by taxing the local population through the control of checkpoints on roads, for instance, or getting into a range of businesses – which in Shan State automatically meant the drugs trade. There are about one hundred such militias in the state; they protect poppy production, and in return for being allowed a free hand to operate by Naypyidaw they pass on some of the profits to government officials as well.

The arrangement suits everyone. These often very rich militia leaders-cum-drug lords have also become essential supports of the central Burmese government control over Shan State.[10] These men who worked openly with the government, being allowed to conduct their businesses legally while keeping out of politics, included the two most notorious "Kings of Opium", Lo Hsing-han and Khun Sa. The former's business, Asia World Company, became one of the country's largest conglomerates, with investments in hotels, ports and much else.

Just as the Shan farmers now export so much heroin, the state itself is awash with the stuff. So much so that the most recent research into drug consumption, carried out by the Dutch-based NGO Transnational Institute, suggests that there is a heroin epidemic in northern Shan State and in Kachin State. Shan State is also home to the largest number of meth labs in the Golden Triangle, makeshift and virtually undetectable premises, often just a bathroom in a house, or a garage. As the former head of UNODC in Burma, Jason Eligh, pointed out to me, *yaba* is so abundant in Shan State because its ingredient chemicals are readily to hand (they are also used when refining heroin from opium), and the pills can readily be produced in an "infinite volume". Shan State alone produces well over one billion *yaba* pills a year.

The Shan elders are aghast at the disintegration of the traditional Shan communities and customs under this tsunami of drugs, trafficking and exploitation. Hkun Htun Oo laments that despite the Shan communities, and in particular the churches, fighting back as best they can, "the Shan children have become drug addicts and infected by HIV". In and around the northern Shan border city of Muse, townsfolk and villagers have taken matters into their own hands. Vigilantes, in effect, have rounded up addicts and dealers and sent them off to rehabilitation camps that they themselves have established.

It is the same in Kachin State. In Myitkyina there are three big drug rehabilitation centres run by the Kachin Baptist Church, as well as a Catholic one and several others on the outskirts of town run by private individuals. The members of the Baptist Drug Eradication Committee snort when I ask them whether they get any help from the Burmese government. If anything, it seems, the authorities are positively obstructive. I visited one of the private rehabilitation centres in Myitkyina, the All Nations Home Ministry, run by the formidable Sarama Lu Lu Tin, a Baptist deacon of greying, close-cropped hair and an admirably sunny countenance. She founded the centre because one of her own three sons had become an addict aged fifteen. He later reformed himself and became a deacon, but had just died at the age of thirty-two of high blood pressure, maybe brought on by his earlier drug habit. In the face of total government indifference to the blight of drugs, she raised her own money to build the centre, on the site of a former cemetery. The money came from Kachin businessmen, and, she told me, "the power of prayer".

The place is built like a fortress, with razor wire atop a steel perimeter wall. This is to stop people getting out, she says. Most of the people inside, almost all young men, have been sent here by their parents, sometimes against their will. Surprisingly, most stay and over a seventy-day course of exercise, massage, hot-salt showers – and prayer, of course – they usually kick the habit. But even so, she knows as well as anyone that when they leave, with no jobs to go to, they might easily slide back into old habits. She knows many who have done just that.

The special regions

Unfortunately, there is no end in sight to the drug epidemic. Regional proposals to free up trade and improve transport, though likely to bring some benefits, are about to make things worse so far as drugs are concerned. As Eligh argues, the local mafias are "the best logistics experts in the world". A new highway or two will suit them fine.

Even if the Burmese government were to have an extraordinary change of heart and sincerely attempt to eradicate all drug cultivation and manufacturing, in any case so much power has passed out of their hands in Shan State that there is probably precious little they could achieve anyway. Not only are there the free-booting semi-autonomous militias to contend with, all with their own symbiotic relationships with local Burmese officials, along the border with China swathes of territory were given up decades ago to separate militias that now operate virtually as independent states.

These are known as the "Special Regions", a legacy of the communist insurgency that nearly toppled the government in the 1950s. Eventually, with the collapse of communism worldwide in the late 1980s the various communist groups came to terms with the Burmese government. They gave up their armed struggles in exchange for the right to run their own mini-states along the border with the Chinese province of Yunnan. These were divided up along ethnic lines. The most notorious is Special Region No. 2, home to the Wa and the fearsome United Wa State Army (UWSA), still probably about twenty thousand strong. The Wa have been heavily involved in poppy production for a long time; the US State Department once calculated the UWSA to be the world's "most heavily armed narco-traffickers".

Just south of this is Special Region No. 4, with its capital at Mongla. This is run by the grandly named National Democratic Alliance Army Military (NDAAM) and Local Administration Committee (Eastern Shan State). About 35 per cent of the population are Wa and the rest are of Shan, Lahu, Akha, Lisu and Loi ethnicities. Here the writ of the Burmese government stops very firmly at the heavily fortified border crossing about an hour out from Kengtung. The Burmese currency is not used in the special region, no Burmese troops or officials are allowed in, and the signs have all changed to the Chinese language.

Essentially, Mongla is a Chinese boomtown within the national territory of Burma, run by the NDAAM mainly for the benefit of the Chinese. The Chinese yuan is the official currency.

One of the main industries is gambling. There is a village solely devoted to tacky casinos just before the visitor reaches Mongla from the Burmese side, and here, hundreds of young Chinese women joylessly pore over the gaming tables quietly moving cards and dice. They clearly aren't getting any fun out of playing against each other, rather they are all following the orders that they receive through their earpieces. For these women are merely proxies for the real gamblers on the Chinese side of the border, who are following the action at the tables on closed-circuit TV monitors.

Mongla is seedy, dangerous and full of prostitutes and drugs. But, as local Shan point out, it also has electricity, jobs and opportunities, unlike Kengtung. There are certainly more construction cranes in Mongla than I saw in the whole of the rest of Shan State. The result is that Mongla is as much a destination for Shan boys and girls seeking any kind of work as it is for Chinese seeking sex, drugs and a turn at the tables. For the Shan, it's not the sort of employment that the old princes would have had in mind for future generations. But, sadly, any more wholesome alternatives for the Shan economy have long been superseded by the Mongla mix of *yaba*, yuan, karaoke and sex. Such has been the fate of the princely Shan States.

PART TWO

REFORM, TO PRESERVE

CHAPTER SIX

An embarrassment of poverty: Burma's collapse

IT WAS MID OCTOBER 2012, and thousands of Burmese had gathered around one of the main pagodas in Mandalay to celebrate the annual *Thadingyut*, festival of lights, at the end of the Buddhist Lent. The streets were crowded with stalls and the trees garlanded with electric lights of every size and colour. People grazed on local delicacies plucked off hot braziers.

From June to October monks and nuns are confined to their monasteries, and since they cannot perambulate around the towns and villages to collect alms, donors come to them instead. This is the time of the "tree of plenty". The pagodas fill up with these metal frames shaped like Christmas trees on which suppliants hang whatever they want to offer to the religious communities, to make merit. The gifts will usually be an assortment of the few possessions that monks are officially allowed to own, such as toothpaste, umbrellas, cups and brooms. But raw cash is also popular, especially in the richer cities such as Yangon. At the Shwedagon pagoda those hoping to make plenty of merit can buy trees festooned with 5,000- or 1,000-kyat notes.

There is always a sense of excitement and anticipation about *Thadingyut*. As well as the monks being confined, lay people are traditionally not allowed to get married during this period. After the full moon of the festival of lights, though, courting couples can finally unite. The atmosphere is one of merry carnival. Outside the pagoda in Mandalay young and old were gathering on open ground for a rare treat, an open-air film show. A young Burmese man was struggling to get the reels onto a magnificent Italian projector, dating perhaps from the 1960s. The pile of spanners and screwdrivers at his side suggested he was long used to going into battle with this ageing beauty.

More venerable still, parked beside the pagoda's entrance, was a lovingly polished red fire engine. It was a British Dennis, an ancient but dignified legacy of colonial times, still on active duty. The attendant firemen explained that the local authorities always asked for the Mandalay fire service to deploy at the festival, considering the hundreds of thousands of lit candles around the city. Fortunately, on this particular night the Dennis wasn't put to the test – the hoses looked distinctly threadbare. The few foreigners gazed appreciatively at this marvellous vehicle, but the reaction of the Burmese was very different. My guide apologised in embarrassment for its age, and the firemen seemed bewildered by our interest. For this fine old Dennis was also a very glaring symbol of just how far Burma had fallen behind the rest of Asia and the world. I had seen a similar one in Kuala Lumpur – in a museum. Here, in one of Burma's richest cities it was still the only emergency service available.

Lies, damned lies, and statistics

By all accounts it was this same profound feeling of embarrassment and shame that eventually persuaded the Burmese military regimes to abandon the nefarious Burmese Way to Socialism in the late 1980s, and eventually to consider more profound change after 2011. The military officers who ran Burma, of course, did very nicely during these years, profiting hugely from the gems, drugs and other trades. They were frequent travellers to the wealthy city-state of Singapore, for example, to shop, park their money and educate their children in the country's expensive private schools. In an important study of illicit capital outflows around the world by the UN Development Programme (UNDP) in 2011, Burma was ranked as the eighth-largest source of capital flight over the previous twenty years. The report estimated that between the 1990s and 2008 approximately $8.5 billion had flowed out of Burma, representing an average of 9.1 per cent of the country's GDP over the period, compared to a developing world average of about half that.

Much of this money would have been laundered through offshore financial centres, away from the scrutiny of foreign (mainly American) or international regulators. The capital leaving Burma, often in simple hard cash, was usually the result of explicitly criminal or illegal activity, such as the drugs trade. As the economic historian Sean Turnell has written, remarkably "this capital flight was also 4.6 times the amount of foreign aid Myanmar received in these years. To put it more graphically, for every dollar of aid received by Myanmar between 1990 and 2008, $4.60 flowed right back out."[1]

This was robbery on a positively Nigerian, or even Congolese, scale, reminiscent of the notorious African kleptocrats Sani Abacha or Mobutu Sese Seko. Burma and some of its sympathisers often complained that its people received a very low share of aid money compared to neighbouring South-East Asian countries such as Vietnam and Cambodia; this was one of the reasons why.

However, especially after 1997 when Burma joined the Association of South-East Asian Nations (ASEAN), the regional political bloc, the country's military rulers were fully exposed, as they travelled around member countries, to the burgeoning gap between the living standards of Singapore, Thailand, Malaysia – even Vietnam – and Burma. Given the litany of Burma's economic mismanagement, corruption, kleptocracy and civil war, as well as the forced expulsion of many of those who had previously produced much of the country's wealth, it could hardly have been otherwise. It is often argued that rogue regimes should be isolated from regional blocs until they reform, in order to give them an incentive to do so. For instance, Turkey is expected to improve its human-rights record to join the European Union. Burma's membership of ASEAN, however, argues the reverse. In this case, regular exposure to one of the most successful economic groupings in the world served to rub the faces of Burma's rulers in their own failures.

Even the most pig-headed of them could no longer deny the terrible reverse in Burma's fortunes since Ne Win's socialist experiment followed by two decades of equally disastrous crony capitalism. The statistics, as far as they could be relied upon, were telling. In 1962, Burma had been one of the wealthiest countries in the region. At that point, Burma's annual income per head of about $670 was more than three times that of Indonesia and more than twice that of Thailand. By 2010, the situation was exactly reversed. The International Monetary Fund (IMF) estimated by that year Burma had South-East Asia's lowest GDP per head, recorded by the World Bank as $824.19 in 2011, equivalent to just

7 per cent of the world's average.[2] The Burmese census of 2014, supported by the UN, showed that average life expectancy was just sixty-seven, the lowest in the region. While at least half the population in Burma still live on less than $2 a day, countries like Malaysia and Thailand are earnestly grappling with the so-called "middle-income gap": how to make the final leap from the top of the developing world to fully fledged first-world status. Singapore, of course, has already made it and now has the highest proportion of millionaire households of any country in the world.

Many countries, whether in Asia or Europe, suffer in comparison to Singapore, a singularly successful economic model. What really must have shocked the leaders of Burma was to see their country being overtaken by the likes of Cambodia and Laos. The former only emerged as a peaceful, (barely) functioning state in the mid 1990s after decades of civil war and foreign invasion, preceded by the ruinous misrule of the murderous Khmer Rouge regime. Yet, by the end of the early 2000s Cambodia was outstripping Burma in terms of GDP per head, as was tiny Laos, another country deeply affected by the South-East Asian conflicts and superpower interventions of the 1960s. Burma, by contrast, had neither been napalmed nor invaded.

Burma's generals spent many years in denial over this precipitate economic collapse. As dictators tend to do, rather than facing the facts they cooked the books. In their anxiety to prove that their country was every bit as tigerish as its Asian rivals, they produced frankly comical figures for the country's growth rate in the 2000s, proclaimed to average 12.2 per cent a year. This was an astonishing figure, outstripping even China. It was completely fabricated.

Today, in the new era of glasnost, ministers more or less admit that the old military regime simply made it all up. Aung Min, a key reformer and ally of Thein Sein, told me in 2013 that now the government relied on "your" (Western) data rather than its own statistics to make decisions. A high priority for Aung Min in reforming the country was clearly to "bring in the accurate use of statistics and data" as part of a general move towards a "new political culture and values". Under the old regime the imaginary numbers were repeated so often that the generals most likely forgot about their dodgy provenance and started believing in them themselves. This is a common pattern in totalitarian regimes; the government's figures would have counted as black propaganda in psy-war terms. More astonishing, perhaps, is the fact that so many foreign agencies took the old regime's numbers at face value, and trotted out the inflated numbers without reflection.

In 2009, a team of economists from Harvard University Kennedy School's Ash Center worked out a more reliable estimate for Burma's supposed growth, based partly on electricity consumption, normally a reliable guide to economic activity, or the lack thereof. The conclusion of the Harvard authors is worth quoting:

> It appears that there was a positive but modest growth of real GDP since 2000. It is possible that per capita GDP growth was close to zero, but more likely that per capita growth was 1–2 per cent per year. This is quite modest for Asia and slower even than the Philippines. If income distribution were becoming more concentrated (say due to the rapid growth of natural gas exports that are controlled by the state), then it is quite possible that most people would have level or even declining real incomes over this period.

Three years later, the team warned, "a comparison of [official] GDP and electricity growth is shown to support our opinion that false reporting has been built into the system and to some extent believed. This is dangerous. You need to know where you are before you know how to get where you want to be."[3]

Even the snakes have gone to China

The Harvard estimates for a possible GDP decline in the early 2000s, even as some countries in the rest of South-East Asia were leaping ahead at 6 per cent or more, certainly chime with my own observations of the country after 2010. They are also broadly in line with other research, once it became possible to start quantifying poverty more accurately (and honestly) after the regime began to reform in 2011. My previous job just before going to Burma had been as Africa editor of *The Economist*, for which I had travelled extensively across the continent. I wrote regularly about poverty and its adverse effects on the life chances and health of ordinary Africans. The poverty I found in Burma by 2010 was in many places just as dire as anything I had seen in Africa. I saw the evidence myself, for instance in 2014, on a trip with representatives of the

World Bank to some of the more remote villages in Kanpetlet Township in central Chin State. At about 5,000 feet in the hills, the Chin were leading an almost medieval existence.

Most Chin are smallholder farmers, growing potatoes and corn mainly for themselves, and yams for export to China. As far as I could calculate, most lived on less than $1 a day. What few farming implements they had ever possessed were long ago sold off to survive the lean times, and there have been many of those. The men hunted animals with ancient muskets, bows and arrows. There was no fertiliser available to increase the meagre yields, and in some villages the crops were being eaten by rats. Snakes, of which there have always been plenty in Burma, used to eat the rats, but there were none left in Kanpetlet. To raise a little more money, the snakes had all been captured and sold to China.

Villagers told me that they could only survive on their own food for about six months of the year and after that they have to improvise. People who had extra food shared it out, others borrowed from relatives. Many just ate less, taking only two meals a day instead of three. Most of the children only ate vegetables and rice. There was barely any meat, once a week at most. The head teacher at a village primary school acknowledged that consequently his charges never got enough protein, vitamins and minerals and were thus usually malnourished, especially during the rainy season. As a government employee he could not admit this sort of calamity directly, but he said enough to suggest that the lack of food must have affected the children's ability to concentrate and learn at school. With so few prospects in these hill villages, many of the young men had left to get jobs in Thailand, Malaysia and elsewhere. Occasionally, they send remittances back to help their families.

Sometimes, these Chin villages received help from UN agencies. The UNDP, for instance, had helped to build and maintain a few schools. The World Bank had also started to intervene, one direct consequence of Thein Sein's reform programme. Despite this, these Chin villagers, the women with their famously painted faces and long, slender pipes, had been all but ignored by the state and federal authorities. One of the villages had written to the state government a few years previously to complain about the rat disaster. An official wrote back, declaring that this was not a disaster, that they were only rats, and there was nothing they could do anyway.

Tellingly, officials from the military regime's governing party, the USDP, had appeared at some of the villages during the 2010 election promising help to build new paths or improve the access roads to some of these villages. Their offers had been taken up; some villagers had even voted for the regime as a result. But that was the last contact most villagers had had with Burmese authority. As all travel in and out of Chin State was extremely restricted by the Burmese government, almost none of the Chin I met had even seen any of the rest of the country, or been much beyond Kanpetlet Township. The Chin did not complain; after all, they knew of nobody else against whom to compare their lives. But these villages were a sorry example of just how impoverished many people in Burma had become over the decades.

Traditionally, the hill peoples have always been the most marginalised in the country and so I might have concluded from my visit to the Chin villages that these were probably the poorest people in Burma. But what I saw in Chin State certainly matched up with what experts on the ground were recording elsewhere in the last decade of the old military regime. Than Shwe's junta denied that there were ever any food shortages in the country, let alone poverty or malnutrition. Yet, surveys of Burma's Irrawaddy Delta and the Dry Zone, in the centre of the country, and normally one of the more prosperous areas, suggested otherwise. Dozens of villages here reported that 85–90 per cent of both farmers and landless families faced "food insecurity and lack of food, even when there was not a drought". Furthermore, the same survey also reported much higher levels of malnourishment and "wasting" in young children than the government allowed.[4]

The wisdom of monks, and the revenge of Nargis

In domestic political terms, this would not have had such critical results as long as the generals continued to hide Burma's relative decline from its own people. Largely cut off from the outside world as they were from 1962 onwards, the Burmese would have had less cause to complain if they assumed that they were doing no worse than anybody else in the region. For many years, consequently, the generals insulated the majority of the population from the outside world, effectively banning international calls, foreign papers and useful Internet sites (in the very few places where the Internet was available). Foreign travel was heavily restricted, except for the elite. Travel inside Burma was also restricted, certainly in the Ne Win years. Tourists were allowed in after the 1990s, on a variety of short-stay visas, to earn hard currency, but the regime did its best to steer them away from local Burmese as well as the poorest, rural areas.

Eventually, however, Burma's military rulers could no longer keep up the pretence. Even if they could fool themselves for a time, there came a point at which it became just too hard to fool everybody else. Michael Montesano, an expert on Burma and South-East Asia, says that with all the advances in technology, television, computers and the Internet, even in Burma there was no longer any way that the generals could "brush this stuff under the carpet anymore".

In this context, it is salient to compare Burma to the generals' close ally North Korea. That country's government oversaw a similarly disastrous reversal in economic fortunes, yet the authorities have done a much better job of shutting out the world. The regimes of Kim Jong-il and Kim Il-sung, the founder of the ruling dictatorial dynasty, acted ruthlessly to sever all contact with the outside world. This was much easier for North Korea because it has fewer borders: a very short one with Russia, a much longer one with China (a loyal if quarrelsome supporter), and the other with South Korea. The regime's main antagonist, could, in different circumstances, have been the source of endless destabilising anti-regime literature and propaganda. But this border with the South is one of the most heavily militarised and tightly sealed in the world.

Burma, however, is surrounded by five different countries, with which it shares extremely long and very porous borders. The border with China alone is about 1,350 miles long. Thus, there has always been a relatively large amount of cross-frontier activity, be it smuggling, tactical support for the militias of the hill peoples, or refugees coming and going. By the end of the early 2000s, there were nearly two million Burmese living and working in Thailand, driven there by the lack of opportunities in Burma. There were also sizeable Burmese communities in Singapore and elsewhere in the region, as well as farther afield. They managed somehow to stay in touch, by many imaginative methods, with their families and friends back in Burma, giving those inside the country a very good idea of how much richer and freer all the surrounding countries were. North Korea's geography and history lent itself to being cut off. Burma proved almost impossible to isolate.

There were also two domestic events that conspired to expose Burma's decrepitude to its own people, puncturing the official view of national success and prosperity. One was the monks' protest of 2007, the Saffron Revolution, and the other was Cyclone Nargis, which hit the south of the country in 2008. Both these contributed significantly to forcing change in Burma by confronting the regime squarely with its own failings, and then exposing those failings to an unusually wide audience.

The monks' protests of 2007 were sparked by the government's sudden removal in August of subsidies on fuel, causing a rapid increase in prices. The government, which had a monopoly on fuel sales, doubled prices from about $1.40 to $2.80 a gallon, and boosted the price of natural gas by about five hundred per cent. These hikes also led to an increase in the cost of food. Soon afterwards, protesters took to the streets to rail against the economic hardship brought on by these enormous price rises. The regime was accustomed, by now, to protests, but uniquely, and much more threateningly, these protests were started and led by thousands of monks.

Ariya, the head of the Shwegug monastery in Mandalay, explained to me in 2014 how the monks had come to start these protests. In Mandalay, the traditional heart of Burma, the *sangha* was particularly influential, so it was here that their dissent was likely to have the most effect. "Every morning monks went to the people's homes for alms, so the monks really knew about the people's problems", recalled Ariya. "The government could not know as well as the monks, because the monks went to people's homes every morning! So, the monks wanted to help their donors. Prices of everything were increasing all the time, so people were really suffering." Indeed, people were suffering so much that they had little to spare for the monks on their morning rounds, so they were going hungry as much as the donors. Thus, the monks started walking slowly around the moated walls of Mandalay's old royal palace asking for *metta*, or "love" in the lexicon of Burmese Buddhism. It was a peaceful demonstration, to publicise hunger and suffering; it had no explicit, or implicit, political purpose. As Ariya explained, "the aim was to pay respect to each other, to love each other, not to be violent or harm each other. People did not have enough food . . . and people did not have any rights, or political rights. So, the monks had to draw attention to this."

For a few tense days the monks were allowed to continue their demonstration, drawing out thousands in support. Nobody was sure how the government would handle this unprecedented rebellion of the *sangha*. Eventually, however, Than Shwe seemed to have made up his mind. Ariya describes what happened next:

> The monks had gathered at one of Mandalay's most famous pagodas. They tried to go out to continue their walk around town, but they were surrounded by people with sticks and batons who beat them back. It was very systematic. Wherever the monks went, these people arrived very fast. My monks and pupils were attacked by these people, and some were injured. The government used the USDP people [in fact, the people from its forerunner called the Union Solidarity and Development Association] and the *Swan Arr Shin*, the people controlled by Aung Thaung . . . the whole city knew about this. The *Swan Arr Shin* are made up of grassroots people: alcoholics, thugs; they were given 3,000 kyat to do anything. They got money for beating the monks, and then probably got drugs and alcohol too. Some are criminals and former prisoners. Lots of people believe that the man who put down the Saffron Revolution was Aung Thaung.

Over the following days the regime swarmed over Mandalay's monasteries, hunting for "terrorists", as the protesting monks came to be labelled, and arresting many of them. Ariya recounted:

> In this monastery there was a donation ceremony, and a man from MI [Military Intelligence] came pretending to be a donor, and enquired about everyone. They tried to do this all the time. In many monasteries some people came in who pretended to have mental disorders, and were selling beans and things to the monks. They would also have a good look around. In our culture, such sellers cannot talk to monks, so these people were very fake.

In Mandalay, at least, no one was killed or seriously injured. In Yangon, it was a very different story. Clearly, discontent with the economic situation in the country had now reached such a pitch that tens of thousands of citizens were prepared to take the risk of protesting. They marched with the monks, and when the police, army and *Swan Arr Shin* went in violently, the result was bloodshed. They shot into crowds of protesters, wounding and killing scores, including monks.

The regime succeeded in quelling the protests. But in deeply Buddhist Burma the killing of monks was profoundly shocking. The regime and its apologists tried to claim that the dead and injured were mostly rogue monks, or people just dressed up as monks – "bogus monks". Or even terrorists. But the truth could not be concealed, that these were genuinely peaceful, non-violent demonstrations with no particular political agenda, to draw attention to widespread hunger and poverty. Than Shwe had always been thought of as ruthless, murderous, coarse and intolerant, but now he was also revealed as a monk killer, and there was no greater crime in Burma. According to Debbie Aung Din Taylor, the Burmese head of an NGO who witnessed these events first hand, "everyone thought that Than Shwe had crossed the line. And he probably thought so too." Just as damaging for the regime, in the new age of digital cameras and laptops, much of the military's gruesome crackdown was captured live on film and flashed around the world in real time. Nobody had any excuse to ignore what was really going on in Burma.

I asked Ariya and his fellow monks in Mandalay whether they had been surprised by the ferocity of the government's action, the shooting and beating of monks. "No", he replied, "they will do anything to protect their power. They are only concerned for their power." Ariya had demanded that the thugs stop the beatings in Mandalay, but they didn't listen to him. "They had no morality. In Burma there are two laws; for those that the government loves, but if they don't like someone, they will use all the laws against him. So there is no *rule* of law here."

Buddhists believe that every evil act will provoke a reaction against the perpetrator, of equal ferocity. When Cyclone Nargis arrived scarcely eight months later, many believed it to be divine retribution against a country that had killed its own monks. Nargis was a tropical cyclone that came barrelling out of the Bay of Bengal and across the Irrawaddy Delta in early May 2008. It was one of the deadliest cyclones in history, causing the worst natural disaster in Burma's recorded past. It sent a storm surge twenty-four miles up the delta, flattening almost everything in its way and killing about 140,000 people. One township alone, Labutta, was thought to have suffered about eighty thousand dead; another, Bogale, lost about ten thousand dead. A further 55,000 people were recorded as missing and many more dead were found in other towns and areas. Damage was estimated at about $4 billion by the UN, making it one of the most costly cyclones ever recorded in the region.

The tragedy was worsened by the response of the government. The emergency services had become so denuded of equipment, modern or otherwise, they were unable to respond to this sort of disaster, leaving the government with almost no means either to help those who had narrowly survived or to rebuild the delta. Instead, therefore, the government tried to play down the magnitude of Nargis, in the hope that its helplessness would not be shown up. But the sheer scale of the catastrophe meant that the awful news inevitably got out. Even the state media had to report it eventually, and as the government proved unwilling or unable to help, it was the Burmese people themselves who stepped up. Thousands of ordinary Burmese left Yangon with their own modest supplies of food, water, clothes and blankets to aid the victims. And, as Taylor, whose NGO was heavily involved in the relief effort, recalls, "When the Burmese went to the villages to help and rescue them, they were shocked by the state of rural poverty." And so the veil was lifted from the official statistics to reveal Burma's true impoverishment.

Worst of all, the government compounded its sins by refusing for a long time to let in any outside aid. Despite requesting help from the United Nations almost immediately, in practice the government held up international, particularly Western, deliveries of aid for days afterwards, partly out of fear that such Western intervention would precipitate a full-scale invasion of Burma and regime change. Certainly some of the Western rhetoric did not help. Gordon Brown, Britain's prime minister, threatened to deliver "forced airdrops", violating Burmese airspace and thus sovereignty, if the regime did not allow foreign aid. Taylor, married to an American, was one Burmese who acted as a go-between for the paranoid generals and the West, striving to reassure the regime that the proffers of aid were sincere, and that the intentions of those offering help were, on this occasion at least, strictly humanitarian.

Nonetheless, it was only about a week after the cyclone hit that a large-scale American airlift, for instance, to Yangon was authorised. It took weeks more for international aid workers to get visas to enter the country and help. Even then, they were only admitted into the affected areas under close military supervision. The delays in delivering relief to the delta undoubtedly cost many more lives than might otherwise have been the case. After the first shock of the event, the military also started trying to block the self-help efforts of the Burmese themselves, in a desperate attempt to pretend that everything was quickly returning to normal. One journalist, Emma Larkin, managed to slip in on a tourist visa soon after Nargis struck and she witnessed the frustrations of the professional foreign aid workers and the local Burmese alike. She writes of the fortnight following Nargis:

> With the majority of international aid workers trapped in Rangoon, the rumours that travel restrictions would be extended to Burmese people were validated by various actions taken by the authorities in the delta. Soldiers at checkpoints started handing out a leaflet stating that it was time to wrap up efforts to help storm victims, as the relief phase of the operation was over and rehabilitation had begun. The text told donors to stop giving aid to people sitting by the road, claiming that they were not real storm victims and had only gathered at the roadside to receive free handouts. From now on, those who wanted to help should contact the Disaster Management Committee in the relevant townships. It seemed a polite enough notice, but it was accompanied by increasingly harsh vigilance. Cars and trucks carrying aid were frequently impounded and their contents confiscated. In one instance, a convoy of twenty trucks was stopped on its way back to Rangoon; the drivers were arrested and kept in jail overnight.[5]

Overall, Cyclone Nargis demonstrated the callousness of the regime and further exposed Burma's poverty and underdevelopment to its own people. It certainly undermined any lingering claims to credibility by the generals. But on the positive side, the episode showed that the Burmese people could mobilise to help themselves, and in fact Nargis proved an important spur to the development of an increasingly active and influential civil society in Burma.

Fantasy economics

But even if it was eventually clear to most Burmese, including the generals in their make-believe world, that the country was economically prostrate, its people short of food, malnourished and usually jobless, there was also the question of blame. Who was responsible for the mess?

The Burmese Way to Socialism had undoubtedly contributed; the nationalisations of 1963/4 had ruined the most profitable bits of the economy and driven out most of the country's entrepreneurs and businessmen. However, the government could not be entirely blamed for the ruinous consequences of Ne Win's Soviet-style command and control economy. After all, Burma's leaders were, to a great extent, merely following the economic policies that were in vogue at the time, championed by many leftists in the West as much as communists behind the Iron Curtain. Despite the Buddhist add-ons to the Burmese Way to Socialism, Burma was essentially in the grip of the economic orthodoxies of the day, taken a little further, even if the generals did not really understand them. The quasi-Marxist economy lasted until 1989, after which it was relaxed and some private enterprise was allowed back into the system. Later on, in the 1990s and beyond, the government could easily blame foreign sanctions for the mess, which obviously starved Burmese manufacturers of foreign markets and investment.

Nevertheless, Ne Win's regime added its own, particularly disastrous Burmese ingredient to the policy mix, for which it was solely and unavoidably responsible – successive demonetisations. These led straight to disaster. The first demonetisation, in 1964, was almost justifiable, but by the time of the third one in 1987, economic management had entered the realms of fantasy.

The demonetisations were a response to the inflationary pressure that quickly built up in the economy as the nationalisations and economic controls of the Burmese Way to Socialism took effect. Amongst other things, this created a huge black market for highly sought-after foreign goods. Rather than easing back on the nationalisations or allowing more private enterprise, however, the regime chose instead to withdraw high-value notes from circulation. Thus, in May 1964, the Demonetisation Act, Revolutionary Council Law No. 7, decreed that all 100- and 50-kyat notes would no longer be legal tender; people would have to trade them in for lower denomination notes at specially designated centres. Unfortunately, this inherently impractical process was so bedevilled by corruption, disorganisation and public ignorance that the result was chaos. It was not only the government's largely imaginary capitalist "speculators" and "hoarders" who were hit by this measure, but ordinary people too.

Balwant Singh, a former government official and Commissioner of Pegu division, left this account of the population's scramble to avoid having their life savings wiped out by government fiat:

> Centres for surrendering the notes were designated. One was . . . next to our house. As all notes were to be turned in within a week of the announcement, a huge crowd formed. The press was so heavy the brick pillar of the centre's gate gave way. Crowds at other locations all over Rangoon were equally large and the arrangements equally poor. The public was hurt and resentful, and tempers boiled over. It was pitiful to see so many waiting their turn in the hot sun – a turn that never came! By evening it was clear that only a small number were going to get to turn in their notes for the promised exchange. The doors of the centre were closed and the crowd told to disperse. An announcement was made that next day; note-changing venue would be the Teachers Training College.
>
> The next day, I got up at 2.30 a.m. to hand in my hoard of 11,000 kyat. When I reached the place, the gates were locked, so many of us climbed the iron railing – a humiliating experience. There were twenty people already in the queue for 1,000 kyat and over depositors. The line for those depositing 1,000 kyat or less was longer. By 10 a.m. I had handed in my treasure and gone home.[6]

He was one of the lucky ones; many others never got their money. Understandably, this debacle profoundly shook confidence in the currency. Thereafter, people preferred to hoard gold or precious stones instead, gravely weakening the formal financial system. The two later demonetisations, in 1985 and 1987, were even more disastrous. The 1985 move was again justified as an attack on unscrupulous speculators, who were supposed to be "manipulating the market". This time 100-, 50- and 20-kyat notes were to be withdrawn, to be replaced by a bewildering system of 25-, 35- and 75-kyat notes. Once again the process of trading in the notes was chaotic, so much so that only about a quarter of surrendered notes were reimbursed. In any case, only a maximum of 5,000 kyat per person per household could be exchanged, arbitrarily wiping out a significant proportion of middle-class savings.

The 1987 demonetisation, though, was the most absurd and damaging of all. This seems to have been ordered at the personal whim of Ne Win, and all three new denominations were withdrawn that had been issued just two years earlier. This time, no compensation whatsoever was offered, and thousands again saw their meagre savings become worthless overnight. Completing the picture that this was the act of a madman, new notes were shortly afterwards issued in multiples of nine (45 and 90 kyat), apparently for no better reason than the dictator's superstitious belief in the power of his favourite number.

Unsurprisingly, no one wanted to hold cash for fear of further sudden demonetisations. Consequently, the demand for black-market goods increased again and inflation ballooned. No one could any longer doubt how utterly capricious and despotic Ne Win's regime had become. That same year, in a desperate bid to attract aid money and borrow at cheaper rates, Burma requested, and was given, "least developed country" status by the UN.

It was the economic chaos precipitated by the 1987 demonetisation that led directly to the widespread protests of 1988. The demonetisations showed clearly the deep incompetence of the regime. Adding this wanton financial vandalism on top of all the other privations that the Burmese had had to bear since 1962 was too much. The tinder was so dry by early 1988 that a tea-shop brawl in Rangoon between students and local youths provided the spark to light the people's revolution that subsequently swept away Ne Win and brought forward Aung San Suu Kyi as the new champion of the Burmese.

CHAPTER SEVEN

The Lady's not for turning: The challenge of the NLD

THE YEAR 1988 WAS a watershed in Burma's history. Mass-protests swept away General Ne Win and the increasingly repressive, incompetent and cruel military regime that had ruled since 1962. The military remained in charge, but were forced to change in order to survive. More importantly, a strong and coherent opposition emerged, the National League for Democracy. The NLD has to this day kept up the moral and political pressure for reform in Burma, even while its leaders have been in turn jailed, exiled or killed.

Out of the chaos and bloodshed of 1988 also emerged the one leader, Aung San Suu Kyi, who would provide the most severe challenge to the regime. For Aung San Suu Kyi and the NLD provided the constant, unrelenting pressure from the grassroots that has contributed significantly to Burma's political shifts from the early 1990s onwards. Just as vitally, she became the international symbol for Burma's struggle for democracy, and thus the arbiter for all Western decisions on the country. This, more than anything, gave her enormous influence over the political landscape. Western-imposed sanctions that the generals needed so desperately to be lifted would only be removed on her say-so. Eventually, the president who most wanted to change the country, Thein Sein, would have to swallow hard and come asking this long-term political prisoner for help.

The Lady returns

As we have seen above, the protests against the regime that started in March 1988 were grounded in the economic distress of a population that had had to endure the demonetisation of the previous year on top of decades of economic mismanagement. Demonstrations sprang up throughout the country, precipitating, in the first case, the resignation of Ne Win and his senior colleagues in July. This came as a huge surprise, and was seen at the time as an impressive victory for the regime's opponents. Not only that, but the government also promised, for the first time, multi-party elections. It seemed, initially, like a Burmese spring. It was anything but.

Ne Win was replaced as president and head of the ruling BSPP party by another general, Sein Lwin, an unpopular crony, who in turn made way for Dr Maung Maung, a more conciliatory figure, in August. He was a constitutional lawyer who had been chief justice under Ne Win. Yet, all the while, since the resignation of Ne Win, pressure continued to build on the streets of Rangoon and other cities for further, deeper change. The anti-government demonstrations reached their climax in the first two weeks of August. But at the same time pressure from army hardliners had also been building, to restore order and clear the streets. There was another shift – some called it a coup – within the military regime when yet another General, Saw Maung, took over from Dr Maung Maung. Then, on 18 September, the army moved onto the streets of Yangon to stop the protests by force. The real shooting had begun, as Ne Win had warned that it would. Altogether, over the course of the following two months of ruthless, bloody repression, about three thousand unarmed people were killed. Any pretence at ruling with popular consent had gone. This was all about coercion and deadly force.

In the midst of the uprising, entirely by coincidence, Aung San Suu Kyi returned from the UK to nurse her dying mother. She arrived in March and by 8 July her mother had recovered sufficient strength to be taken home to the family compound on University Avenue on the shores of Inya Lake. This house had been given to the family by a grateful nation in honour of her father General Aung San; all the families of the Thirty Comrades had been so rewarded. (General Aung San's own home, where he lived from 1945 to 1947 as he negotiated Burma's independence, is now open to the public as a museum, after having been closed for many years by the military regime.)

Before July 1988, Aung San Suu Kyi had barely lived in Burma. Born in 1945, she lost her father to an assassin's bullet aged two, after which she received her early education in India where her widowed mother had been appointed ambassador. Later she was educated in Britain, at St Hugh's College, Oxford University. Here she met and married her husband, the Tibetan scholar Michael Aris, and settled down into the comfortable life of middle-class academia. They had two boys, Alexander and Kim (named after Rudyard Kipling's fictional hero), and lived in a family house in one of the university-city's grandest Victorian crescents.

She visited Burma regularly and certainly maintained a strong interest in her father's life and Burmese politics. She even travelled to Japan to study the most controversial period of Aung San's career, when he worked with the Japanese. But she never showed any desire to live in Burma. Events were soon to change that. When Aung San Suu Kyi was in Rangoon in June 1988 she could scarcely avoid the turmoil and bloodshed going on around her. Unarmed young men were shot right outside the hospital where she was nursing her mother.

Although she did not take part in these demonstrations, her standing as the daughter of General Aung San meant she was quickly drawn into the political arena. Asian politics are dynastic, and so people naturally looked to her for guidance and leadership. No one else of stature had yet emerged who could bind together the burgeoning variety of people now opposed to the regime – disenchanted military officers, students, bankrupted shopkeepers, intellectuals and more. As the man of the family, Aung San Suu Kyi's elder brother might have been expected to fill this role, yet he lived in America, showed no interest in politics and came to be deeply estranged from Aung San Suu Kyi and the rest of her family.

Aung San Suu Kyi had the steel her brother lacked, she had the name and the pedigree, and she was on the spot. Asked by many to speak out, she made her debut speech at the Shwedagon pagoda on 26 August 1988. This slight, pretty woman of forty-three, watched by her husband and sons alongside hundreds of thousands of others, quite unexpectedly proved that she could electrify a vast crowd with the power of her words.

Her speech that day has defined her politics ever since, and set the agenda for the opposition to military rule in Burma. In a direct riposte to Ne Win and the generals who had fought in Aung San's army for independence against the British, she called the ongoing protests in favour of democracy, "a national crisis that could in fact be called the second struggle for national independence." She quoted the powerful words of her revered father: "We must make democracy the popular creed ... the only ideology which is consistent with freedom ... an ideology that promotes and strengthens peace." The delighted crowd roared, clapped and celebrated; democracy had found its voice. She ended by telling of her own "strong attachment" to the army, as, literally, a child of the institution, yet it was time to "get rid of the one-party system ... free and fair elections [must be] arranged as soon as possible."[1]

The opposition team

Thereafter, a coherent opposition movement began to form around her, which quickly came to be called the National League for Democracy. Its leadership reflected the breadth of the resistance that Ne Win had provoked. Foremost among them was Tin Oo, a veteran of Aung San's Burma Independence Army who had been decorated for valour. He was the voice of those who had followed and fought for Ne Win and Aung San against the British in the belief that they were forging an enlightened and democratic Burma, only to be deeply disillusioned by the reality of Ne Win in power. When I met with Tin Oo in 2014 he seemed to be as ramrod straight, dignified and politically engaged as he had ever been. In many ways he, more than anyone, embodied the hopes and disappointments of modern Burma. We talked in his cramped little office in the noisy, chaotic headquarters of the NLD in central Yangon, his voice sometimes barely audible above the din of trucks splashing through the pot-holed, monsoon-lashed street outside.

He was born in Pathein, the biggest town in the Irrawaddy Delta, surrounded by the gentle paddy fields of the country's principal rice-growing area. He left high school in Pathein just as the Second World War started. Like many of his generation, he desperately wanted to join Aung San's Burma

Independence Army to drive out the British, but was at first turned away for being too young. The Japanese attack on Burma at the end of 1941 over-rode such tenderness, and the seventeen-year-old was duly enrolled in the successor to the BIA, the newly formed Burmese Defence Army (BDA) under the nominal control of Aung San. The young Tin Oo was trained for seven months by Japanese officers. He graduated in November 1944 as a second lieutenant in the BDA. He supported the switch to fight for the advancing Allies against the Japanese in March 1945 and ended the war as a company commander.

Tin Oo stayed on in the army after the war and was assigned to one of the three battalions of the Burma Rifles that made up the very small military force that, in his view, saved the government of the newly independent country in 1948. His battalion commander was Ne Win, whom he came to admire for his patriotism and military nous. Under Ne Win's patronage as head of the armed forces after 1949, Tin Oo rose rapidly through the ranks. By his mid twenties he was a Lieutenant Colonel and had become one of Ne Win's most trusted officers. "Ne Win and myself were father and son; we had great affection for each other", recalled Tin Oo. "I admired Ne Win during the insurrections [of 1948–9]", he said, although he was also aware that the head of the army was "very ambitious".

Even after Ne Win's coup in 1962, Tin Oo continued to climb up the bureaucracy, becoming head of the army himself for two years during the mid 1970s. All the time, however, Tin Oo was increasingly aware of how much damage Ne Win's dictatorship was doing to the country, politically and economically: "All the work of the era of parliamentary democracy was undone, all the stuff that we had achieved. Everything began to go downhill from 1966 . . . the failures started, and Ne Win himself became more and more suspicious of the generals under him."

Almost inevitably in the closed, paranoid world of Burma's military politics, suspicions fell on the favourite son himself – "just like Orwell's *Animal Farm*", reflected Tin Oo. It didn't help either that as student street protests started against the regime in 1974, the demonstrators began chanting Tin Oo's name as a possible alternative to Ne Win. That had probably been the final straw for Ne Win. In 1976, Tin Oo was forced to resign, and in the following year he was arrested and jailed.

On his release he spent two years as a monk, and then took a degree in law for the following five years. When the protests of 1988 started, at first Tin Oo did not want to get involved. But, as with Aung San Suu Kyi, others pulled him in. His name carried enormous prestige, especially among all those other former military men who had been cashiered or locked up by Ne Win. So he was persuaded to head a new outfit called the All-Burma Patriotic Old Comrades' League. This represented, in effect, opposition to the military regime from within. Tin Oo gave a well-attended speech in Rangoon, just after Aung San Suu Kyi. Other former military men also flocked to the cause, such as the dissident general Aung Gyi and Kyi Maung, a colonel who had also fallen out with Ne Win.

Very quickly, Tin Oo and his fellow soldiers decided that they could not bring down the regime on their own, so they joined forces with Aung San Suu Kyi and the students and intellectuals who had gathered around her. It helped that Tin Oo had known her father – and from the start he admired her tough qualities.

The most prominent of the intellectuals around Aung San Suu Kyi was Win Tin, another member of the new central committee of the NLD, officially founded in September 1988. He was a highly principled and combative journalist, fiercely opposed to Ne Win's regime. Myint Myint Khin, a left-wing female barrister and associate of Win Tin's, also joined the central committee. They adopted as the NLD's emblem the fighting peacock; during the struggles against British rule it had been used as a symbol by Aung San and the students.

The NLD was from the start, therefore, a very diverse mix of people. Peter Popham, one of Aung San Suu Kyi's biographers, has written:

> The NLD has always been more a "united front" than a party, a bundle of aspiring politicians with different ideas and backgrounds, bound together by the desire to end military rule and by belief in Suu and her charisma. It had little of the ideological glue that defines a party in much of the world, and but for her it would surely have broken into several warring factions long ago.[2]

There was nothing that the founders of the NLD or anyone else could do about the massacres of September 1988, nor the military clampdown that followed them. Thousands of students and activists were forced to flee Rangoon, to avoid the military's dragnet. Many went to the border areas, where some joined the rebel ethnic militias to take up arms against the Burmese government, now their common enemy.

One such was Ko Nyi Nyi Kyaw. Now an activist in Mandalay, in one of the city's tea shops in 2014 he told me how he had got involved in the 1988 uprising in Mandalay:

I was twenty-two and before the shootings in 1988 I had never been involved in politics; I was never interested. After graduating from high school I attended the technological institute in Mandalay. I studied engineering and wanted to go to sea. Some of the teachers there inspired me to take part in politics . . .

On 7 August a lot of flyers were around to advertise a protest on 8 August. At 10 a.m. that day, groups of youths came out onto the streets, but the army attacked them with cars and trucks. The army tried to run them over . . . my friend, a 19-year-old, his name was Kin Maung Wyn Salim, was the first person shot dead that day. There were two shot dead. I saw this happening. My friend's body was on the road, covered in blood. So, people were very angry and gathered around again, so the army fired again. There was a lot of blood on the ground. This made me very angry . . . the army were treating his body like a dog. That changed my life.

I started protesting. Then the monks came out to join the protests, for three days. Then the students of Mandalay University. I was in the engineering school compound when one army battalion forced its way in. I was tortured and had my teeth kicked out. We were transmitting news about the protests from the school compound and the army thought that we might be making weapons as we were engineering students. Fifty-six students were eventually arrested, and I was held for seven days. When we arrived at Mandalay prison it was very empty, and after that about fifty people arrived every day, including those with mental diseases and skin diseases – lepers. I thought the army did this intentionally, to cause trouble; I was put in a cell with lepers.

During the few weeks of August and early September before the final military crackdown on the 18th, Ko Nyi Nyi Kyaw, like others, enjoyed a brief spell of open political activism, organising the students into a more concerted opposition to the government. But after the next round of shootings and beatings began on the 18th, he took the decision to flee, beginning his new enforced life as an underground activist. He, like thousands of other students, headed for the hills along the eastern borders, hoping to link up with the existing ethnic militias to translate their political protest into a new armed struggle:

> I went from Yangon to Mandalay by train, and then from Mandalay to Myone, and then from there to Laiza on foot. That took ten weeks, dodging army patrols. The reason I went to Kachin State is that there was a communist army there, but the students only joined the ethnic groups . . . We worked with the KIA. My group in Laiza was about five hundred . . . in the whole country there were about 30,000 such students. In Laiza, we got rice and salt from the KIA, we got some money, a monthly salary, and also military training and weapons. We also got some advanced training, like using mortars.
>
> The main reason the students went to the borders was to train and to protect themselves. We still wanted to carry on our civil rights movement, but not by arms. We were only holding arms for democracy. People respected the armed students. The area where I commanded was near Bhamo. There were Shan and Kachin communities there . . . and a lot of Shan youths joined us too.

Ko Nyi Nyi Kyaw thus became one of the leaders of the students radicalised by the events of 1988. In 2005, they formed into a more coherent organisation called the 88 Generation. This pro-democracy group shared many of the same aims as the NLD, and there was a great deal of crossover between the two in terms of ideas and personnel, but they remained distinct. Many students, like NLD members, chose to become exiles abroad, often in Thailand, rather than remaining in Burma with the ethnic militia groups. The big Thai towns nearest to the Burmese border such as Chiang Mai and Mae Sot thus became hosts to increasingly large and diverse Burmese exile groups.

The events of 1988 shook the military regime to the core – from now on it was to be confronted by not only the armed ethnic militias that it had been fighting since independence, but also by a large, angry, organised and sometimes armed political opposition. The following year, in 1989, a nervous and clearly uncertain new military government, anxious to find some common way forward (only to save its own skin), declared that it would hold elections to a new parliament. This body would then draft and vote on a new constitution. The regime did everything it could to cripple the opposition's chances of doing well in the poll. The NLD's leaders were all picked up and imprisoned; Aung San Suu Kyi herself was placed under house arrest in July 1989. The government now also introduced a new rule that she could not stand as a candidate for president because she was married to a foreigner. All forms of campaigning were effectively banned, and in any case under the prevailing martial law it was illegal for more than five people to gather together. The occasional party broadcast had to be preapproved by the censors. Naturally, the government picked the most auspicious date possible for the poll, 27 May 1990, a veritable profusion of lucky nines.

Despite all this, the result was a landslide victory for the NLD and their, by now, wildly popular leader. The party took 392 of the 492 seats on offer. Voter turnout was 72.6 per cent. The regime's proxy party, the National Unity Party, came second in terms of share of the votes, with about 22 per cent, but fourth in terms of seats, with just ten.

This electoral humiliation came as a tremendous shock to the regime that, for reasons still unclear to this day, had badly underestimated the NLD's popularity. Confronted with this incontrovertible vote of no confidence, the government simply refused to convene parliament, effectively nullifying the result.

It should be remembered that the 1990 vote was not a general election in the normal sense of the term; it was for a parliament to draft a new constitution, so the NLD was not denied an explicit mandate to govern the country. Nonetheless, it was a clear demonstration of the opposition's popularity. By not convening the parliament as promised the State Law and Order Restoration Council, or SLORC, as the regime had rebranded itself, denied the NLD the right to have the largest say in framing the new constitution, a right that it had won overwhelmingly at the ballot box. Thereafter, there were no elections until the largely rigged general election of 2010. In between, the military regime attempted to snuff out the opposition threat by force, and to develop a new constitutional settlement on their own.

Insein, pronounced "insane"

To crack down on the NLD, during the twenty or so years following 1990 most of its leaders were arrested, rearrested, jailed and tortured. Aung San Suu Kyi was famously subject to several long periods of house arrest in her lakeside home. On the occasions when she was released, she was never allowed to stray far from Yangon. In 2003, her convoy was attacked by the thugs of the *Swan Arr Shin* and she narrowly escaped with her life.

Her fellow leaders suffered much worse than house arrest, such as co-founder of the NLD Win Tin. I met him in the small converted garage and outhouse that passed as his home, just a year or so before his death in 2014, aged eighty-five. Win Tin lived here courtesy of a friend and supporter, as he himself had lost his house, salary and almost everything else during his many years in prison. Sitting on a small chair, conveying a slightly donnish air surrounded by books and papers, he reflected on all that he had lost and gained during his long, hellish years of incarceration.

As one of the founders of the NLD, Win Tin had been picked up and imprisoned by the authorities early on, in July 1989, and had subsequently served almost twenty years in the notoriously harsh Insein prison. By some accounts Win Tin was the longest-serving political prisoner in the world. As a close colleague of Aung San Suu Kyi and a fierce and longstanding journalistic critic of the regime even before he formed the NLD, he was singled out for special treatment in prison; he was, by his own account, branded a communist, a hardliner, the puppet-master of Aung San Suu Kyi. Consequently, the prison guards, together with officers from military intelligence, tried to break him, subjecting him to the vilest and most humiliating treatment that they could devise. He was kept in solitary confinement for most of the time, only being allowed out to see other prisoners during his increasingly frequent visits to the prison hospital. Win Tin was never allowed to read or write in his cell. He spent five years in a special block run by military intelligence where he was interrogated over and over again, but at very irregular intervals, sometimes once a day, sometimes once a month, to keep him disorientated. "At the beginning of the sentence, they asked questions for days on end, and to tire me out I got no sleep and little food", he recalled. If his interrogators were especially disappointed with the answers they were given, and they usually were, he was incarcerated in the part of the prison where the Alsatian guard dogs were trained to fight. Here, he was forced to sleep on the floor of a tiny kennel, surrounded by the constant barking and howling of the dogs. On one occasion he had to endure this for a full seven months. All the time, his persecutors wanted him to renounce the NLD and Aung San Suu Kyi, and to confess to ulterior motives for wanting to sabotage the regime. He was promised that if he did so he would be released. He was offered other inducements, such as being allowed to travel abroad. He refused all these blandishments, telling me that "I couldn't give in, because others were looking up to me as the leader of the party."

As I spoke with him in 2013, Win Tin remained as defiant and unyielding as ever. The streak of righteous stubbornness that sustained him in prison was still very much in evidence. He habitually wore a blue prison shirt to remind the world that although he had been released, many other political prisoners remained behind bars. Speaking in fluent and well-honed English, he was intellectually sharp, his eyes sparkling with curiosity and engagement behind large, owlish glasses. Physically, though, he had suffered terribly. He had lost a testicle after an operation for a strangulated hernia performed in a dirty prison hospital cell, and then lost his teeth after repeated beatings. He was refused dentures. He also had two heart attacks in prison, but was frequently denied medical treatment and Red Cross visits.

Yet, throughout he remained unbowed. On one occasion he sent a dossier to the United Nations detailing the abuses, torture and terrible conditions in the prison. The Burmese authorities punished him for this with another seven years in jail. But eventually, he got his way and was released on his own terms, unconditionally, in September 2008, as part of a general amnesty. It was his personal victory over the regime, and he immediately returned to lampooning the generals and their satraps in his newspaper columns. Win Tin also set up a foundation to provide medical care for former political prisoners.

Almost the only relief he got in prison was thanks to the petty larceny and corruption that infested every corner of the military government. "As long as you can give a bribe, you could do anything", he remembered.

> The prison guards were very corrupt, they would accept anything, food, or money, to do things, like sending messages in and out. Every fortnight we got provisions from home, and sold this to the rich people in the hospital. The rich prisoners got to live in the hospital, where you were relieved of ordinary duties, and these rich people bought sugar, biscuits and more from the other prisoners. The profits from this went to the prison guards, and they smuggled in paper and pens, so we could write at least. We even got a portable radio in . . . but could only listen in the morning and evening, to a bit of the BBC.

Another stalwart of the NLD is Win Htein. When I met him in 2012, it was hard to comprehend that the seventy-one-year-old had spent almost one-third of his life in prison. He remained sprightly, humorous and almost unfeasibly cheerful, betraying few signs of his long confinement. Indeed, he seemed to be enjoying life, having just been elected as one of the new NLD MPs to the federal parliament in the same set of landslide by-elections that had seen Aung San Suu Kyi elected as well.

Like Tin Oo and many of those who helped to start the NLD, Win Htein had been in the army himself, only to be forced out in 1977 on suspicion of having being involved in a plot to overthrow Ne Win. I talked with him outside his small government-assigned hut in the capital Naypyidaw. He was the oldest of the new intake of forty-three NLD MPs, and clearly revelled in his position as the parliamentary party's elder statesman. His new status was reward enough, he told me, for all the sacrifices he had made. A full half of the new crop of NLD MPs were "jailbirds", he proudly told me. Win Htein had been imprisoned on three separate occasions for a total of exactly twenty years and two months; from 1989 to 1995, from 1996 to 2008 and again briefly until his final release in 2010. He served in five prisons around the country, including Insein. Before 2000, he recalls, conditions were particularly grim; he was kept in solitary confinement the entire time, only after 2000 was he allowed to mix with other prisoners. He was beaten frequently by the ordinary criminal inmates, who were assigned to oversee – and humiliate – the political detainees. When he was first imprisoned he was also tortured by military intelligence, the same outfit that paid such close attention to Win Tin.

Women members of the NLD were not spared either. As mentioned earlier, Khin Lay had been a student at a dysfunctional Yangon university in the early 1990s, and started working for Aung San Suu Kyi a few years later. In 2000, she accompanied the NLD leader on a tour outside Yangon and was subsequently arrested by the police. She was thrown into Insein, where she spent four months. Khin Lay was kept with three other women in a cell measuring no more than eight square feet. They were let out only twice a day, for fifty minutes in all. Khin Lay remembered particularly the brutal and relentless interrogation sessions by military intelligence:

> I did five days of interrogation non-stop. I could not sleep, and had to sit on a high stool with no back for the whole day. I fell off the chair. I was allowed to eat but could not wash, and was handcuffed to go to the toilet. I was blindfolded a lot of the time. Some MI asked me questions very politely, some very rudely. They just wanted to torture us . . . they already knew all the answers. It was all men asking the questions, other women felt very threatened. My mother died during my detention, but I was not told.

Revolution by hook, bus and money

With most of its leaders locked up or under house arrest, many of its cadres in exile or hiding in the jungles along the Burma/Thai border, there were few left to keep the NLD going. The party was infiltrated by government informers and stooges at every level, and all comings and goings from its headquarters, a ramshackle set of buildings in central Yangon, were closely watched by plain-clothes police. Party members ran grave risks, and they did so only by leading a life on the run, always trying to stay one step ahead of the authorities. Many of these shadowy, secret supporters of the party constituted a new generation of the NLD. They were too young to have participated in the 1988 protests, and so their paths to political consciousness were usually very different from their NLD elders. Indeed, given the tight official restrictions on news and information from the early 1990s onwards it could hardly have been otherwise.

Take Nay Chi Win, for instance, who was to prove one of the most able of the new generation of NLD activists. At the time I spoke to him in 2013, he had just set up the party's first research department, on a shoestring budget from the floor of his sparsely furnished apartment in downtown Yangon. He was co-ordinating a young team that was also producing briefing documents for the senior party leadership. Each member of the team had a particular subject to cover such as the environment or religious freedom. However, Nay Chi Win had not always been so determinedly political, as he recounted for me:

> I was born in 1980 in Yangon, in the township of Twantay, on the other side of the Yangon River. I went to school, and wanted to be a university student – but in 1998, after I graduated from school, they were all closed. But why? This was my first political question. Up to age eighteen I knew little about politics; I knew only the basics, about 1988 and that Aung San Suu Kyi had won the Nobel Peace Prize, but that was about it. My family explained more, and then a friend, a woman, secretly gave me the UN Declaration of Human Rights, in Burmese, and she asked me to read it secretly or else I would be arrested. I read it, but did not understand much of it in Burmese. But it did start me questioning.

It says much about the Burma of the 1990s that Nay Chi Win and his friends considered they had to read the UN Declaration of Human Rights, to which Burma was officially a party, in secret. Nay Chi Win had three brothers, and it was at this point that their mother suggested that one of them should help Aung San Suu Kyi, and that whoever did so should be supported by the other boys working in the family businesses. As Nay Chi Win had just read the UN document, he was considered the most qualified to volunteer for the Lady, as Aung San Suu Kyi came to be known. In exchange for being supported by his family (for however long it took to bring about democracy in their country) he agreed to forego any share in the family inheritance. This was considered to be a serious sacrifice, for the family businesses included a video-rental store and a small fish farm. His mother worked as a nurse.

But how to start his life as a secret political agent? His mum did not know where the NLD headquarters were, and neither did anybody else in the family. So Nay Chi Win asked at the local tea shop, where someone fortunately happened to work for the NLD on social projects, weighing malnourished children. From here Nay Chi Win joined a fortnightly NLD reading circle, which included Tin Oo, who became like a second father to him; this was the start of his real political education. He also attended English classes at NLD headquarters, where he first came to the attention of the not-very-secret police watching the building. He was sent to the British Council to learn more English.

From here on, together with a small network of NLD activists, Nay Chi Win worked tirelessly to get the word out, and to keep the NLD message in front of the public. In so doing, he launched not just one, but three revolutions, as he recalls:

First there was the hook, or bulldog clip, revolution. Our job was to attach NLD statements and leaflets to the bulldog clips that hung down from people's apartments in Yangon. We did this after dark, every day. Sometimes we had only fifty leaflets maximum, because of a lack of money. We did not have a printer, or computer; sometimes these leaflets would be handwritten.

Then there was also the bus revolution. Two people in a bus would start talking about the NLD and political events, pretending that they had heard the news on the radio, so that people could hear them. We were stopped many times by secret police or informers, but we could claim that we had just overheard it on the radio.

And there was also the money revolution. We wrote things on a kyat banknote, and then handed the money over in shops to spread the word. Sometimes we were stopped by police, but we could claim that we did not know where the money had come from.

During all this time, Nay Chi Win was living a precarious, hand-to-mouth existence, often sleeping rough, at the train station or in the night market. If he could hide away in friends' apartments, he says, he preferred living in the richer areas of downtown Yangon, "because most neighbours were Muslim or Chinese, and so were not involved in politics". Here, therefore, he could be relatively safe from informers.

He was nearly caught three times, and in December 2008 was accused of being linked to the Democratic Voice of Burma, an exile opposition news organisation. On the run again, this time he coloured his hair and dressed up as a punk to confuse the police. From now on his main job for the NLD was to serve as the link between the incarcerated leadership in Yangon and the leadership in exile abroad – so he spent most of his time in a downtown Internet café. He had befriended the owner, who let him do his work there. Questioned by the police as to why he rarely left the café, he claimed that all his family were women and that he had no job, so he was bored and didn't want to go home in the evenings. It was Nay Chi Win who managed to get messages from Aung San Suu Kyi, then under her last period of house arrest, out to the exile NLD movement almost every fortnight. He was the courier – a vital link with the outside world.

By this time he had dedicated a decade of his life to Aung San Suu Kyi and the NLD, but had so far never actually met the Lady in person. She was eventually released from house arrest in early November 2010, and two days afterwards Nay Chi Win was taken round to the famous house on Inya Lake to meet her at last. Theirs was not an overly sentimental encounter. He did not want to pose for photographs with her, as most people did, and she wanted to get on with the job of revitalising the NLD. She seemed to know very little of the NLD, Nay Chi Win recalls, other than the fact that it was in a dire state. "It's very important to set up the party", he remembers her saying.

With the Lady released, and the NLD once again starting to operate as a fully legal political party the following year, Nay Chi Win's clandestine life could come to an end. In 2012, on his own initiative, with the help of an even younger cohort of students and political activists, he started to set up the NLD's research department, this time in the open, with no restrictions. His mother, who had inspired him to work for the NLD in the first place, gave up her job as a nurse and closed down the family video-rental business so she could dedicate her own life to the NLD. She is now the local NLD information

officer in their home township so Nay Chi Win's brothers complain that consequently they now have to support two political activists in the family. "It's
better not to have democracy", they joke.

It is a moot point in the family, however, whether the progress Burma has
made since 2010 does constitute a genuine democracy. The original deal was
that the brothers would support Nay Chi Win until democracy was achieved.
At the moment he is on half pay. It's probably as accurate a measure as any of
the point Burma has reached.

Retribution, revenge and Buddhism

How did those NLD leaders who were imprisoned for so long survive, and
emerge in such apparent good spirits? Even more remarkably, very few of the
NLD people to whom I have spoken since their release – often after ten or
fifteen years in prison – show the slightest desire, or need, for revenge against
those who incarcerated, tortured and humiliated them. This must take a
remarkable degree of self-restraint, at the very least. How have they managed
these feelings, and why do they seem less preoccupied with retribution than
other dissidents released from jail elsewhere in the world?

Win Htein told me that it was his Buddhist faith that had "spared" him
any thoughts of revenge against his jailers. Since 2012, as an MP in the federal
parliament in Naypyidaw, he regularly encounters those in the army or the
military regime who had been personally responsible for jailing him, such as
the interior minister. But, Win Htein said quietly, he tries not to be angry with
them. He just says hello and walks on. Win Htein told me that this is part of
his Buddhist practice. A desire for revenge, for retribution, comes from feelings of anger and hate, he said, and "anger is like fire, it will consume you and
you yourself will suffer". Prisoners like him had already suffered enough, and
it was time to move forward.

Khin Lay put it in similar terms. "We have been tortured", she said, "but
we are the free people, we are spiritually free. They [the army] will feel threatened, they are the ones who will be spiritually imprisoned." She referred to the
self-correcting mechanism of Buddhism, of good and bad karma: "If you do
bad things, you will suffer bad things. So, Than Shwe will suffer after he passes

away . . . he will definitely suffer. Karma is a self-regulating mechanism, and will take care of Than Shwe and people like that automatically . . . they will suffer for the killings of the monks."

Nobody in the NLD, Win Htein argued, wants to exact revenge on their former tormentors and persecutors, no one wants to take them to court or drag them before war-crimes tribunals. Is the irrepressible Win Htein, though, perhaps uniquely strong willed? Maybe, but many other NLD former detainees share his attitude. Take Myat Thu, a very different creature from Win Htein. Much younger, thoughtful, and rather frail looking, he was imprisoned twice for his democratic activism, first in 2000 for two years and seven months, and again in 2008. He was finally released in May 2011 in one of the first mass-releases of political prisoners that marked the start of Thein Sein's reforms. He too spent time at Insein prison, but was then moved, and incarcerated deep in the jungle in Burma's interior.

Here, he told me, living conditions were very bad. The cells had mud floors and he slept on a bamboo mat. Insects and snakes periodically fell from the roof. Myat Thu was in solitary confinement for six or seven months at a stretch; he lost some of his hearing after brutal interrogation sessions and later developed cardiac problems. Yet, Myat Thu professes no desire for retribution. On release he dedicated himself to building a better democracy in Burma, acting as an informal pollster at the landmark by-elections in April 2012. He also returned to his academic studies, winning a highly prized scholarship to the London School of Economics to study political science. He went on to help found the Yangon School of Political Science.

Tin Oo was the most vehement on the subject. Although he was imprisoned at Insein, as the former head of the army he was treated better than most during his time there. He was kept in solitary confinement, with no books, but he had two small rooms, a bedroom and an anteroom. His two-year spell as a monk following his first imprisonment in the 1970s had been particularly instructive. "I meditated mostly", he told me simply. Tin Oo remains determined that the NLD should not seek any revenge on their tormentors, or countenance any violent struggle against Burma's military rulers. For this was the very quality that distinguished the NLD from its opponents, as Tin Oo argued to me:

Our policy from the beginning was to renounce violence or any armed struggle as an instrument of policy . . . if we are burning for some sort of revenge, we will achieve nothing. The people will only say that the NLD is the same as the military people. We have suffered great loss, but we do not seek any retribution. Victims should be compensated, but we seek no revenge . . . we never think about it. People must work harmoniously, all together, whatever their past . . . I feel happy, as long as I can see the liberty of my country again. We want peace and harmony restored for our people.

In this sense, Tin Oo was reflecting Aung San Suu Kyi's own deeply held creed of non-violence, inherited from the thinking and practice of India's liberation hero Mahatma Gandhi. Aung San Suu Kyi had studied Gandhi's writings closely during her time in India and all her actions as leader of the NLD have been deeply imbued with Gandhi's thinking.

Not everyone in Burma, however, accepted Tin Oo's and Aung San Suu Kyi's arguments for non-violence. It was one thing to use such tactics against the British in India, so the argument ran, but the British could just walk away from India, as they eventually did, to slip the consequences of their rule. Burma's generals were in a very different situation. They had nowhere to run to, so they had no option other than to cling to power by any means, no matter how violent and repressive. By this calculus, the moral strength of non-violence among their opponents was less persuasive. To this day many of the armed militias of the ethnic groups tell me that their main difference with the NLD is a fundamental disagreement over violent resistance versus pacifism.

Certainly, the Buddhist convictions of men like Tin Oo and Win Htein, their willingness to cast aside any desire for revenge, has helped Burma's political transition since 2011. There will be no Gaddafi-type gangland executions or humiliating Mubarak-style trials in Burma, even if the NLD does eventually come to full power in the country. Neither, in all probability, will there be any tribunals such as those in Cambodia involving former Khmer Rouge leaders, dragging on for years at the cost of millions of dollars in a chronically poor country. Some in the West have been outraged by the prospect of Than Shwe and his cronies "getting off scot-free". But it is hard to find many Burmese who feel the same. They want to move forward.

One NLD activist with whom I discussed this compared their situation to that of post-apartheid South Africa. There, the new black-majority government led by Nelson Mandela set up a "Truth and Reconciliation Commission" as part of a wider attempt to heal the wounds left behind by fifty years of brutal white-minority rule. My NLD interlocutor observed that the reason the commission was generally regarded as such a success is that it could only hear testimony: it could not press charges or sentence perpetrators. "The trick", he argued, "is to forgive, but not to forget. We are burying a bitter past for a better future." This has been one of the NLD's most admirable and remarkable contributions to Burma's transition.

Win Tin, the man who continued to wear his prison shirt until his death, was less convinced than others about the virtues of relinquishing all desire for retributive justice. He felt no "personal grudge against the military or the generals", he told me, but he could never forgive the military as an institution for imposing so much suffering on the people of Burma. He thought that too many people, especially the NLD icon Aung San Suu Kyi, were too willing to forgive the military. The evils of the military regime, Win Tin told me firmly, should not simply be brushed under the carpet, as if nothing had happened. "The generals have to repent and make some sort of apology to the people", he insisted. If they did not do both of these, and genuinely change their policies to forge a democratic Burma, then they should be sent off to war-crimes tribunals.

Furthermore, Win Tin was also very clear-sighted about what fifty or so years of authoritarian military rule had done to the Burmese people, and to the NLD itself. Talking to me in 2013, in the middle of the stuttering transition process, he warned that people had generally underestimated the effects of the decades of military thought control. The relentless brainwashing and Burmanisation in the schools, all the white, black and brown propaganda, had, he said, corroded the Burmese people's sense of independence and liberty.

"We are like cattle", he declared, and went on unflinchingly to point out how this attitude could be seen most starkly in the unquestioning deference shown to Aung San Suu Kyi, to the detriment of both herself and her party. He remarked how nobody dared to question her, or to volunteer opinions in any way contrary to hers. "We have lived for fifty years under military rule, and people now have a habitual behaviour of not talking out in front of people senior to them", he observed. "This attitude is a reverence for the authority figure, because of the long reign of the dictatorship in Burma." He noted how there was almost no discussion in the NLD about the constitution or other serious matters – everybody, he said, just waited for the Lady to speak. "This is bad for the NLD, bad for democracy and bad for Burma", he said. Win Tin insisted that members of the NLD should maintain an activist attitude, always challenging and questioning authority, whatever its shape or form. Only then could Burma start to become a real democracy. "We are not cattle", he urged. "We should be able to speak out."

CHAPTER EIGHT

Change from the top:
Than Shwe to Thein Sein

THE TRAUMATIC EVENTS OF 1988 dramatically transformed the political and economic landscape of Burma. Despite the unrelenting repression of the NLD and other opposition groups after 1990, when the election result was so baldly ignored, the regime did nonetheless begin to change course. Most obviously, the SLORC, the name for the successor regime to Ne Win's government, abandoned the Burmese Way to Socialism, and it also began to develop what it called a "seven-step road map" to constitutional government, what General Than Shwe would later characterise as "discipline-flourishing democracy". With the economy crumbling and a popular uprising threatening at every turn, the government was in an economic and political cul-de-sac. It was time to change direction, whilst also conceding as little as possible to the regime's opponents.

To acknowledge that the government itself believed it was working towards reform from the early 1990s onwards is important in understanding all that has happened since. In the minds of the quasi-civilians who served under the reforming President Thein Sein, they were merely carrying out changes initiated by the previous government of Than Shwe. The only startling thing about Thein Sein is that, to most people's surprise, he dramatically speeded up the pace of the reforms. In this sense the political transition of the last few years has been very much a top-down affair, initiated and implemented by the regime – with, in the latter stages, the vital participation of Aung San Suu Kyi. This has been both the strength, and the weakness, of the entire process. More than anything, this distinguishes the Burmese transition from the "people power" revolutions of the Arab Spring, the fall of communism in Europe, the toppling of Indonesia's President Suharto and the Philippines' Ferdinand Marcos, to name but a few examples.

Crony capitalism

Take the economy first. Almost as soon as Ne Win's successors in the SLORC, later renamed the State Peace and Development Council (SPDC) in 1997, took over, they began to roll back the highly centralised bureaucratic economy of the Burmese Way to Socialism. Laws were introduced to clear a space for the limited reintroduction of private enterprise and a market economy. The first new private bank since 1963 was established in 1992, and by 2002 a further twenty-one were in business.[1] The Myanmar Agricultural and Rural Development Bank Laws was supposed to organise a proper system of rural credit for the first time. A new central bank was also established. Foreign investment was encouraged, especially from Asia. Thai, Singaporean and Japanese capital, in particular, began to flow into the country. Crumbling old hotels and other assets that had passed into government hands under the 1963 nationalisations were sold off and spruced up by foreign capital. The old colonial Strand Hotel in Yangon, for instance, which had been neglected virtually to the point of collapse under government control, got a makeover and reopened its doors in 1992.

However, no one mistook this new economic landscape for a Western-style free-market system. It was more a case of crony capitalism, or even military capitalism, as almost all the new banks and businesses set up in the 1990s were run and owned by the friends and associates of the ruling generals. Sometimes they were even owned directly by the military itself, through its newly founded holding companies. This was the only way that a business could get a licence to operate, and in return the new businesses were expected to help the government and do its bidding.

This was certainly the case for Burma's banks. Sean Turnell has studied this in some detail. Of the biggest private banks founded after the early 1990s, two of the most notable, Myawaddy Bank and Innwa Bank, were owned directly by a military holding company. The chairman of Myawaddy was usually a senior military officer, a member of the SLORC/SPDC. Likewise, Innwa Bank was owned by the military's other holding company, the Myanmar Economic Corporation. The other bigger banks were usually set up by businessmen considered close to the SPDC. One such was Kanbawza Bank, founded in 1994 by Aung Ko Win.

Consequently, some of these banks were considered to be heavily involved in the money-laundering and drug-trafficking activities of regime members. Myanmar Mayflower Bank, for example, might have introduced the first ATM machines to Burma, but the bank was known to one and all simply as the "Poppy Flower Bank". Many of these sorts of banks were also heavily involved in the regime's prestige projects, such as building Than Shwe's new capital at Naypyidaw.

Some of the other industrial conglomerates that rose to prominence during these years, such as Asia World Group founded in 1992, were also closely linked to the regime, and sometimes to the narcotics trade. The founder of Asia World, for example, was Lo Hsing Han, an ethnic Kokang Chinese who died in July 2013. At one time he controlled his own private militia. Asia World won contracts to expand Yangon's international airport and also participated in several of the more controversial Chinese-led dam projects. The other most famous conglomerate is Max Myanmar, founded in 1993 by a tycoon called Zaw Zaw, well known for his ties to the military. Thanks to his friends, Max Myanmar won contracts to do much of the building work in Naypyidaw.

Several adverse consequences for the country flowed from this particular brand of crony capitalism. Most obviously, since it was all run primarily for the benefit of a small club of people at the apex of Burmese society, very few others saw any benefit. Despite the profusion of new private banks, for instance, lending rates remained too high for the vast majority of the people to afford. Thus, by 2010, still only about 10 per cent of Burma's population had a bank account. And as so many of the new banks and businesses were connected to the regime, and suspected of money laundering and other offences, they were almost all subject to American and Western sanctions from the mid 1990s onwards. At the time of writing, many of them are still subject to the same sanctions.

Furthermore, as most of the new banks and other financial institutions were managed by former, or even current, military people, there was a critical lack of professional expertise to run the system efficiently. There was also very lax regulatory oversight. All this contributed to a severe banking and financial crisis in 2002/3 that nearly wrecked the whole economy (again). The crash was triggered by a classic run on the banks, stemming from people's understandable lack of confidence, leading to a liquidity crisis and a currency shortage. It also impacted the real economy; businesses went bust and employees went unpaid for weeks or months. Even by the beginning of Thein Sein's reforms in 2011, the country had barely recovered from this. The crisis also dampened enthusiasm for any more economic reform. After 2003, there was almost no forward movement in the direction of restructuring the economy.

More discipline than democracy

The regime's attempts to reform itself politically went rather better than its fumbled stab at economic change. As early as 1992, the SLORC convened a "constitutional convention" to try and initiate a broad-based discussion about Burma's political future. The NLD did participate at first, but withdrew in 1995. The process was then moribund until 2004, when the SPDC restarted it with the seven-step road map to democracy.

This proposed a clear succession of steps to a new political settlement: reconvening the national convention; moving to the implementation of a "disciplined democracy"; drafting a new constitution; adopting that constitution via a referendum; holding legislative elections; convening the new parliament; and then forming a new government and other constitutional bodies. According to Burmese officials, the whole process was implemented as promised. The constitutional convention took place as a road show moving around the country to gather views. A referendum was held in 2008, just after Cyclone Nargis; one of the reasons that the government's response to the cyclone was so poor is that it was mainly focused on holding its referendum. This duly endorsed the recommendations of the convention. In 2010, a general election was held to elect a new parliament. Then in 2011, the military government led by Than Shwe resigned, to make way for the newly elected democratic government and new president, Thein Sein. As a bonus along the way, Aung San Suu Kyi was finally released from her last period of house arrest just after the elections of 2010.

Thus, "each step of the road map has been fulfilled", argued Léon de Riedmatten to me in 2013. De Riedmatten worked in Burma throughout the early 2000s, for the UN and other international agencies, often interacting closely with the government. "So, nothing very surprising in all that, it all went to plan. Than Shwe is the architect of the existing democracy, there is no doubt about it." Although, continued De Riedmatten, this was an "imposed democracy", without any contribution from the people. Indeed, the most salient feature of this imposed and "disciplined democracy" is the way in which the military's predominance was cemented into the new constitution. Most obviously, a full one-quarter of the seats in the lower house of parliament were reserved for unelected military officers, and as Section 436 of the new constitution ruled that most amendments to it required 75 per cent of the MPs to vote for the change, this effectively gave a lock on power to the *Tatmadaw*.

Government sympathisers argued that this was not uniquely onerous – Pakistan and Bangladesh also had such provisions – but these countries have hardly been beacons of good governance, let alone democracy. What is for sure is that the arrangements clearly signalled that under its new democratic disguise the *Tatmadaw* was in fact intent on maintaining its power. Moreover, the 2008 constitution further entrenched the special status of the military within the nation. Accorded even more legal privileges by the new constitution, the *Tatmadaw* became virtually a state within a state, beyond the reach of civilian authority.

On top of this, most notoriously, there was Clause 59(f). Than Shwe, who had a particular dislike of Aung San Suu Kyi, probably inserted this very narrowly focused provision into the constitution specifically to stymie the political aspirations of his most feared opponent, then languishing under house arrest for Clause 59(f) that barred anyone whose spouse or children were foreign citizens from running for president. Aung San Suu Kyi's late husband, Michael Aris, was a British academic, while her two sons were born in Britain and hold British passports. Such is her popularity that there was a good chance Aung San Suu Kyi's party was going to wipe the board in the general election in late 2015. But the president is then chosen by MPs. Were it not for Clause 59(f), freshly elected NLD lawmakers would surely quickly elevate Aung San Suu Kyi to the presidency. As it stands, this scenario is impossible under the 2008 constitution, and in the years running up to the 2015 election the army's MPs stubbornly refused to contemplate any change.

In mid 2013, for instance, after months of deliberation a 109-member parliamentary committee charged with gathering opinions on constitutional change issued a report purporting to show that most Burmese were against changing this clause. In all, the committee, dominated by the MPs of the military's proxy party, the USDP, claimed to have received 28,000 letters about proposed changes to the constitution, but fully 100,000 signatories, so the committee claimed, opposed change either to Clause 59(f) or to provisions that guaranteed the armed forces their 25 per cent of the seats in parliament. By contrast, allegedly, a mere 592 signatories favoured scrapping the clause. This was all disputed by the NLD, of course, but it proved that the military were determined to cling on to all the safeguards that Than Shwe had bequeathed to them.

This is a consequence of top-down reform. The new constitution might have made some concessions to the opposition and to democracy, but it still left the political system heavily weighted in favour of the military. Just as pertinently, it may also be true that many in the military saw Burma's transition *ending* in 2011, after the 2010 elections and the elevation of Thein Sein to the presidency, as this was the final implementation of the new disciplined democracy. All that has happened since, on this reading, could just be an irritating and irrelevant coda for many of those in power in Burma.

Of course, the way that the new constitution was drafted was unacceptable to the NLD and its sympathisers. The NLD boycotted the referendum on the new constitution in 2008, and the elections in 2010. But this decision split the party, with some arguing that opposition forces had to take any opportunity, no matter how slight, to express dissent against the government. A breakaway faction of the NLD, calling itself the National Democratic Force (NDF), chose to participate in the 2010 elections, and won sixteen seats. Its MPs have never been forgiven for what many in the NLD saw as a betrayal of the party's principles.

Most of the other political parties did compete in the 2010 election. The Shan Nationalities Democratic Party came in third nationally, winning fifty-seven seats. Nonetheless, with no competition from the NLD, the exclusion of several other minor parties from the election by one means or another and no official media coverage for the opposition, the overwhelming winner was the military regime's newly formed proxy party, the Union Solidarity and Development Party (USDP). It won 59 per cent of the seats in the lower house of parliament. Combined with the 25 per cent of seats reserved for military officers, this gave the government about 84 per cent of the seats in the new parliament. Discipline indeed.

Those from the Burmese opposition and ethnic parties who participated in the 2010 elections believed that it was worth doing so. Many thought that, despite the obvious limitations, the "space" (their favourite word) for opposition politics had widened and that the government was even sometimes willing to listen to them in the new parliament. A member of the Shan Nationalities Democratic Party, the biggest of the minority ethnic groupings, argued that although the election was rigged, his people now had "time and room to prepare" for the following election in 2015. The NDF also urged patience. Their leader, Khin Maung Swe, who was imprisoned by the regime for sixteen years, told me: "We had so many demonstrations on the streets, but with no results. So, now we have moved our fighting to the parliament."

But despite the elections, the government, locked away in its fortress at Naypyidaw, was still not talking to anyone who disagreed with it, let alone political opponents like the NLD. It was attempting to reform in a vacuum. Outside the closed ranks of the military and government insiders, very few Burmese (or foreigners) took the claims of reform seriously, and no one believed it would lead to anything substantial. However, there were some who wanted to get the government talking with people who could really help it to change – if there was anyone in Naypyidaw willing to listen.

The Third Force – breaking the impasse

Hla Hla Win was born in Yangon in 1981. She was educated at one of the best high schools in the capital, which is to say that she learned almost nothing, but being bright, ambitious, forceful and articulate, she managed to win a scholarship to go abroad for her undergraduate degree, to William Penn University in Iowa. Deprived of the opportunity to study anything very much in her own country, she was, by her own account, a "greedy student", taking "minor" courses in a host of subjects, languages, reading, education as well as her major. Returning to her own country in the mid 2000s, she "wanted to change Myanmar", to use the knowledge that she had gained abroad to help her country.

But how to do that? Like many of her generation she was too young to have participated in the demonstrations of 1988, so she had not been swept up by the feverish enthusiasm for the NLD and Aung San Suu Kyi. At the time of her return, the NLD seemed to be achieving little anyway. Politics was at an impasse, with the military regime and the NLD locked in a depressing stalemate. Surveying the apparently futile political scene back home, many of her friends who had also managed to study abroad just stayed away. For a time, this seemed like the correct decision. Hla Hla Win, alongside the few who now were returning, searched and failed to find the right opening. But that all changed in November 2008 when she met Nay Win Maung, the man who was to play a key role in driving Burma's transition.

At that point Nay Win Maung was forty-six, clever, articulate and intense, a chain-smoking journalist and political activist who had graduated in medicine from Yangon University. He was passionate about his work, Hla Hla Win recalls, "but was not interested in power or money". He did a four-month course at Yale University in 2004. Some people who worked closely with him described him as inspirational, and also as an obsessive. Amongst many other things he was a publisher of two weekly magazines, one called *Living Colour*, a business journal, and the *Voice*, but his principal activity by then was running an organisation that he and six others had founded in 2006 called Myanmar Egress.

This think tank, for want of a better way to describe it, was to be an institutional locus for all those like Hla Hla Win who had become frustrated and disillusioned by Burma's political gridlock. They wanted an alternative to the unrelenting oppression of the military on the one hand, and the stubbornness of the NLD on the other. Thus, Egress, and similar bodies, came to be known as the "Third Force" in Burmese politics. The name itself – Egress – expressed what the seven founders wanted to achieve, meaning a "way out" (in Greek) of the political deadlock.

From the very beginning there was an element of subterfuge about Egress. The real aim was to try to enlarge the political space in the country for discussion and dialogue, and then to try to change the political system. But, as one of the founders told me, Egress was billed rather more blandly as a "capacity development centre", so as not to arouse the suspicions of the military. Its overt task was therefore educational, holding classes on topics such as leadership, economics, social entrepreneurship, civil society and comparative constitutional models. These were all subjects that were not explicitly political per se, but that could nonetheless be used to examine and think about politics by those attending the classes. The Egress offices shared a building with a shabby hotel, the Thamada, just up from the downtown area of Yangon. There was a small library, stacked with photostatted books (the real things being largely unavailable in the generals' Burma). One of the main teaching rooms was named in honour of J. S. Furnivall. Hla Hla Win eventually became head of English-language teaching at Egress. It was the opening she had been looking for.

As Hla Maung Shwe, one of the seven founders, told me, "we wanted to change the country; to develop skills and capacity for nation building". Unlike the NLD, which rejected all signs of change in the military regime of the mid to late 2000s – the seven-step programme to democracy and the elections of 2010 – Egress was prepared to exploit any opportunity for change in Burma, no matter how unlikely the source. Their belief was that they had to work with whatever was on offer from the government. If they participated in the processes of constitutional reform initiated by the military, then they might at least be able to influence it a bit in the right direction. Thus, remembered Hla Maung Shwe, they were well aware that the 2008 constitution, for example, was hardly democratic, but they could use its provisions to get to the election of 2010 and do more from there. "If you rejected it completely", he argued, "then the road to reform would be very long."

Hla Maung Shwe was unusual among the directors of Egress in that he was the only one who had formerly been a member of the NLD. He had been imprisoned for just over a year by the regime. The other board members were essentially academics and/or businessmen. The latter were to provide the new organisation with some start-up money, but foreign foundations also provided funding. As well as seeing what they could do in Burma, Egress wanted to forge links with the extensive exile community. For by now, many of the sons and daughters of Burma's middle classes had been educated abroad and were mostly based either in America, with an impressive concentration of talent at Harvard University, or in Chiang Mai. Many associated with Egress or other Third Force organisations had based themselves in Thailand's second-largest city. Egress wanted to harness this impressive array of talent to rebuild the shattered country. By now, some of these exiles, even those who had been radicalised directly by the 1988 democracy protests, were just as frustrated by the political impasse as those who had remained in Burma.

One of their number, Aung Naing Oo, for example, had fled to the jungle after the 1988 killings and had then gone on to found a non-governmental organisation in Chiang Mai. He studied at Harvard University and earned a master's degree in public administration, and so became a key member of the so-called Harvard Group, a group of exiled intellectuals and academics. By the beginning of 2011, however, when I met him, he had long abandoned his earlier support for sanctions and other punitive action against the generals. Sanctions, he told me then, had only isolated the country, and "the more isolated the country is the more the generals and their families can control everything." As for the NLD, he thought that Aung San Suu Kyi's "resistance is a political cul-de-sac, and won't help Burma". If the opposition had negotiated with the military after the 1990 elections, he reflected, "Burma could be a step closer to democracy by now." He, like many of his peers, had decided that a new approach was needed.

Egress certainly aroused the government's suspicions. Military intelligence frequented it in order to nose around. They even filmed some classes, but clearly didn't feel too threatened. For, importantly, although the directors of Egress were clear in their mission that they wanted the military government to change, people like Nay Win Maung were themselves scions of that very same military establishment, affording them a measure of protection.

His parents had both been teachers at the Defence Services Academy in the former British hill station of Pyin Oo Lwin (formerly Maymyo), his birthplace. His parents had therefore taught most of the Burmese military leadership, particularly the generation of generals who were to lead the democratic reforms after 2011: Thein Sein, Shwe Mann and Aung Min. They had therefore known of Nay Win Maung as the son of their respected teachers. Hla Hla Win told me that this alone "established trust" between them and the director of Egress. Nay Win Maung thus became a vital bridge to the military regime – a reformer, but one whom the generals could trust. He was the "go-between", as Hla Hla Win put it, "the only man who knew everyone".

Even so, it was only serendipitously that the generals discovered how their teachers' son could now teach them. In 2007, military intelligence arrested Nay Win Maung for writing about politically sensitive issues in his magazines. Agents cleared out his office, and took his computer and papers to go through back at headquarters. But if the government was expecting to find evidence of subversive behaviour, they were proved wrong. In fact, two of Nay Win Maung's policy papers turned out to be positively constructive. It was stuff that the government, bereft of ideas and yet anxious to move forward after years of isolation, could well use. In the words of his associate Khin Moe Samm, "after a few days he was let go, but they [the military] asked him to continue writing these kinds of things, and to pass them to the government secretly, so nobody would know." The military, naturally, did not want it to be known that they were taking advice from an outside source, and an NGO at that.

The principal figure in the government who took an interest in what Nay Win Maung had to say was Shwe Mann, who was to emerge after 2011 as the boldest reformer in Thein Sein's government. Shwe Mann graduated in 1969 from the Defence Services Academy, where he had been taught by the Egress director's parents, and worked his way up the ranks, from major in 1988 to general in 2003. By 2007, he was a joint chief of staff of the *Tatmadaw* and the third-highest-ranking member of the regime.

After Shwe Mann had discovered Egress, his youngest son Aung Thet Mann (also known as Shwe Mann Ko Ko, born in 1977), who owned one of the country's few wireless providers, was consequently assigned a delicate task by his father. He was discreetly to attend classes at Egress to learn more about the political mechanisms and economic policies that a reforming government might be able to use. This became an important back channel for spreading ideas from Egress and the rest of civil society to the government.

Thereafter, Egress was given licence to teach and lecture on ever more previously controversial subjects, and at the same time their advice was increasingly sought out by putative reformers in the government. While the 2010 election was boycotted by the NLD, Egress was eagerly embracing what it saw as an opportunity to intervene in politics for the better. They offered much more explicitly political classes to those people who would stand in the 2010 election. A lot of the ethnic-based political parties that fought in the election beat a path to Egress, for classes on public policy, civics, political leadership and much else. Altogether, Egress claimed to have trained about ten thousand people in the run-up to the election. Military intelligence was certainly intrigued, again coming round to have a close look at the "voter education" programme.

Many in the NLD, particularly, criticised Egress for cosying up to the junta, of "sucking up to the regime" in Hla Hla Win's words, of giving it a veneer of respectability by allowing it to use the language of reform without the substance. Many saw the election of 2010 as a trap, to seduce unwary opponents into legitimising a parliament that in reality would merely act as a rubber stamp for the junta, with its built-in military majority. Hla Hla Win received threatening emails from Burmese at home and abroad, accusing her of being a traitor to the cause, and more. She was unmoved, seeing this as another unfortunate example of just how dangerously polarised politics had become. Nonetheless, a thick skin was required.

Fortunately, Egress not only had a bridge to the military regime in Nay Win Maung, it also had a bridge to the NLD in Maung Shwe. The former member of Aung San Suu Kyi's party ensured that despite the mutual antagonisms Egress was never cut off completely from Aung San Suu Kyi and the NLD: they all met up amicably enough soon after she was released from house arrest in November 2010. After the 2010 election, the Egress directors also met openly with Thein Sein, with Soe Thein, a former admiral and reform-minded minister, and with Shwe Mann. These ministers were all shopping for ideas, and they talked extensively about nation building, how to reconstruct Burma's shattered economy and how to begin a political dialogue with the opposition.

Maung Shwe understood that they could only achieve any of this with the co-operation of the international community, and the key to winning that support was to win the endorsement of Aung San Suu Kyi. So, it fell to him to broker the crucial meeting between Thein Sein and Aung San Suu Kyi in August 2011. At Naypyidaw, beneath a portrait of General Aung San, the two former adversaries shook hands and posed for photographs. Neither party has given an account of exactly what was agreed, but it's safe to assume that Thein Sein offered to legalise the NLD and release political prisoners, among other political reforms, in exchange for Aung San Suu Kyi promising to encourage Western governments to lift sanctions and to end Burma's diplomatic and economic isolation. This encounter kick-started the reform process, making it a truly broad-based movement across the political divide. It was not a simple task to set the meeting up, with Aung Min and Soe Thein working on it from the government side, but it proved to be the single most critical point in the whole transition. To that extent, Egress had lived up to its name, to find a "way out".

As the reform movement gathered pace after the meeting between the president and Aung San Suu Kyi, so Egress was asked for more and more expert advice and guidance from the government. Thein Sein and his like-minded ministers became aware of how ill informed they were in exact proportion to how quickly they opened up to the outside world. Some of the requests to Egress from Naypyidaw became increasingly frantic. The most memorable was for box sets of *The West Wing*, the 1990s fictional American TV series about life on the staff of an American president. It had been used as a teaching aid in Egress classes, and now, belatedly, the military regime needed to find out in a hurry how democracy was actually supposed to work.

That was about the last thing that Nay Win Maung confided in me, as by January of 2012 he was dead of a heart attack. The smoking certainly hadn't helped, but then, as he told Hla Hla Win, he only had ideas when he smoked, and he had a lot of ideas. He left four young daughters. At his funeral, many of the reforming ministers who had worked with him left their condolences, saying that they had lost a teacher.

A Burmese Spring? Thein Sein and the reformers

Despite how good Egress was at its job, none of its endeavours would have come to anything if there had not been some ministers in government receptive to its message. Indeed, until Shwe Mann showed an interest no one could be sure that anyone at a senior level did actually want genuine change, disciplined or not. But once Shwe Mann came forward, it was clear that some of his colleagues were also looking for a way out of Burma's poverty and isolation. There weren't many of them, but enough to begin a process.

The most important, and unlikely, reformer turned out to be Than Shwe's handpicked successor as president, Thein Sein. Formally voted into office by the vast military majority in the newly elected 2010 parliament, he started his new job in March 2011 and soon proved that appearances can be very deceptive. Slightly stooping, bespectacled, frail and soft-spoken, in contrast to the burly, brutish-looking Than Shwe, he looked like anything but the ex-general that he in fact was. Equally, there was nothing in Thein Sein's resumé to suggest that he would be anything but a model of the repressive military men who normally ruled Burma. He had risen through the ranks obediently doing the bidding of his masters. He had been appointed general and prime minister, and thus Than Shwe's heir apparent, in 2007.

However, immediately on becoming president he gave a series of three remarkable speeches that marked him out as very different from his predecessors. The speeches were his inaugural to the new parliament on 30 March 2011, another that he gave to ministers in the new government and a further one to the Central Committee for Progress of Border Areas and National Races. As one Burma expert, Richard Horsey, has noted, these were all carried in full by the state media, so they were designed to be read and digested by as many Burmese as possible.[2]

Rather than just reeling off the usual inventory of fictitious successes, Thein Sein, for the first time, acknowledged that things had gone badly wrong in Burma, and that many people did not support the government. He admitted that there was deep poverty, as well as corruption. Furthermore, to rectify all this, he argued that the regime would now have to work with "good-hearted political forces" beyond the government – meaning, quite obviously, the NLD. And the regime, he admitted, would also have to enlist the aid of international organisations, such as the hated foreign NGOs, to "improve the socio-economic status of the people". With three strokes Thein Sein had up-ended four or more decades of official lying, evasion and double-talk. Immediately, people in organisations like Egress took notice. The Americans also registered the change in tone, being anxious at this point to open a new dialogue with the regime.

This was remarkably candid, even brave, stuff from the president. But it remains a mystery as to why he poured all this out at this particular point. He was well into his sixties when he gave these speeches. Had he believed these things all the time, but just kept them close to his chest during his rise up the bureaucracy? As Than Shwe's handpicked successor, had he been given the go-ahead to admit to all these failures by the strongman himself, who had presided over them? Certainly, Than Shwe never seemed to contradict anything his successor said or did. We can only assume that the former dictator tacitly endorsed the dramatic change in rhetoric and policy. Maybe there was an agreement between the two men, whereby Thein Sein was allowed a free hand as president as long as he swore not to hound and scapegoat the former president and his family, as had happened to Ne Win (see below).

In this sense, Thein Sein, for all his apparent forthrightness, remains something of an enigma. He was born in a village in the Irrawaddy Delta, into a poor family, so he must have had a better idea than most of his moneyed peers in the upper ranks of the army of what it was like to be poor in Burma. More than most, he would have known how ordinary people had suffered under the incompetent, unjust economic policies of the military governments. Certainly, one of the most heartfelt passages from his first presidential speeches was when he said: "There are still many people whose lives are a battle against poverty, whose lives are a hand-to-mouth existence, and many unemployed people."

As well as being unusually concerned with the poor in Burma, Thein Sein remained, by most accounts, surprisingly honest. He had not enriched himself unduly through his political connections on the way to the presidency, and neither had he, as far as is known, been entwined with the grimy, corrupt drugs and gems trades, despite having been stationed in Shan State for several years.

No tawdry YouTube videos of lavish family weddings have appeared around Thein Sein. In his character, at least, he seems to have been strangely untouched by the selfishness, viciousness and inhumanity of most of those around him.

Could this be why Than Shwe picked him? We will probably never know. Thein Sein certainly became an eager consumer of Egress papers on economic reform and restructuring, showing a rare willingness to listen to anyone who was prepared to offer constructive advice. Again, this was a sea change from his predecessor, who preferred the security of living in a sealed world of syco-phants and yes-men.

Vitally, as the new president had suggested in his inaugural speeches, he personally was open to enlisting Aung San Suu Kyi's help in changing Burma, and to giving her concessions in order to achieve this. In this matter, he took a very different attitude to Than Shwe. Some speculate that Than Shwe's animosity towards her could have been caused by jealousy. As the man who, by his own lights, had introduced democracy to Burma, Than Shwe was exasper-ated by the attention Aung San Suu Kyi got for her own stand for democracy.

Indeed, there is still a lot of conjecture as to exactly why Than Shwe, the brutal military dictator, ever decided to dismantle, even in a limited and controlled way, his own architecture of centralised control. There was the economic misery that his regime had caused, but perhaps also the need to establish a beneficent legacy, to outshine Aung San Suu Kyi, and to counter-balance the killing of the monks in 2007. But the most persuasive argument is that he did not want to end up like his predecessor Ne Win, or his family. After Ne Win's resignation in 1988, the ex-president enjoyed a great deal of background influence for a time, but then fell out with the regime in the late 1990s and died a disgraced man under virtual house arrest in 2002. Furthermore, he saw members of his family also arrested and imprisoned, and even sentenced to death, for an alleged plot to overthrow the regime (although subsequently they were all released). It is said that Than Shwe was also obsessed by the fall of Indonesia's strongman President Suharto, swept away by a mass-uprising in 1998. Following this argument, Than Shwe engineered the transition mainly to end the centralised, arbitrary rule that could so easily crush an ex-president. In short, Burma's new democracy was to be the dictator's exit strategy.

If so, the strategy has paid off. Than Shwe continues to live in Naypyidaw, after what has been in many ways a remarkable departure from office. His successors have left him well alone, and even the NLD, which might have been expected to call him to account for crimes against humanity and corruption, has ignored him. He very seldom makes any public appearance at all.

There is no doubt that Thein Sein has made an enormous difference at the top of government. Even those who sympathised with his ideas inside the government bureaucracy never expected him to move so fast after taking over the presidency. Ye Htut, an ally and later minister of information, admitted to me:

> The speed of reform surprised us. That depended on the president, and that took us by surprise. We were living in a very centralised system for many years, and so did not know how to change. When [Thein Sein] was elected president we were very happy. We understood he would reform, but expected him to take a year or two to consolidate his power, but in fact he moved after three or four months.

Ye Htut, like others, was startled by the honesty of Thein Sein's inaugural speeches.

A senior official, who did not want to be named, also attested to Thein Sein's personal contribution to reform. The president "was a genuine person for change", he told me, "even if some of his cabinet are not willing to change." Thein Sein took a particular interest in anti-poverty programmes, rural development and the issues that he had raised in his inaugural speeches. My friendly bureaucrat was working on one such project that had been approved by the president within three weeks of it being presented to him, a wondrously short amount of time in Burma's lumbering bureaucracy. But, he warned, "if the president doesn't support a project, little gets done."

Rivals, reformers and refuseniks

Shwe Mann, who had taken the first interest in Egress, was probably the second most important figure in the reform process. He must have been expecting to get the top job himself in succession to Than Shwe. Missing out on this in 2011 fuelled an obvious rivalry with the new president, creating a noticeable tension at the heart of the new government. Appointed the Speaker of the lower house of the new parliament in January 2011, he rapidly established the new legislature as a rival power base to the president's office.

Those who knew him best were sure that Shwe Mann was, in the words of one, "using parliament to launch his own presidential bid in 2015" – and sure enough in June 2013 he declared his intentions to run for the presidency. Even so, Shwe Mann's political ambition had one very dramatic and positive consequence: it gave parliament a far greater prominence and significance in the reform process than anyone would previously have imagined possible. For when hundreds of freshly minted MPs arrived in January 2011 to take up their seats in the gaudy new parliament building, nobody took them very seriously. The vast majority were either unelected military MPs, comprising the army's 25 per cent bloc, or members of the army's proxy party, the USDP. Surely, most presumed, this was going to be more of an echo chamber than a debating one.[3]

At first, this was true. MPs struggled to be heard at all, let alone hold ministers to account. But under Shwe Mann that quickly changed. He ensured that proper debates happened, to scrutinise proposed legislation, and he set up specialist parliamentary committees with wide-ranging powers to probe into the darker recesses of the generals' Burma. Parliament thus began regularly to challenge the presidency over legislation and official appointments. In September 2012, for example, an overwhelming majority of MPs from all parties of both houses of parliament voted to impeach the nine judges of the constitutional court. Appointed by the president, the judges had tried to clip the wings of the parliamentary committees, yet they were all forced to resign. Another matter, the passing of a vital new foreign investment law, also became a bone of contention between the presidency and the legislature. Drafts passed back and forth between Thein Sein's office and parliament with, on this occasion, the army MPs trying to protect their own financial interests against the more investor-friendly instincts of the president. It all started to look a little bit like *The West Wing*.

Another contribution to the changes in parliament was the landslide victory of forty-three NLD members of parliament (among them Aung San Suu Kyi) in the April 2012 by-elections. These seats had become vacant as newly appointed ministers relinquished them in order to take up their government jobs. In a major test of Thein Sein's commitment to reform, fulfilling his side of the bargain struck with Aung San Suu Kyi the previous August, these by-elections were allowed to be free and fair – and the NLD swept to victory in every seat they contested bar one. It was a similar sort of triumph, if on a less grand scale, to the one in 1990, but on this occasion the government honoured the result and Aung San Suu Kyi and her colleagues were allowed to take up their seats. And when they did, it certainly gave parliament a jolt.

The NLD started to propose bills, something previously viewed as an impertinence for a non-government party. One bill, which didn't get very far, would have forced cabinet ministers to reveal their financial assets. The NLD also became adept at using parliamentary committees to scrutinise ministries and policies. All this was supported by Shwe Mann, who also got on much better personally with Aung San Suu Kyi than did Thein Sein. A significant appointment for the leader of the NLD came when she was made chair of a new fifteen-member parliamentary Committee for Rule of Law, Peace and Stability. This gave her a very useful official perch from which to pursue her favourite themes.

The presence and irreverence of the NLD seemed to embolden the USDP members, too. One of the NLD's parliamentarians, Win Htein, observed that MPs from the USDP were admitting to him that they were delighted that a boring chamber had become livelier. Gradually, testing the boundaries, USDP MPs could become just as inquisitive and critical as their NLD colleagues. Take the new parliamentary Land Investigations Committee. This began work to look into the widescale practice of land-grabs, whereby military and government officials and their cronies arbitrarily seized land. MPs from several parties fanned out across the country taking evidence about these flagrant abuses of the law. Soon they were reporting that some 5,670 hectares (14,000 acres) had been seized in Mon State alone. It was almost unprecedented for the regime to be challenged in this way.

Behind Shwe Mann, the next most important reformer was Aung Min. A former major general, he started off under Thein Sein's presidency in the modest role of minister for rail transport, but he soon emerged as the key government negotiator in the regime's efforts to sign ceasefire agreements with all the ethnic militia groups. This quickly became one of the most cherished objectives of the new government, thus elevating the importance of Aung Min; in 2012, he became a minister in the president's office from where he could concentrate full-time on his job as chief negotiator. Acknowledging his success in his role, the EU, Japan and the UN together provided funds for a new Myanmar Peace Centre in Yangon, which essentially acted as a secretariat for Aung Min's multiple-track negotiations with the Kachin, Karen, Mon, Chin and others. By the end of 2013, he had managed to sign ceasefire agreements, all more or less holding, with every significant armed group except the Kachin. Finally, in March 2015, he even managed to sign a tentative agreement with the Kachin. These were major achievements.

All those I have spoken to from the ethnic groups who have negotiated with Aung Min praise his honesty, frankness and sincerity. Aung Min himself seemed very open-minded on how to reach an accommodation with the army's bitter foes. He started to talk about the great unmentionable, federalism, and accepted that there would have to be new guarantees of equal rights for all. His team also began looking at new power-sharing and resource-sharing arrangements, for instance to redistribute wealth from richer to poorer states in a new federal set-up. All heady stuff for a rather gruff Burmese military man.

The limits of change

When I saw Aung Min in his office in Naypyidaw in September 2013, flanked by aides and translators, he repeated what had become the mantra of the new government: "Without peace, no democracy; and without democracy, there will be no development." Finally ending Burma's many civil wars had thus become a priority in order to achieve, as the end goal, economic development. It was a telling formula. Democracy was not an end in itself, but merely a means to bring about economic growth – a belief that all the government reformers shared.

Like President Thein Sein in his inaugural speeches, Aung Min was refreshingly honest about Burma's problems. He talked to me about underdevelopment and poverty, and even offered a clear-sighted critique of the education system, "which needs more brain-storming and political thinking" than rote learning.

But here again, Aung Min was thinking along utilitarian lines, with better education considered simply as a means to achieve economic growth. "Every country in the world is trying to become richer. The economic issue is most important", he said, "we need a political system that can bring about economic development to make our people richer – we need to reduce the poverty rate from 26 per cent to 16 per cent."

Not surprisingly, given the importance accorded to fixing the economy, the technocrats brought in to run financial institutions such as the Central Bank came to play key roles. Winston Set Aung was educated in the West, and was drafted in to work in the ministry of planning, after which he became vice-governor of the Central Bank. There he helped to oversee a reform of the banking sector and started planning for the opening of a stock market, with technical help from Daiwa Securities Group and the Tokyo Stock Exchange. Soe Thein, the former admiral, younger than Thein Sein and Aung Min, emerged as another key reformer. As one of the so-called "super ministers" in the president's entourage he assumed overall responsibility for the government's economic reform agenda.

At the top of government, therefore, was a good handful of very dedicated, able and open-minded reformers. Led and inspired by Thein Sein, they managed to achieve a remarkable amount in a short space of time. However, there are strong caveats as to how much they wanted to achieve, and as to how much they could have been expected to achieve.

To take the first caveat. As Aung Min had explained to me, democracy was seen as a means to an economic end rather than a virtue in its own right. The reformers felt obliged to deal with the NLD only in exchange for money, investment and Western technical expertise. But, ideologically, they remained clearly divided from Aung San Suu Kyi, whose overriding object was to achieve a functioning, Western-style democracy. This is why, to the Burmese military mind, democracy must be disciplined; it had to serve a very limited purpose – economic recovery – and little more.

It should also be acknowledged that the reformers' limited goal of economic rather than political change is much more in line with regional norms than Aung San Suu Kyi's vision for her country. The formal prioritisation of economic growth over freedom of expression, human rights and democracy is the governing principle of Singapore, China, Vietnam, Cambodia and Thailand, to name but a few. It would be strange if the generals looked very far beyond these sorts of countries for the model of what a (slightly) new Burma should look like.

As to the second caveat, it has become increasingly clear that those within Burma's government who are committed to even this limited reform agenda are few in number. Most in the army and bureaucracy had done relatively well out of the old ways, and are deeply reluctant to change, especially if it means sacrificing their extremely privileged economic and political positions in the country. Take the senior official I spoke to who told me all about his salary and his admiration for Thein Sein. He told me that he shared the president's "great sense of urgency to catch up with the rest of the world, to have a more democratic government and more progress". And, like many, he had been pleasantly "surprised at first [after Thein Sein took office] how quickly things changed". But, he added, he had been deeply "disappointed at how few were prepared to follow the president's lead". Speaking to me in 2014, over three years after Thein Sein had taken over, my insider lamented that there had been no "genuine change. Most people in government have not changed. We should say frankly, no." This meant that frustrated reformers like him were constantly battling against the bureaucracy. In his words the changes in Burma were "in fact quite fragile".

That is a good word to describe the reforms. Many of the former military officers who comprise Burma's governmental and business elite followed Thein Sein's lead only reluctantly, and only as far as they really had to. My senior official reckoned that fewer than half the government bureaucrats he knew supported reform. Another official told me that one-third supported reform, another third were adamantly opposed to it, and the final third were sitting on the fence waiting to see who would come out on top.

CHAPTER NINE

A new "great game":
The geopolitics of change

THE INTERNATIONAL CONTEXT TO Burma's reforms was just as important as domestic political concerns and two countries in particular have played an outsize role in Burma's evolution over the last couple of decades: China and America. The former, of course, sharing a 1,350-mile-long border with Burma, has loomed large in the country for many centuries, and several hundred thousand of Burma's ethnic hill peoples live on the Chinese side of the border. America has more recent historical connections with Burma, through the Baptist missions and through the support of the Kachin and Karen Levies for American forces during the Second World War in the Allies' fight against the Japanese.

But Burma has been, as well, a frontline between America and China, an area of confrontation between the two most dominant powers in the Asia-Pacific region. In the 1950s, the CIA backed the anti-communist forces of Chiang Kai-shek who had retreated into Burma's border regions in Shan State. The CIA hoped that Chiang's KMT might be capable of launching a decisive counter-blow against the communists from these Burmese bases. In the context of the Cold War, defeating Chinese communism was the over-riding imperative of America, and the fact that shipping in arms and money to the KMT further enfeebled an already dangerously weak Burmese government was considered to be little more than collateral damage. The CIA only gave up the struggle in 1961, but by then the KMT had contributed mightily to the political destabilisation and disintegration of the Shan States; it had even started its own opium-growing there.

By the early 1990s, communist China was clearly the prevailing force in Burma. The burgeoning economic superpower rushed to exploit its puny neighbour's vast natural wealth and as China rushed headlong to became the second largest economy in the world so its demand for oil, gas and hydro-power merely increased. To most Burmese, meanwhile, the untold quantities of Burmese wood, jade, rubies and gold that ended up for sale in the border towns of China represented nothing less than the wholesale plunder of their country. Consequently, the glaring inequality in the relationship between Burma and its vast neighbour became one of the main reasons that President Thein Sein's new government changed tack after 2011. China had squeezed too much out of Burma, and in the absence of a countervailing influence from the West due to sanctions, its embrace had become suffocating.

Everything is for sale

The story of disenchantment in the Burma-Chinese relationship can be told through the town of Ruili and the city of Kunming in China's Yunnan province. The first used to be a sleazy little border settlement on the Chinese side of the Burma-China border, the latter is the capital of what used to be one of China's poorest regions, a backwater, far removed from the urban tiger economies of the Chinese littoral.

How all that has changed. Ruili is now a rapidly expanding, conspicuously rich entrepôt, much the same as Kunming many hours' drive away. The provincial capital now has a shiny new American-designed airport, the coun-try's fourth largest, alongside other typical signs of China's new prosperity – vintage wine stores and an Aston Martin showroom. Kunming is being promoted as the destination of choice for millions of domestic Chinese tourists, largely on the back of Yunnan's proximity to Burma, with what are regarded as its exotic hill tribes and mountains of jade. Indeed, much of the new wealth of Ruili and Kunming stems from the Chinese region's trade with Burma, and in particular the jade from Kachin State. There are thousands of shops selling jade products in Ruili. Hundreds of thousands of Chinese dealers, shoppers and tourists flock here to buy the stuff, and it's not just pendants and trinkets on offer. There are statuettes, boxes, sculptures and more; almost anything, in fact, that can be worked in the green stone.

The jade is certainly extremely expensive in Ruili. On a visit to one cavernous showroom in the centre of the town, the Everything is Good jade company, I was quickly steered towards one particular lump of black rock among the many thousands on display. It looked innocuous enough, only about a foot square. But a small slash on one side, revealing a translucent green and purple interior, betrayed its true worth: this was the highest-quality jade from Burma, and to discerning Chinese customers that means the best in the world. After quite a lot of haggling over currency conversions, my translator worked out that the price tag for this particular rock was $1.2 million.

All the jade in Everything is Good had been brought over the border from Kachin State. Young boys were on hand with little water-spray bottles to moisten the surface of the countless rocks strewn throughout the premises, some the size of boulders, after which a small flashlight was held against the surfaces. A small patch of green or purple will then be revealed, indicating the value of the rock. To spice things up, the shop offers jade betting; the customer can buy a whole rock blind, and then have it cut open on the spot. If there is a lot of purple, it will be worth more than he bought it for. If not, he can always have another go. It's a game that appeals to the twin Chinese passions of gambling and jade.

Then there are the teak products, made from the equally highly prized Burmese rosewood. The huge, freshly felled trunks arrive in Ruili from across the border and are then transformed into almost anything, of any size, in the Ruili workshops: beds, sofas, lamp-stands, Buddhas, even fishponds. Towering over the entrance to one wood shop I found the *ne plus ultra* of tasteless, wasteful woodwork, a lion colossus, eleven metres long and four metres high. It took a year to make, consumed two entire trees and was on sale for over $1 million (see plate 14). The proud owner expected it to end up in a hotel lobby in Beijing or Hong Kong, like its two predecessors.

There are thousands of small-scale Burmese traders with licences to deal in jade, gems and wood in Ruili and the surrounding region. Interestingly, about three thousand of those are thought to be Burmese Muslims, including Rohingya, using their kinship networks around the region to their advantage.[1]

However, the local Burmese populations where the jade and other gems come from see hardly any of the profits from what is sold at Ruili – working conditions in the mines are terrible, the pay miserable, and there have been many recorded examples of forced and child labour. This gets to the heart of the imbalance in the cross-border trade, and with it the fundamental inequality in the Burma-China relationship. For the Burmese argue that while Chinese businessmen in Yunnan make fortunes marking up their imports, often in collusion with corrupt Burmese officials, most locals benefit very little from it. Not surprisingly, therefore, the Chinese have become extremely unpopular in Burma, especially in Mandalay and the north of the country where most of the jade, teak, rubies and other stones are sourced. Chinese businessmen are seen as robbing the Burmese, Kachin, Shan and others of their birthright – literally, the wood, stones and water among which many generations of their people have lived. It's one of the few issues on which the Burmans and all the ethnic groups in Burma can wholeheartedly agree.

And while the Burmese watch their fast-diminishing reserves of teak, jade and marble disappearing up the Burma Road into China, so too they are seeing the Chinese destroying some of the most beautiful parts of their country to build pipelines and dams. For China's rapidly developing economy has looked to Burma to satisfy its growing energy requirements.

In 2009, for example, the China National Petroleum Corporation began building major oil and gas pipelines right across the middle of Burma, from the Chinese-built port terminus of Kyaukphyu, in south-west Rakhine State, all the way to Kunming, via Mandalay and Lashio – a distance of some 480 miles. The pipelines were accorded a very high strategic priority by the Chinese. To get oil and gas into the country from producers in Africa and the Middle East, the pipelines provided a vital alternative to the choke point of the Straits of Malacca, prone to piracy and terrorism and even, possibly, a hostile blockade. The cost of the two pipelines combined was about $2.5 billion, and they started operating towards the end of 2013. Yet, they were built with no regard for the damage inflicted on the local environment along the way. I followed the pipelines from Mandalay up to the Chinese border while they were being built, and the carnage was obvious. The objections of local villagers had mostly been ignored.

As well as the pipelines, even more controversially there were dams. Burma has been targeted by all five of China's state-owned power companies, keen to find new sources of cheap, renewable and not too distant energy. Construction contracts began to be signed in the early 2000s, and the first of the new big dams, Shweli River 1 Power Station, began operating in 2009. Several more Chinese-funded dams were built on the Salween River that drains down from the Himalayas on the China-Burma border, crossing into Burma proper in northern Shan State. According to one source, at least forty-five Chinese multi-national corporations have been involved in approximately sixty-three hydropower projects in Burma, including several substations, transmission and electrification projects.[2] The biggest and most costly of these projects was going to be the Myitsone dam, agreed between the Burmese government and the China Power Investment Corporation in 2006 (see Chapter Four).

The Chinese fondly believed that the Burmese would welcome all this development in their impoverished country. From 2008 to 2011, the total Chinese cumulative investment in Burma jumped from $1 billion to nearly $13 billion. Much of this, about $8 billion, was accounted for by the three biggest Chinese projects, namely the pipelines, the Myitsone dam and the opening of a huge copper mine at Letpadaung, also in the north of the country. Just between April and August 2010, as these projects were all moving ahead at full steam simultaneously, Chinese spending in Burma amounted to two-thirds of China's investment in the country over the whole of the previous two decades.[3]

Moreover, all this came on top of years of further Chinese assistance to Burma, for building roads, bridges and other such infrastructure projects. The Burma-China relationship at the government-to-government level had also been solidified by a close military and strategic relationship. Since the 1990s, China had become the main supplier of arms to Burma, selling jet fighters, naval ships and other hardware. China has also helped to train the Burmese armed forces. In exchange, China may have been allowed access to Burmese bases on the coast of the Bay of Bengal, giving it a watchful presence in the Indian Ocean and farther afield, although there are no actual Chinese bases on the coast. At the United Nations, China, a permanent member of the Security Council, had also occasionally given Burma's pariah military regime diplomatic cover in the face of hostile resolutions and criticism from the Western powers.

"Stupid, stupid, stupid"

This all worked very well for the Chinese. In the absence of any foreign commercial or diplomatic competition in Burma after the mid 1990s, when Western sanctions began, China seemed to have carte blanche to do what it wanted in the country. China's monopoly hold on Burma's political economy meant that it virtually dictated the terms of the relationship between the two countries, and in particular the terms of trade.

Yet, in focusing on government-to-government contact alone in the name of "non-interference" – China's official policy of respecting a foreign government's right to pursue any policy it wants regardless of the consequences – the Chinese completely missed the resentment building towards their presence in Burma. The result was that what the Chinese took to be a solid, mutually beneficial relationship with the Burmese exploded in their faces – with long-term consequences for Burma, the balance of power in South-East Asia, and the way that China deals with poorer countries.

The flashpoint for all these simmering tensions was the Myitsone dam. As we have seen, the cancellation of this project by President Thein Sein proved to be very popular in Burma, but in China the suspension of the dam was greeted with utter astonishment. The Chinese were given no forewarning. Probably never before had a country that was regarded as a client state turned round and delivered such a public rebuff to the People's Republic. Soon afterwards, I went to visit the foreign policy scholars at Beijing's various university schools and departments of foreign relations to gauge reactions. These are the approved voices of the Chinese government, licensed to articulate opinion in a rather freer manner than the government bureaucrats. One such, Zhang Xiaomin, an expert on development economics, told me that the suspension of the dam had been "a complete shock to the Chinese government", forcing them to think "very seriously" about its relations with Burma, and other nations too.

Zhu Feng, a professor of international relations at Peking University, went into more detail, analysing where China had gone wrong in Burma. He told me that the "alarm bells were ringing" about how the Chinese should carry out all aid and development work in Burma and other poor nations. In retrospect, explained Zhu, the mistake in Burma had been to focus only on building relationships with government officials, without paying any attention to "domestic political nuances". In other words, the Chinese had mistaken government co-operation for public acquiescence, an easy mistake for authoritarian regimes to make.

This was a direct consequence of the official doctrine of non-interference. In Burma's case, certainly, this had amounted to little more than a pretext for deliberately ignoring Burmese public opinon because it suited Chinese interests to do so. The Chinese had habitually derided the Western practice of attaching conditions to their aid and other assistance programmes, calling it "meddling" or even "neo-imperialism". But in sticking to the non-interference policy so scrupulously, Zhu argued, China had missed the vital "shifts in policies, words and political thinking" that they might have picked up had they listened to voices other than the government's and engaged the country at a local level. This was "stupid, stupid, stupid", said Zhu: "It's a big lesson, and we have to learn from it." It also demonstrated that "we are a premature power", he added, yet "to grow into a man". Indeed, Western critics of China's foreign policy had used the 2008 Beijing Olympics to make much the same point, except in more exaggerated form. They seized the opportunity to protest against China's support for murderous regimes in both Burma and Sudan, dubbing it the "genocide Olympics".

At the very least, non-interference encouraged wilful ignorance. The Chinese I talked to in Ruili knew almost nothing about Burma, other than the fact that it was poor and, many believed, dangerous. No one I questioned had ever heard of Aung San Suu Kyi, nor did they show any inclination to find out more about the country.

Chinese visitors to the border town are positively discouraged from crossing over into Burma, the very source of all the jade and jewels that they pick up on their shopping trips. Instead, bizarrely, a miniature Burma has been built for their benefit just on the Chinese side. No need to fret about all the scary stuff just over the frontier, here one can stroll in safety around a surreal Burma theme park, complete with gaudy plastic replicas of famous landmarks such as the Shwedagon pagoda and the Golden Rock. There are spooky mannequins of smiling monks, and, most disturbing of all, a small-scale house inhabited by real "live" ethnic minority people. Two Padaung women, with gold rings binding their necks, stand motionless, mournfully waiting for their photos to be taken in exchange for money. Here, Burma is orderly, picturesque (depending on your taste) and wholesomely Buddhist. It is also in China, which is perhaps the way the Chinese like to imagine it, as a kind of obedient dependency. Little wonder, then, that the Myitsone dam affair came as such a shock, or that many Chinese remain perplexed as to why the Burmese do not display more gratitude for Chinese investment in the country.

All in all, the democratic transition in Burma, as far as it goes, has been a searing experience for China. But at least they seem to be drawing some of the right lessons. Chinese overseas aid and development policies, for instance, have undergone an official overhaul in recent years, partly in response to the Burmese imbroglio and also to China's involvement in some African countries. Increasingly, that involvement has been criticised by Africans as well as the usual meddling Westerners. The Chinese government is now telling businesses – especially its state-owned companies – operating overseas to be more respectful of local customs and people, and to invest more in what the British and Americans would call "corporate social responsibility". Thus, the China National Petroleum Corporation, which built the oil and gas pipelines across Burma, has belatedly been constructing schools in villages near the pipelines. In this way Burma itself has had its own, if more unwitting, impact on its giant neighbour.

Enter Obama

Above all, the Chinese foreign-policy experts I spoke to agreed that China's stumble was going to be Washington's gain. For to compensate for the loss of Chinese goodwill, the Burmese government was bound to turn to the West, and particularly America.

But although the Chinese acknowledge that their country's previous free hand in Burma will diminish, the scholars I spoke to were unwilling to concede that the Burmese government might have turned to the West out of their own free will, out of self-interest. Rather, they attributed this realignment entirely to the malign intentions of an America that wanted above all to contain the rise of China in a strategically vital region. Many Chinese thus see the renewed American interest in Burma as the culmination of a sinister long-term plan to detach Burma from the Chinese sphere of influence. A Western-dominated Burma, they theorise, could only threaten China. One Chinese expert, for instance, worried to me that if America managed somehow to lead Burma to democracy, this would in some way "influence the situation in China", as if the virus of voting might spread over the border.

However, although the American, and Western, rapprochement with Burma in recent years has been one of the most significant factors in the country's recent reforms, this process has been a good deal more pragmatic than the Chinese allow. It was fortuitous, almost, that just as the Burmese were looking for a way to prise their country away from their giant neighbour that the Americans were looking for a way to re-engage with Burma.

As we have seen, following the failure of the generals to honour the results of the 1990 election, America had gradually heaped trade embargos and other sanctions onto Burma. The economic and diplomatic assault was led by Congress, beginning in 1990 when it passed the Customs and Trade Act, enabling the president to impose new sanctions on the generals (although the then-president Bush refused to do so). In 1992, America symbolically withdrew its ambassador (although still maintaining its embassy, consequently headed by a mere chargé d'affaires). Then the Republican-controlled 104th Congress of 1995–6 passed the Free Burma Act, introduced by Republican Senator Mitch McConnell, which called for tough economic and trade sanctions on Burma, as well as on countries that traded with it. Senator McConnell remained the most militant congressional advocate of a hard line against Burma throughout the following years. McConnell was a member of the Southern Baptist Convention and so was concerned not only with the brutal suppression of the NLD and the democracy movement but also with the attacks on the Christian Kachin, Karen, Chin and others.

Finally, in 1997, despite doubts about the effectiveness of such action, President Bill Clinton imposed the first sanctions on Burma by banning most new American investment in the country. America also used its clout to exclude

Burma from multilateral financial institutions such as the IMF and the World Bank. The following administration of President George W. Bush denounced the Burmese regime at every turn, and imposed new economic sanctions, as well as trading and visa restrictions, of its own. The European Union imposed an arms and technology embargo in 1990, followed by visa and other diplomatic bans on Burmese officials from the mid 1990s onwards. Other Western countries acted similarly; Canada's Special Economic Measures Act of 2007 stopped all Canadian exports and imports to Burma and prohibited any financial dealings between Canadian and Burmese firms and banks. As far as the West was concerned, from the late 1990s onwards Burma became effectively isolated. Human rights activists also campaigned for individual companies to disinvest in Burma, and many did. Only a few big companies stayed on, most prominently Germany's DHL and France's Total Elf.

Yet, a decade later, by 2008/9 or so, many American politicians and officials were arguing that sanctions had failed. Most obviously, they had not persuaded the Burmese regime to change its ways. Worse, the sanctions might have encouraged Than Shwe and his lackeys to behave even more callously than they might otherwise have done by forcing tham into the hands of the Chinese, who cared less about human rights and democracy than the West. The Democratic Senator for Virginia, Jim Webb, was one of those who argued that it was therefore time to try something new, and as chairman of the congressional Subcommittee on East Asian and Pacific Affairs he was in a good position to do something about it. At a subcommittee hearing on the hill in September 2009, he summed up America's dilemma from the viewpoint of a sanctions sceptic:

> Our isolation of Burma has resulted in a lack of attention to the region's strategic dynamics. Burma remains flanked by India and China, and is widely seen as being increasingly under China's sphere of influence. I believe that the political motivations behind our isolation of Burma were honourable, based on a desire to see democratic governance and a respect for human rights inside that country. At the same time, the situation we face with Burma is an example of what can happen when we seek to isolate a country from the rest of the world, but the rest of the world does not follow. Through the limits of our diplomatic and commercial ties, we have

also limited our connections with the people of Burma and prevented them from seeing the best that a free society can offer. We limit aid for their development and intellectual exploration. Moreover, we limit opportunities to push for positive change, because we do not talk directly to the government in charge. So the question, quite frankly, is whether this approach has brought Burma closer to democracy than when sanctions were first imposed.

In referring to the "rest of the world" that was not following America's lead on Burma, Webb was not only discussing China, and maybe Japan, which remained very engaged with Burma throughout this period, but also the countries that made up ASEAN. This is the main regional grouping, based in Jakarta, to which Burma had been admitted in 1997. ASEAN had taken a very different approach to Burma, one that undoubtedly influenced American thinking as regards its own policy towards the country.

In respect to it's policy towards Burma, ASEAN was led by Singapore, Thailand and Malaysia. Not uncoincidentally, these countries were also amongst the largest foreign investors in Burma. Tiny Singapore and medium-sized Thailand were, for example, well ahead of America in terms of their volumes of trade. As distinct from American and European attempts to force change in Burma through isolation, ASEAN championed what diplomats liked to call a policy of "constructive engagement" with the country. Singapore, for instance, cultivated contacts across a wide range of sectors, at the official and military level, with academic and research institutions, with business and finance. Burma's generals were allowed to come and go freely to the wealthy island state.

Singaporeans who supported constructive engagement, such as Tan Khee Giap, an associate professor at the Lee Kuan Yew School of Public Policy and a frequent visitor to Burma since 2000, argue that this approach was in tune with the values of Asia in general. Asians had a humble dream, Tan told me, that all Asians "will be educated and have a roof over their heads", and all Asian countries should be helping each other to achieve this dream. It was the "politics of aspiration that would change Burma", he insisted, not sanctions. Singapore thus had an obligation to continue helping the people of Burma to better their lot economically, and this trumped concerns about human rights. Like others I met in ASEAN, he was, in his own words, "disgusted by the double-standards of the West over Burma". Stabbing his finger in my direction, he said heatedly: "You are the last person to be qualified to speak about it [human rights], after all the colonial oppression and bullying of Asia."

Proponents of ASEAN's constructive engagement pointed to some concrete successes for the policy. Quiet, behind-the-scenes diplomacy by ASEAN, for instance, managed eventually to persuade a very suspicious Burmese regime to let in aid after Cyclone Nargis in 2008. ASEAN took the lead in forming a so-called "Tripartite Core Group" together with Burma itself and the UN to lead post-Nargis reconstruction efforts.[4]

But it is also true that this approach failed to encourage any obvious change in Burma's political system during the early 2000s. Nor, as we have seen, had most ordinary Burmese benefited much from the economic links that ASEAN and other Asian countries had maintained with Burma. If anything, Burma had fallen even further behind the rest of Asia during the period after 1995. This was partly attributable to sanctions, but mostly to the parasitical, dysfunctional style of crony capitalism that prevailed in Burma during those years. Certainly, there is little evidence to suggest that, at least on an economic level, constructive engagement came anywhere near helping the Burmese fulfil their Asian dream. Clearly, only a dramatic change in the regime's policies and access to large-scale external funding and expertise from the likes of the World Bank, the IMF and Western aid agencies could get the Burmese economy out of intensive care. But that was impossible under American sanctions.

So, with few results to show either for sanctions or Asia's constructive engagement, one of the first decisions of the new administration of President Barack Obama in early 2009, prodded by the likes of Webb, was to order a comprehensive review of America's Burma policy. This was led by Kurt Campbell, the new Assistant Secretary of State for East Asian and Pacific Affairs. Not surprisingly, this review came up with a mix of the previous policy and the ASEAN way – to maintain the sanctions, but to open up dialogue with the Burmese leadership. This new approach was to be called "pragmatic engagement". The policy, as Campbell expressed it, was to "test the intentions of the Burmese leadership and the sincerity of their expressed interest in a more positive relationship with the United States."[5] All this was run past Aung San Suu Kyi, whose opinion carried enormous weight in Congress and with American officials.

Indeed, even as Campbell was outlining this new policy in public, in practice it was already in full swing. In August 2009, Webb, for one, had already paid the first official visit to Burma by an American legislator for almost a decade. He was allowed to visit Aung San Suu Kyi under house arrest and also met Than Shwe, a sure sign that Burma was at least receptive to the American feelers that were being put out. Other American envoys perceived the same change: just as America was exploring a way out of its own diplomatic cul-de-sac on Burma, so the regime was trying to extricate itself from China. The Burmese leaders, it was clear, were groping around for ways to change and needed American help, but were unsure how to obtain it.

Campbell visited Naypyidaw for the first time in the autumn of 2009. Little came of it, but he was assured that change would come. A new American special envoy to Burma, Derek Mitchell, paid his first visit in early 2011. As he recalled later, he wasn't even sure whether he would be given a visa at the time, but when he did arrive in Naypyidaw he was told very firmly that Burma was now devoted to the democratic path, and that the regime wanted a much better relationship with America. Mitchell duly replied that this was possible, but dependent on concrete actions by the regime, such as the release of political prisoners. Up to this point, therefore, there was more aspiration than action on the Burmese side. It took the appointment of Thein Sein in March of that year to change the relationship definitively. Mitchell recalls that from reading the inaugural presidential address it was obvious that "this guy was different". Now, "there was something here to test." Thereafter, the president swiftly responded to the American demands for action to show his good faith over reform.

The Asia pivot – a new "great game"

Thus, the American re-engagement with Burma came about as a consequence of both countries changing, fortunately at the same time. The Burmese regime was anxious to bring in the United States to break its dependence on China; America had become frustrated with the apparent failure of sanctions. It also helped that in his inaugural address as president, Obama declared that he would extend a hand to pariah regimes that were "willing to unclench their fist", showing that America was ready to take a fresh look at old, intractable problems. In the end, Obama got a sweaty palm to clasp in Burma.

There was also the "Asia pivot" to consider. As well as a willingness to talk to "rogue" or "evil" regimes, in Washington parlance, another leitmotif of the Obama administration was to reorientate America's foreign policy away from fighting futile, expensive and unpopular wars in the Middle East and Afghanistan, and towards the Asia-Pacific region. Obama's officials judged that most of the world's economic growth was forecast to take place here in the twenty-first century. But the region was also the locus for the greatest emerging threat to American security in the new century – China. In practice, the pivot amounted to beefing up America's existing alliances in an effort to reassure China's nervous neighbours, such as Vietnam and the Philippines. This has been called by many a new policy of "containment", and detaching Burma from China's orbit seemed an obvious potential gain for this strategy.

American officials like Mitchell, however, resisted this notion of a new containment policy. They argued instead that America had to "up its game in the region" as Asia assumed ever greater economic and thus diplomatic importance. "Our allies thought we were distracted in the [early] 2000s", Mitchell told me, so "we had to reassure our allies in the region." Furthermore, there was a "competition in terms of values and rules" in Asia, he argued, between America's brand of a free society and the "Beijing consensus" of market capitalism coupled with political and social oppression. America had to stand up for its values, argued Mitchell, but this was not "necessarily being anti-Chinese". Thus, the American "change in policy on Burma had been all about Burma, not about China. Burma has decided to change, and they are responding to China . . . not us."

Mitchell was right, up to a point. The Chinese were certainly wrong to see the turn of events in Burma as the culmination of some long-term American conspiracy, specifically to turn Burma against China for geopolitical and strategic gain. As Mitchell warned, "the Chinese misinterpret all this at their peril

. . . it's easier for them to blame the superpower, because that makes them the victims." Nonetheless, it is also true that the Asia pivot invested the American re-engagement with an urgency and intensity that it might not otherwise have had. Indeed, in retrospect it is evident that America probably moved too fast in that re-engagement, especially in terms of ending sanctions.

Once President Obama and his secretary of state Hillary Clinton had got the green light from Aung San Suu Kyi to deal with Thein Sein, events moved with bewildering speed. Aung San Suu Kyi only met Thein Sein to agree on political reform in August 2011, yet by the beginning of December Clinton was in Burma for probably the most momentous foreign visit of her four years at Foggy Bottom. On 1 December, wearing flip-flops and a *longyi*, the traditional Burmese sarong, President Thein Sein welcomed the secretary of state to his gaudy throne room in Naypyidaw. It was the first visit by a top American official to Burma for fifty-odd years.

Relations were cordial, with Thein Sein anxious to explain to Clinton how he was trying to transform the country from an impoverished one-party state into something rather better. A "workmanlike" discussion (according to the Americans) was followed by a light lunch of braised abalone and black-pepper mantis prawns. Later the same day Clinton travelled to Yangon for her first meeting with Aung San Suu Kyi, during which the American's unfeigned admiration was clearly in evidence. Within twenty-four hours, therefore, Clinton had put her official imprimatur on the country's transition process. She had endorsed Thein Sein's government while publicly legiti-mising the leader of the opposition as an equally important partner in the country's reforms.

This was a defining moment for Burma, after the decades of Western sanctions. Both sides came bearing gifts. For her part, Clinton promised the return of the World Bank to Burma, to assess the country's many economic needs and consequently to start lending again. For his part, Thein Sein reaf-firmed his commitment to democracy, promising to hold free and fair by-elections the following year, in which the NLD would be allowed to compete. Other American envoys had also regularly demanded prisoner releases, and these were now carried out with surprising swiftness. By 2013, within two years of Thein Sein taking power, most political prisoners had been released.

Following Hillary Clinton's trip, Senator McConnell's visit in 2012 was also very significant. America's most fearsome critic of the military regime met Aung San Suu Kyi in Yangon and, as it had been for Clinton, this was clearly a very emotional moment for him. Persuaded the changes in Burma were for real, he pushed for the subsequent lifting of congressional-led sanctions.

But it was Clinton's trip that really made the difference. The transformative moment was her public meeting with Aung San Suu Kyi at her old lakeside home in Yangon. After the rounds of meeting government ministers in austere Naypyidaw, Clinton and her team jetted down to the very different world of vibrant, ramshackle Yangon. Clinton and Aung San Suu Kyi had a private dinner the first evening, during which they quickly bonded, but it was the next morning that they met publicly, in front of reporters, at Aung San Suu Kyi's home.

Up until a few months previously, no photograph of the ex-political prisoner, not even a mention of her name, had been allowed in any Burmese papers. Yet, here she was meeting the representative of what had until so recently been the regime's sworn enemy, in front of a crowd of local and international press. Expectations were soaring.

Aung San Suu Kyi's compound, set idyllically on the banks of Inya Lake, has become almost as iconic as the Lady herself. This was where she had endured the long years of house arrest. The building was the backdrop for those few images by which the world remembered her during that time, photographed as she occasionally appeared over her high front gate to wave and speak to cheering supporters. For Clinton's visit, the place had been spruced up. Cyclone Nargis had inflicted terrible damage to the compound in 2008, felling trees in the garden and damaging the roof of the house. Now the porch, where Aung San Suu Kyi and her guest were to pose, was given a fresh lick of paint. Fresh flowers lined the garden footpaths. More vexing recent additions were in evidence too. A new razor-wire fence had been erected only two weeks previously on the lake side of the garden – a precaution, I was told, on account of Aung San Suu Kyi's new accessibility and the changing times in Burma.

Clinton arrived just after nine in the morning, and was ushered into the house with her team. On the other side of the table were the NLD leader and senior officials from her party. After a long discussion, the two women finally appeared for a photocall and brief speeches. At first their body language was quite stiff and formal. Aung San Suu Kyi expressed herself "happy" with America's engagement. It would make the way ahead "clearer", and encourage the process of democratisation. She also reminded her audience that democratisation was just one of many things that Burma needed; a cessation of ethnic civil conflicts and the rule of law were vital too. Clinton, now full of smiles, then thanked the Lady for her "steadfast" leadership, and promised that America would now "work to be a partner with Burma". Finally, the two embraced each other warmly. It certainly seemed a very sincere moment. The cameras whirred. The defiant old house was witnessing a great liberating moment.

After this, it seemed, new freedoms came thick and fast. Censorship, for the most part, was lifted, more prisoners were released, and conversations about political subjects became less hushed. The reforms received a tremendous, spectacular jolt forwards. Weary foreign investors and businessmen gained reassurance. Even the visit of Obama himself to Burma, almost exactly a year later, felt like something of an anticlimax after Clinton's triumph. The US president touched down for six hours, during which he crowded in an inordinate amount of glad-handing, sightseeing and speechifying. As he told his awestruck audience at the University of Yangon: "When I took office as President, I sent a message to those governments who ruled by fear: we will extend a hand if you are willing to unclench your fist. So, today I've come to keep my promise and extend the hand of friendship."

By 2014, apart from maintaining a blacklist of about a hundred regime cronies, almost all American sanctions had been dropped. But despite the blessing of the world's superpower, how far were Burma's rulers really willing to change?

CHAPTER TEN

Burma's future and the ghosts of the plural society

TWENTY OR SO MILES outside Myitkyina in the village of Wai Maw, I was strolling around the compound of the Baptist church with a young Kachin, La La Hkawng Dau, known helpfully as "Jack". It was October 2014, and the head of the Christian Leadership Training Centre was telling me all about his ambitions for the future.

For now, this Baptist church was still very much a refugee centre, a consequence of the war that had broken out again between the KIA and the Burmese army in 2011. Neat rows of makeshift bamboo huts lined one part of the compound. Behind them were the emergency latrines and some basic washing facilities. The church here was putting up over one hundred Kachin refugee students; these were the boys and girls being educated partly at the local government schools and partly at the Baptist centre itself.

In the very near future, Jack was hoping to start educating the refugees, as well as other Kachin boys and girls, entirely at the Baptist mission. In other words, he would be reopening the original mission school that had been closed down by Ne Win's government in 1964, together with all the other such schools in the country. Jack was very excited by the prospect, and plans were well in hand. He was conducting workshops on the curriculum, and training teachers. He hoped to recruit twenty of them, giving the new school an average class size of about thirty, as distinct from the hundred-plus at the local government school. Learning would be student-centred, with teachers following more what their charges wanted to learn about, and there would be plenty of

English-language instruction, and music. Indeed, we wandered around to the accompaniment of a tuneless din emanating from one of the huts, the youngsters already getting to grips with their cheap Japanese electric keyboards. Jack was hoping to open another such school at about the same time.

It all sounded very enticing, but, as Jack acknowledged, it was also going to be illegal. For in Burma's highly regimented system, all children have to go to the woeful government schools. But Jack argued, if the Kachin Baptists did not take action for themselves their "future generations would be lost". Already, he lamented, the local Kachin culture had almost disappeared. Furthermore, the Burman-dominated schools system was producing children "who can't write or speak properly. Only a few students can write, aged sixteen or seventeen, in Burmese or Kachin."

So, Jack was taking matters into his own hand, and it only took a short walk outside the compound, across a patch of dirty, open scrub, to see what the alternatives were for his pupils. Here, scattered among the grass, were the telltale signs of the local drug addicts. This patch was cleared every day or two by volunteers, but even so the ground was still littered with the discarded plastic wrappings of needles and syringes. The syringes themselves had all been tossed over a wall into the garden of the local Catholic school, where they were all plainly visible. Jack himself did not allow any of his pupils to leave the Baptist compound, in case they were seduced into taking drugs or drinking. Drugs were, of course, very popular in Wai Maw, Jack explained, and could be bought easily. "No one is arresting the dealers. Some are arrested, but can pay about $1,000 to be released." It was a common refrain in the area.

Tiny cracks of freedom

Before the reforms of Thein Sein's government, Jack argued, it would have been ridiculous even to contemplate reopening a mission school. Now, though, "we can do this because we feel a bit freer; before, we could not do anything." This is very much the story of contemporary Burma. All over the country people are taking advantage of the new political atmosphere, of a new tolerance, to get on with their own initiatives and help themselves. Generations' worth of pent-up entrepreneurial, social and intellectual energy is now being released, regardless of the government's old rules and regulations. Burma is in a state of flux, and no one is sure what the new political dispensation really is anymore. Thus, more and more people are testing the new political boundaries, waiting to see what happens, always wondering if, or when, the push-back will come from the authorities.

Jack, for instance, admitted to me that many Kachin parents were worried about what might follow if their children went to his new school rather than the government high school. What about that vital end-of-school certificate that they would need to go on to other government-run colleges in Burma? Not to worry, said Jack. If the government got rough about it the kids would just go on to the Baptist schools and colleges in India, as they had always done. At least they would be properly educated there. He was optimistic, anyway, that his mission school would open on time and be allowed to function. He said that eleven similar schools had already opened in Shan State, and the government had not interfered with them so far. Whether this was out of incompetence, indifference or even something rather more high-minded, nobody could be sure.

It was much the same story in Myitkyina itself. A new shop had just opened off the main square, opposite the entrance to the *manau* festival ground, selling T-shirts, mugs, diaries, key rings and anything else emblazoned with the symbols of the KIA. The slightest public display of these would have been unthinkable only a year or so earlier. At the very least it would have invited immediate and harsh retribution from the Burmese military. Now, teenagers were happily motorbiking around town flaunting the crossed swords of the KIA on their shirts and scooter helmets.

Down by the Irrawaddy River, not far from the government compound, the Humanity Institute (HI) opened in 2012. Much as Jack hoped to save Kachin children from the clutches of the government with his mission schools, so the HI hoped to do much the same for Kachin students. The local government-run Myitkyina University is, by common consent, abysmal. Its corridors have passed into local folklore for the number of used needles that pile up on the floors. The HI, therefore, set up by local Kachin businessmen and teachers, hoped eventually to start up a new, separate university to rival the government one. Nbyen Dan Hkung Awng, the young, dynamic and very articulate Kachin founder and director of the institute, explained to me that the HI also wanted to give an "updated education" in place of the university's archaic system of rote learning. As well as this, the HI had an explicitly Kachin nationalist agenda; all courses were to be taught only in Kachin and English, to the exclusion of Burmese. The purpose of the HI, he argued excitedly, was "to regenerate Kachin culture".

Like almost everything else in Burma, the HI required a licence to operate. When I visited him in 2014, Nbyen Dan Hkung Awng said that he had applied for the appropriate licence in June 2012, but had not heard anything since. In the meantime, he said, he was just "going ahead anyway". He said that he now had a bit more political space in which to operate, so, like Jack, he was seizing the opportunity, making the most of this moment of official ambivalence.

Next door to the HI, in a glorious house right on the bank of the Irrawaddy, lived one of the elder stateswomen of the Kachin, Ja Seng Hkawn Maran. Her father had been the second chairman of the Kachin Independence Organisation, and she herself was a leading member of the Kachin Women's Association modelled on similar such Maoist groups in China. She too was testing exactly how serious the new Burmese government was about genuine change. She and other Kachin business people had formed a new company, the Kachin State Public Company Limited, to run utilities and other such businesses for the Kachin. They would thus provide services for the Kachin, such as electricity, that the Burman-run state government had never done adequately.

The company had revived two old hydroelectric plants, and in a novel form of public-private partnership this had been done in conjunction with the Burman-dominated state government. Another project was to revive the decrepit railway service from Mandalay to Myitkyina, previously the lifeline between Kachin State and the rest of Burma. Under the Burman-run company that had previously operated it, Ja Seng Hkawn Maran told me, the railway had been corrupt, slow, unreliable and expensive. So, she and her investors had bought a three-year contract from the state government to run an improved line that would bring tourists up to Kachin State and also restore some pride in the Kachin's ability to run their own projects. Their glossy new brochure for the railway promised, among other attractions, that "Services will be given by employees with eager mindsets different from previous era"; "Water/Electric lights will not be in shortage and there will be cleanliness services of toilets"; and "Electric fans and sweet melodies and beautiful songs will be entertained throughout the journey."

She had already trained sixty staff with the requisite "eager mindsets" to start on the new railway – but when I met her they were still waiting for the state government to hand it over to them, a month after it had agreed to do so. "So they are still not doing what they say", Ja Seng Hkawn Maran reflected. And it was much the same story with the hydropower plants. There were still great difficulties with the Burmese state authorities in the new public-private partnership. This was more evidence, for her, that "they don't really want to change". Nonetheless, she reflected, "we are pushing at the door whenever we have a chance."

It is a very different story, of course, for big business in the newly reforming Burma, particularly in the strategic national sectors such as telecoms, oil and gas. This is where the government most wanted to attract foreign investors and so Naypyidaw has positively rolled out the red carpet in its eagerness to get new companies up and running. Bringing foreign money and expertise into these sectors had, after all, always been one of the main points of the reform process. After a well-conducted and transparent bidding process, for instance, the all-important new telecoms licences were awarded to two foreign companies, Norway's Telenor and Qatar's Ooredoo. For the first time these two will provide mobile coverage for most of the country, at an affordable rate, in competition against the existing government-run network. The consumer, a novel concept in Burma's political economy, should be the main beneficiary of such competition.

Where the government itself has not been taking a lead, however, it's a different story, especially in the hill areas. As Ja Seng Hkawn Maran reflected, the local Burman authorities still seemed very unsure as to whether they wanted "to give a chance to other people". In Kachin State, perhaps, it was not surprising that the Kachin should still find it difficult co-operating with the local Burmese authorities. After all, technically the KIO were still at war with the Burmese state when I went there in 2014. In Karen State, matters should have been improving more rapidly after a landmark agreement to stop fighting was signed in January 2012. But talk of a "peace dividend", let alone any wholesale economic improvement, still seemed to be out of reach when I visited Hpa-An a couple of years later.

One obvious testimony to the historic ceasefire was the smart new Karen National Union office along one of Hpa-An's main roads. It was adorned with photographs of Karen leaders with President Thein Sein and his underlings, all smiles and handshakes, unimaginable only a few years back. Here was the evidence that there had been some real change in Burma over the last few years. There were also some small signs of economic development. Overlooking the Salween River in one of the few picturesque bits of town, the foundations were being dug out for a smart new hotel, for instance. This wouldn't attract much attention anywhere else in contemporary Burma, as there are now scores of new hotels going up in Yangon and Mandalay to cater for the surge in tourists, but in Hpa-An it was a big event. And, on the face of it, this should also have been a bit of indisputably good news, as the new hotel promised hundreds of rela- tively well-paid jobs in a city where regular employment remained scarce.

If only. In fact, the hotel had become yet another symbol of the ongoing political confrontation between the local Karen and the central Burmese authorities. For most Karen, I found, were in fact opposed to the hotel, for the simple but overriding reason that they had not been consulted. The local Karen member of the state parliament, a formidable, strong-minded woman call Nan Say Hwa, argued hotly that the hotel had been "imposed" on Hpa-An by the governor, one of the usual Burmans appointed by the central govern- ment in Naypyidaw. Nan Say Hwa argued that this man never listened to "people's advice or desires". In this case, she said, the businessman who had put up the money for the hotel was a crony of the governor. Had they been consulted at all, Nan Say Hwa continued, the local Karen would have demanded that the hotel should not have been built on a pitch where many of them played football, and where General Aung San had given a famous speech before his murder in 1947.

Thus, what should have been an economic opportunity for Hpa-An had become yet another source of political conflict. In this sense political change has been lagging badly behind the modest economic progress in the new

Burma, for the old structures of central Burmese control over the Karen and other hill peoples have barely changed since President Thein Sein's reforms began in 2011. There might have been some increase in democracy at the centre, in elections to the federal parliament for instance, but the political and administrative architecture of central Burman control over the whole of this extremely diverse country has scarcely been touched. It seems that, for all its ceasefires, Burma's ostensibly reforming government has yet to learn anything very much about how or why the country's political structures need to be overhauled. Little wonder, then, that at the KNU office in Hpa-An, a Karen, Major Saw Shee Sho, remained sceptical of the government's willingness to change fundamentally the way it governed the country, now or in the future. "Fighting could be over", he told me wryly, "Or maybe not. Meanwhile, we are keeping our weapons."

The dark side of Burma's new democracy

Nonetheless, in the cities, town and villages of the central Burmese plains there is no doubt that a greater degree of political and intellectual freedom has prevailed since 2011. With the end of newspaper censorship and more access to the Internet, ordinary Burmese now have a much better chance to learn about their country, and the world, than at any time since independence. There is more freedom of expression and thought than for decades. Especially since the Clinton visit at the end of 2011 and the by-elections of April 2012, political parties have been allowed to operate more or less as normally. Khin Lay, for one, the former NLD activist imprisoned in Insein, told me that she celebrates the new freedoms for what they really are: "Now we can sleep very well at night . . . In the past, the police mainly came at night, unannounced, and we were always hearing the knocking at the door, or motorbikes . . . this is the happiest thing [about the reforms]. In the past, I had to take sleeping pills to go to sleep, but no more."

But there has been a much darker side to Burma's progress since 2011, and one that might yet undermine all the best-intentioned attempts by reformers both at home and abroad to change the country for the better. Appropriately, this aspect of Burma's story over the last few years began in Sittwe (formerly

Akyab), the capital of Rakhine State. The accumulated hatreds and resentments from the colonial era deeply influenced all the most malevolent and divisive policies of the Burman generals after 1962. But, sadly, even in this new era of a supposedly reforming Burma, those same hatreds and resentments are still being exploited, this time by a desperate Burmese government anxious to face down the electoral threat from Aung San Suu Kyi and the NLD.

In June 2012, Sittwe erupted in a bloody orgy of killing, destruction and looting as the majority Rakhine population turned on the Muslim, mainly Rohingya, minority. This was repeated, albeit on a slightly less destructive scale, in October of the same year. Altogether, about ninety people were killed and over 100,000 Rohingya displaced during the two episodes. Those Rohingya who had escaped from Sittwe were forced to live in hastily built refugee camps a few miles outside the town.[1] When I visited Sittwe just after the second outburst of violence, it was clear just how thoroughly, almost surgically, the Rakhine had driven the Muslims from their midst. The charred remains of a Muslim house would smoulder in between immaculately intact Buddhist houses on either side. Mosques had been burned to the ground, and a state of apartheid had effectively been declared. No movement was allowed in, or out, of the Muslim quarter in the centre of the city. Similarly, no Muslim refugees were allowed into Sittwe from the squalid refugee camps just beyond the town's boundaries. At the time of writing, these camps held about 140,000 people. The Rohingya refugees' only means of escape was by sea, and so tens of thousands have been taking to ancient, ill-prepared fishing boats to try to reach the Muslim communities in, mostly, Malaysia and Indonesia. Hundreds have drowned as these vessels have sunk, capsized or just disappeared in one of the greatest and least reported tragedies of our age.

As we saw in Chapter One, the imposition of the plural society in Sittwe was particularly loathed by the Rakhine because it involved an influx of both Burmese and Indians, mostly Muslims, to take over many jobs in the state, as well as foreign rule by the British. Rakhine relations with the Rohingya Muslims have stayed tense and occasionally incendiary ever since. There have been periodic bouts of extreme violence and also the enforced expulsion of many thousands of the stateless Rohingya in the 1990s.

Every Rakhine I met in Sittwe, particularly the unrepentant bigots of the Rakhine Nationalities Development Party, the main political representation of the Rakhine (now the Rakhine, or Arakan, National Party), seemed to have a dusty old pamphlet or video purporting to demonstrate the stark reality of the "Muslim threat". This threat took many forms, apparently; that the Muslims were having so many children that they would soon take over Burma; that all Muslims had been to terrorist training camps in Pakistan or Afghanistan; and that all Muslims wanted to destroy Buddhism. Clearly, the Rakhine had been reared on a fantastical diet of anti-Muslim rhetoric, which partly accounted for the fanatical and bloody defence, as they saw it, of their homeland in Rakhine State. Many believed that just as previously Buddhist Indonesia (witness the famous temple of Borobudur, they argued) had been overrun by Muslims, so the same could easily happen in Burma.

Furthermore, they were encouraged in all these beliefs by those most respected members of the Burmese community, the monks. One day in Sittwe I witnessed a large, angry mob demonstrating in the main street against Muslims. They had been provoked, according to them, by the news that a Muslim relief organisation was trying to set up an office in Burma to help the Rohingya victims of the sectarian violence. These sorts of protests were not uncommon, but what caught my eye about this particular one was that it was being organised by monks. Shockingly, the saffron-robed holymen were corralling the crowds along Sittwe's main street. This was the intersection of the *sangha* with the most chauvinistic and nationalist elements of Rakhine Buddhism, and it was clearly a potent mix. One stoked-up protestor spotted me looking on and rushed over. Joined by a couple of mates, he demanded to know what religion I was. Fortunately, I could honestly tell him that I wasn't a Muslim.

The violent ethnic cleansing of Sittwe was most likely sparked off by the rape of a Buddhist Rakhine woman by Muslim men. Soon after a similar chain of events began to be repeated throughout the Burman heartlands. In most cases, the killing, burning and looting of Muslims and their shops and properties also occurred in the centres of the plural society, in towns and cities like Meiktila, an important railway-junction town north-west of Naypyidaw, and Mandalay. Allegations of the rape of a Buddhist woman by Muslim men sometimes sparked off these events.

Take Mandalay, where Muslims account for about 10 per cent of the population. A young and gentle Muslim friend, whom I shall call Harry, described what happened there in the first days of July 2014. In the weeks before, there had been a surge of hate-speech among the Buddhist communities, not only against Muslims but also against Aung San Suu Kyi and the NLD. On 1 July, the rabblerousing leader of the more nationalist, anti-Muslim monks, Ashin Wirathu, from one of Mandalay's monasteries, posted a report on his Facebook page that a Muslim man had raped a Buddhist woman near Naypyidaw. The man accused of the rape had a tea shop on the corner of a street in the centre of Mandalay. Soon afterwards, a crowd of Buddhist Burmans surrounded the premises shouting threats and trying to force it to close. Harry, watching, described what happened next:

> About thirty or forty men and women turned up on motorbikes. They were outsiders, no one had seen them before. They were shouting "Kill all Muslims" and "This is our land, not your land". The police did not intervene at first, but later tried to disperse the crowd. All night, groups of people were going around Mandalay shouting and screaming this. At 5 a.m., a Muslim man was attacked and killed by a mob on his way to prayers.

A Buddhist man was also killed. Harry talked sadly about the aftermath of the violence: "A lot of people don't trust each other now. Buddhists are afraid to go into Muslim tea shops and Muslims won't go into Buddhist areas. So, the town is more divided now. That is the effect of the violence."

Ever since 2012, there have been constant attempts to ratchet up divisions and hatred between Buddhists and Muslims. The outsiders on bikes who had turned up screaming racial abuse on 1 July had carried out similarly provocative tours of Mandalay before, only since no one had been killed on those occasions the news hadn't been picked up. Social media and Twitter had become easy conduits for the most unlikely and inflammatory rumours and slurs. Mandalay, for instance, is English-Premier-League-mad and most monks (for some strange reason) support Manchester United. But a post on Facebook a few years ago pointed out that since the American (and Jewish) owner of United, the late

Malcolm Glazer, had a beard he must be a Muslim. Loyal Buddhists were thus urged to transfer their allegiance to another club. Harry himself had at one point become a Facebook victim. His girlfriend happened to be a Burman Buddhist, and this too had been posted up on Ashin Wirathu's Facebook page. As a result, Harry and his girlfriend found themselves blacklisted by Buddhist landlords who wouldn't rent an apartment to a mixed-religion couple.

Many people in Burma believe that these attacks were co-ordinated and encouraged by the government, in conjunction with nationalist monks like Wirathu and other elements. All the attacks followed a similar pattern and they have all taken place since 2012. The date is not a coincidence. This is when Sittwe erupted, but it was also the year when the ruling party began to feel most threatened by the NLD after the party's dramatic triumph in April's by-elections, when Aung San Suu Kyi was elected to the national parliament. These two events became linked, as the principal aim of the anti-Muslim violence has been to exploit the existing ill will against Muslims, as demonstrated at Sittwe, to counter the enduring electoral appeal of the NLD. Elements of the USDP, it seems, have tried to scare Buddhists into believing that Muslims are about to take over Burma, whilst then reassuring them that only they, the USDP, will truly stand up to defend their "race and religion".

Aung San Suu Kyi, by contrast, by advocating universal human rights and the rule of law, can be depicted as being a friend of Muslims, and thus, by default, an enemy of Buddhism. This is nonsense, but in a political environment dominated by ignorance, rumour and innuendo, this campaign has had an effect. The political aim of the hate campaign against Muslims is to chip away at Aung San Suu Kyi's popularity among her core supporters, Burman Buddhists, and thus reduce her electoral appeal, at the general election due to be held in 2015, and thereafter. It is the politics of fear – or democratic politics, Burmese-style.

As one Muslim activist explained the anti-Muslim assault to me, "the main target is the NLD, and Muslims are the scapegoats". In the lexicon of American electoral politics, the agenda of "race and religion" has thus been turned into a wedge issue, a ploy to try to separate Aung San Suu Kyi from her natural supporters, or base. Republican strategists in America have used the issue of gay marriage in a similar way in presidential and congressional elections, to scythe more socially conservative, grassroots Democrats away from the Democratic leadership.

No one is sure who has been orchestrating the anti-Muslim, anti-NLD campaign. The bully boys of the *Swan Arr Shin* are thought to be the main agents provocateurs, the mysterious outsiders who turn up in places like Mandalay to stoke up feelings, shout slogans against Muslims and possibly kill a few of them. Aung Thaung, the close friend and henchman of Than Shwe, known to be close to the *Swan Arr Shin*, has been fingered by the Americans. He was blacklisted by America just before President Obama's second visit to Burma, for an Asia summit in November 2014. "By intentionally undermining the positive political and economic transition in Burma, Aung Thaung is perpetuating violence, oppression and corruption", read his official US Treasury citation. The psy-war arm of military intelligence has been publishing anti-Muslim material for decades, so it is possible also that some of the current material being circulated emanates from the military. Aung Thaung is also known to be close to some of the monks of Mandalay, and has been connected in particular to the most notorious of the chauvinist, nationalist monks, the poisonous and outspoken Ashin Wirathu.

The numbers game

Born in 1968 near Mandalay, Wirathu is the widely acknowledged leader of the 969 movement, the most prominent anti-Muslim organisation among the *sangha*. The movement is virulently anti-Muslim, chauvinistically pro-Burman and very nationalistic. Wirathu has been quoted as saying that "[Muslims] are breeding so fast and they are stealing our women, raping them". He has also said that most of Burma's Muslims are "radical, bad people". Many cars and shops in Burma are now plastered with a 969 sticker, to show support for the anti-Muslim monks. In its most recent, post-2012 incarnation, the movement probably originated from among the monks in Mon State, although its intellectual antecedents, if we can call them that, are much older. 969 might at first have been a spontaneous movement, in support of the Rakhine against the Rohingya in Sittwe, but it was quickly exploited by the authorities.

The number 969 has a distinctive meaning in Buddhism. The first nine stands for the nine special attributes of the Lord Buddha, the six for the six special attributes of his Buddhist teachings, and the last nine represents the nine virtues of Buddhist monks. The numbers are also intended as a direct counter to the Muslim number 786. Across South and South-East Asia, Muslims represent the phrase "In the Name of Allah, the Compassionate and Merciful" with the number 786. It is often displayed in shops and businesses to show that they are Muslim-owned. Some Burmese Buddhists, however, see the number as further evidence of the Muslim conspiracy for world domination. After all, the belief goes, the digits add up to twenty-one, clearly demonstrating that Muslims want to conquer the world in the twenty-first century. "Are you serious?", I asked the monk in Mandalay who told me this. "Yes", he replied, "lots of non-educated people believe that." The number 969 is intended to be the numerical nemesis of 786.

There is no doubt that the 969 movement is well funded and well organised. It has its own weekly newspaper (possibly a product of the psy-war department), which regularly attacks Islam and other religions such as Christianity. Wirathu was jailed in 2003 for hate-speech, after inciting a crowd to kill Muslims in revenge for a Muslim allegedly killing a Buddhist woman, but he was conveniently released in early 2012 as part of a political-prisoner amnesty. Monks in Mandalay to whom I spoke in 2014, none sympathetic to Wirathu, pointed out that whereas before he was nothing more than a small-time religious bigot, after his release from prison in 2012 his rhetoric took on an explicitly political tinge, especially in terms of his attacks on Aung San Suu Kyi and the NLD. Wirathu and his acolytes have often mocked the symbol of the NLD, the fighting peacock, or *Khut Daung* in Burmese. Wirathu calls it the *Mut Daung*, or Muslim peacock.

The monks I spoke to attributed this sort of political slur directly to the influence of Aung Thaung. At one monastery in Mandalay, a senior monk explained it to me thus: "Wirathu wants to be famous. He met Aung Thaung in his temple, and after that he changed. Before he was talking about just religious issues, and after meeting Aung Thaung he started talking about politics and the NLD."

The monk pointed out that since 2012 Wirathu and other 969 protagonists have enjoyed almost complete freedom, unlike the rest of the population – "the government allows them to do anything they like." Many of the allegations on

Wirathu's notorious Facebook page, the main conduit for his hate-speech, are usually no more than cleverly concocted and provocative lies. The post on 1 July about the rape of a Buddhist woman, for instance, which sparked off the violence in Mandalay, rapidly turned out to be a complete fabrication.

The 969 movement has also inspired a wider Buddhist organisation called the Association for the Protection of Race and Religion, known as *Ma Ba Tha* in Burmese. This is a more broad-based affair and is consulted by the Ministry of Religious Affairs on draft legislation affecting issues of "race and religion". This movement is supported by the money of one of the regime's wealthiest cronies, Khin Shwe, head of the Zaykabar Corporation and also a government MP. He has founded a Buddhist support group called Sasana Nogghaha; one of its aims is to establish a small prayer-room or meeting-hall for Buddhists on virtually every street corner of Burma's big cities. With plenty of money available, some of these corner buildings in Mandalay, for instance, are very elaborate. Here, monks circulate Buddhist-nationalist propaganda, encouraging the prevailing anti-Muslim sentiment.

In 2014, President Thein Sein himself asked parliament to draft legislation based on four proposals for new laws that emanated directly from the *Ma Ba Tha*. Thus, the president has become closely associated with their agenda. All the proposals sought to limit further the rights of Muslims in Burma and to divide Muslims from the Buddhist majority. Much of the proposed legislation, especially the prospective Buddhist Women's Special Marriage Bill and the Religious Conversion Bill, would violate even the existing Burmese constitution, let alone contravene international norms on human rights.[2] When the UN Special Rapporteur for human rights in Burma attacked the four proposed laws for just this in early 2015, she was savagely denounced by Wirathu. According to press reports, he called her a "bitch" and a "whore".

Divide and rule?

The monks of Mandalay are, on the whole, well-meaning and thoughtful people. They can see straight through Wirathu, and understand the anti-Muslim campaign for what it really is. Sadly, though, such are the appalling levels of ignorance among most, particularly young, Burmese, that the lies and rumours circulated by the 969 movement have been believed all too easily. In a society where for decades there was almost no media available except for the few desultory government-run press and TV outlets, few have the wherewithal to analyse social media, for instance, critically and objectively. Furthermore, the drip, drip, drip of fanciful and malicious propaganda merely reinforces many people's existing prejudices.

So, unfortunately, argues Ko Nyi Nyi Kyaw, the 88 Generation (see Chapter Seven) activist from Mandalay, the 969 movement and all the chauvinistic Buddhist propaganda "has had a big effect". He himself has had cause to follow this closely as, unusually for an activist of that generation, he is a Muslim, a descendant of the Kaman group that migrated to serve under the Burmese kings in Mandalay over three hundred years ago. He has been targeted by the authorities for being a Muslim just as much as for being a pro-democracy activist. After he was arrested during the pro-democracy demonstrations in 1988, he says that his interrogators from military intelligence were mostly concerned with his faith, not his politics; "Mother-fucker *Kala*, why are you involved in Myanmar politics?", they shouted.

Even now he seems to be of great interest to the authorities. We were talking in a rather seedy tea shop in Mandalay. Most of the other customers were young, very scruffy and obviously impecunious, except for one middle-aged Burman in an immaculately pressed *longyi* and radiantly white shirt. Even I clocked him as he sat down at the nearest table to us. Sure enough, after an hour or two of eavesdropping, he left, exchanging pleasantries with Ko Nyi Nyi Kyaw on his way out. "Special branch", said the latter. "He's often in here. Now we can talk properly."

Ko Nyi Nyi Kyaw runs an organisation called Metta (meaning benevolence, or love) to promote inter-faith reconciliation, but he acknowledges that this has become hard going. The 969 movement has been "very successful in the villages and the towns . . . nearly every Burmese person believes that this is a Burman, Buddhist country . . . and isolation from the rest of the world had fuelled this. Now there are few monks who have been to other countries, so everyone has this mindset." He is very pessimistic about the future: "Inter-faith work has not worked. It is very difficult to confront this. It is silly to say that we can defeat this campaign."

Many would agree with him. He argues that as people turn against the NLD under the sway of all the anti-Muslim propaganda, so it will be harder now for the party to win as many votes in the epicentres of the plural society – like Meiktila, Rakhine State and Mandalay – as they might have done before. Indeed, there is plenty of evidence that the "wedge" is working all too well within the NLD itself. Nay Chi Win, the head of the party's research department, told me that there have been several instances of Buddhists turning against Muslims within the party. He cites one occasion when some members of an NLD township committee came to him for advice. A number of their fellow Buddhist committee members were trying to expel the Muslim members of the committee, and they were trying to stop this. However, they were afraid to do anything themselves "for fear of being called pro-Muslim". In the end, Nay Chi Win told me, he stiffened their nerves and prevented the expulsion of these Muslims.

But this is not how it always goes. Muslim leaders say that already plenty of Muslim NLD members have been kicked out of the party by their Buddhist colleagues. Aung San Suu Kyi herself and the elder statesman Tin Oo go round local party committees to talk about the virtues of tolerance and fraternity, but this seems to have only a limited impact. Nay Chi Win is surely right that at least some of those provoking anti-Muslim sentiment within the NLD will be government informers and provocateurs. Since the NLD has no central registration system or record of who has joined the party, it's almost impossible to weed these people out, he says.

"This is a plot to win the election on a race and religion platform", says Nay Chi Win. But seeing the plot so clearly does not necessarily mean that it's easy to foil. He explains the political dilemma of Aung San Suu Kyi: "It forces her into a corner. If she sticks up for the ethnic minorities, she will lose popularity, as the government will accuse her of being pro-Muslim. If she says something against the Rakhine community, then she will be accused of racism. So, she must just insist on the rule of law."

That sounds all very well, but for many in the West it amounts to not speaking out at all, and that carries its own cost. Many of her supporters have been disappointed, to say the least, by her overly cautious comments on the mass-killings and ethnic clearing of the Rohingya since 2012. Equally, she has been criticised for not defending the Muslim minority more generally, just as she has also been strongly attacked by the Kachin for not standing up for them as they were being shelled and bombed by the Burmese army before the ceasefire in early 2015. These are the dilemmas of a former icon who used to transcend the political fray, but who now has to operate as a humdrum politician in an environment that has been carefully designed by her opponents to thwart her.

Her aides reassure everyone of her private sympathy for Burma's Muslims, but argue that it is very difficult for her to say much. She must know that it is the single issue that could yet prevent the NLD eventually coming to power, as they should have done all those years ago. Would she want to jeopardise winning future general elections, beginning in 2015, by speaking out more forcefully against Burman Buddhist violence and hate-speech? The hope is, as Nay Chi Win argues, that there will always be a silent majority of Burmese Buddhists who have no taste for 969 and their anti-Muslim propaganda, and who will always vote for the NLD regardless. Maybe, but it's also true that the government, the USDP and the massed ranks of the military, who want to cling on to as much of their power and privilege as possible, think that this electoral strategy could be enough to damage, if not completely stop, the NLD. It has been noticeable how USDP members of parliament and ministers have become gradually more recalcitrant over further reform as the "race and religion" strategy has developed, particularly since 2013. The government flatly refused to give any concessions to the NLD over the constitution, for instance. The success of the 969 movement and the anti-Muslim, anti-NLD propaganda emboldened them, in part, to dig their heels in. No longer do they feel obliged to accept that the tide of history is inevitably against them.

The regime's hardliners have also been helped by the fact that the West has thrown away the significant leverage that it used to have in Burma. In the year or so after Clinton's visit, the West had considerable power over both the quality and quantity of reforms, swapping sanction lifting for prisoner releases and so on. But the sanctions were lifted too quickly, and too comprehensively. Europe, in particular, gave up all sanctions (except an arms embargo) in one go. America and Europe never carried much of a big stick in Burma, and now they have thrown away all the carrots too. So, the West's ability to influence events has subsequently diminished. Calls by Obama for a reboot of the stuttering reform programme during 2014, for instance, went almost entirely unheeded; the West could now be safely ignored.

In retrospect, it seems that the Obama administration was too anxious to prove its good faith in offering to come to terms with its most obdurate opponents. America found that it had to start reimposing selective sanctions against Aung Thang in 2014, as the situation in Burma gradually deteriorated. But it's very unlikely that this sort of sanction will have any effect on the direction of Burmese politics. It was a case of too little, too late. The Burmese generals must have calculated that the West had by now invested too much political, emotional and financial capital in the country since 2011 for there to be any large-scale rolling back of the West's support for Thein Sein's government.

If we could just muddle towards a Malaysian-style political system, the USDP must think, that would be an acceptable outcome of Thein Sein's reforms. In that case an ethnic-majority (Burman) party would win electoral hegemony by recasting politics entirely around the defence of the power and privileges of that majority, just as the Malays have done. In which case economic growth would be achievable without giving way to any profound political change.

Unfortunately, the opposition to this "race and religion" agenda has not been as strong as it might have been. Aung San Suu Kyi's relative silence on the matter has damaged her reputation among the minority ethnic groups in the country. Very few among the leaders of the Kachin, Karen and other groups would support her politically anymore, as they feel that she has let down the ethnic groups generally in not backing minority rights more against the Burman-dominated government. Likewise, Aung San Suu Kyi's warm words towards the army, in honour of her father as the founder of the *Tatmadaw*, have also been badly received among those who have spent decades being used as human minesweepers. Doubtless, she must not antagonise the army unduly, as it will still have a large say in the country's future whatever happens, but, the argument goes, she didn't have to go quite so far out of her way to give it her blessing.

In all, it often seems that the qualities that won Aung San Suu Kyi so much admiration as the persecuted opposition leader from 1988 to 2010 – her obduracy, steadfastness and courage, as well as her willingness to put country before family – have served her less well in more recent years. Since the NLD was legalised in 2011, she has struggled to convert the party into a functioning, democratic institution, ready for government. Aung San Suu Kyi has proved poor at delegating, and there has been almost no attempt to establish a wider leadership group around her, to spread responsibility for policy making. There is no formal "shadow cabinet", or ministers-in-waiting with their designated portfolios. On the contrary, power is tightly held in a small cabal around Aung San Suu Kyi, causing resentment amongst the wider party. Mass-campaigns have been organised in support of changing the constitution to allow her to be elected president, but there have been no similarly wide discussions on any aspect of NLD policy. Too often, her legendary stubbornness can now come over as arrogance and inflexibility. There has also been little attempt to foster a younger generation of leaders who must step in soon to take over from the old guard.

All this has left the party weaker than it should be, especially given the enormous popular goodwill towards it, and also towards Aung San Suu Kyi personally. As a result, there has been less push-back against the generals' "race and religion" propaganda than there might have been. Contrary to what must have been expected after Aung San Suu Kyi's release from house arrest in 2010, certainly since 2012 it has been the more recidivist wing of the USDP that has been largely setting the political agenda in Burma, not the world-famous leader of the NLD. Most strikingly, the NLD has failed to pick up the mantle of Aung San Suu Kyi's father and articulate a detailed vision for a modern Panglong agreement, of a confederated Burma, to rival the generals' sour and fearful defence of the status quo. Indeed, overall the diehards in the USDP have succeeded remarkably well in slowing down the impetus for change in Burma since the glory years of 2011 to 2013, and everyone must share some of the blame for that.

The victims' victims

And what of Burma's Muslims, the scapegoats in this deadly political game? Like the Palestinians in one sense, they are the victims' victims, in this case of the Burmese, and in their turn of the British. The Rohingya, of course, are paying a terrible price for the anti-Muslim mania that has been whipped up, but it is affecting other Muslims too. Burma's Muslims are proud of their tolerance and moderation, their Sufi traditions and their respect for other religious communities. They are, in this sense, the best that the plural society still has to offer contemporary Burma. But Muslim leaders like Dr Myint Thein, director of an Islamic Institute in Yangon, argue that all this could fray, or even be lost, if young Muslims feel an increasing need to mobilise and fight back against the Buddhist-nationalist onslaught. He fears, rightly, that if the Buddhists attack the Koran and continue defaming the Prophet, as the 969 movement does, then it will become correspondingly easy for extremist Islamist terrorist groups like Indonesia's Jemaah Islamiyah "to recruit young men, unemployed and poor, to the cause, young men who have seen their houses burned down and their family members killed. Until now we have seen no such connections, but if these ultra-nationalists [Buddhists] continue like this, it will happen."

Myint Thein tells me that he writes letters to Shwe Mann, Thein Sein and other ministers to warn them of this, but "they do not reply strongly, they say they don't want to discuss it." With good reason, perhaps, as this may be exactly what they want. Outbreaks of mainstream Islamic terrorism in Burma would suit the 969 movement perfectly, as it would confirm all their most lurid warnings about the Muslim threat. One knowledgable source told me that in the new looking-glass world of Burmese politics, military intelligence is already working in the shadows to help Muslim organisations that are raising Muslim consciousness and awareness, in the hope that this will just provoke a bigger anti-Muslim backlash from Buddhist-nationalists.

Obviously, it would be a terrible tragedy for Burma, and the region, if this cycle of violence and intimidation were to continue. It's a horrible irony that thousands of young Muslims in Britain and France rush off to fight for extremist groups like Islamic State despite all the political and material benefits that they enjoy, whilst Burma's Muslims receive almost nothing from a country that constantly rejects them, yet remain almost entirely unradicalised, either against the Burmese state or in favour of the worldwide jihad. The Internet might change that, but for now, the Rohingya aside, theirs is a remarkable record of restraint in the face of endless provocation.

Yet, there are already faint signs of a new militancy among some Muslims in Burma in response to 969. One Muslim group called Tablighi Jamaat, founded in India in the 1920s, has been gaining followers. It is a very mild form of the more rigorous Middle-Eastern strains of Islam, and is now organised in cities like Mandalay as a form of Muslim self-defence.

I met one of the better-known Tablighi Jamaat activists, Ka Win Naing, in front of his hardware store in Mandalay. Lean and earnest, with a thin wispy beard and dressed in a neat *longyi*, he stressed to me that he firmly identified himself as a Burmese. "Islam teaches us to love where we are born", he explained, "so as a Muslim born in Myanmar, so we love Myanmar." Yet, the authorities made it impossible for him to be Burmese, he said, as much as he wished to be so. Despite the fact that he was born in Mandalay, he was still identified as an Indian on his national registration card. He had asked to be Burmese, he said, but was told that as he was a Muslim, he could not be Burmese; he had to choose between being an Indian or Pakistani. So now, he felt, turning to Tablighi Jamaat "was the best response to the racism". Becoming more religious, praying and working together with other Muslims, could save them.

What else could he do, he asked? His life, after all, was dissolving around him. He had been renting this same hardware store for seventeen years, but had just been given a year's notice by the Buddhist Burman owner. He in fact got on very well with this man, Ka Win Naing said, and the Burman would have liked to have continued renting the premises to him, "but he had been threatened by the monks of 969".

Another victim, another scapegoat, of the new democratic era. Burma might be changing, and often for the better, but it will come at a price, to be paid by anonymous, law-abiding, hard-working, patriotic men like Ka Win Naing. If he and others like him leave Burma now, this will be another generation of well-connected, ambitious and relatively wealthy businessmen and shopkeepers lost to the country, as happened after 1964, just when the new reforming Burma needs these people the most.

Epilogue

As I WRITE THIS from the comfort of my hotel room in Yangon, hundreds of people from Burma are drowning off the coast in the Bay of Bengal. It is May 2015, and over the last few months about thirty thousand Rohingya have been fleeing western Rakhine State in flimsy boats, hoping to make shore in Indonesia, Malaysia or Thailand, to start a new life. They pay traffickers thousands of dollars for the trip, yet so many don't survive the ordeal. Still more have been turned back by unwelcoming governments.

The plight of the Rohingya boat people has been capturing world headlines; the BBC and CNN have been running film reports from alongside, on top of and even inside the traffickers' filthy old vessels for weeks. Everyone in the world, it seems, has something to say on the subject – except for the Burmese government.

For a long time, they were entirely silent on the matter, with the government-sanctioned news media, both print and electronic, following suit. Eventually, weeks into the escalating crisis, ministers could no longer avoid the international clamour and were obliged to comment. Even then, however, it was only to condemn the people smugglers and traffickers who, they claimed, were at the heart of the problem. Of the Rohingya themselves, and of the desperate poverty, discrimination and anti-Muslim hostility that were really driving them into the sea, there was still not a single word. Parroting the excuse that the Rohingya were not officially citizens of Burma, or one of the 135 officially recognised ethnic groups, officials washed their hands of them, carrying on as much as possible as if nothing had happened. On one particular day, when the crisis peaked, with Indonesia and Malaysia finally caving in to international pressure to accept some of the thousands of Rohingya adrift at sea, Burma's TV news led with President Thein Sein accepting an international award on behalf of the country's rice growers at Naypyidaw.

The whole episode was terrible for the Rohingya, of course, but it was also worryingly reminiscent of the old days more generally. Not only was there the news blackout of this uncomfortable subject, but the government's callous indifference to the suffering of the Rohingya reminded many of their attitudes towards the victims of Nargis in 2008, just as the increasing persecution of the Rohingya echoes the treatment of all the ethnic minority peoples of Burma during the most oppressive periods of military rule. Similarly, the militant anti-Muslim sentiment of today, partly stoked by forces within the government itself, recalls earlier eras of sectarian violence.

In other words, although Burma has certainly progressed since 2011, when President Thein Sein took over, in important respects little has changed. Of course, there is now infinitely better mobile phone coverage, there are more banks and more restaurants, and even the venerable old roads of downtown Yangon have been resurfaced. But the country, it seems, still has to come to terms with its very difficult and bitterly contested history; the mosaic often seems to be as broken as ever. There is now plenty of the long-cherished "development", but who is benefiting? In Rakhine State, for instance, it is going almost entirely to the Rakhine people rather than being shared with the Rohingya. Thus, development will further entrench the ethnic divide rather than help to bridge it.

The Rohingya are an extreme case, of course, but as this book has demonstrated, all the supposedly official non-Burman ethnic groups have suffered the same sort of discrimination and oppression as the Rohingya have. In this sense, the legal niceties have never mattered much. Little wonder, then, that it has taken so long to sign ceasefire agreements with the Karen, Kachin and others, or that the start of real political talks could still be a long way off. Ordinary Burmans are often surprised that these groups take so long to negotiate with, but that is only because much of the modern Burmese state's aggression has taken place well out of sight of the Burman-majority heartlands; it is real enough.

These considerations make it hard to be too optimistic about Burma's future. The country will have elections, maybe even free and fair, and it might even, eventually, evolve into some sort of limited federal structure, honouring the original promise of its founding father, General Aung San. But on the current trajectory, these Western-style political mechanisms might only serve to disguise the country's underlying divisions rather than resolve them.

Take federalism, for instance. It's a concept that often gets bandied around as a solution to the country's ethnic divisions, to devolve political power to Kachin or Rakhine States, for instance, in order to empower the Kachin and Rakhine enough to keep them within the union of Burma. Yet, no country in the world, with the possible exception of India, has ever tried a federal system based purely on ethnicity. And anyway, in every Burmese state there is a multiplicity of ethnic groups, several of whom would fear that their rights and language would be trampled on by a newly empowered dominant group. The Rohingya, it's safe to bet, would suffer even more were the Rakhine to have greater control over their state.

The much more difficult alternative, but the only viable one in the long run, is for Burma to embrace its extraordinary diversity, for as this book has argued, in the contemporary world this should be its greatest strength. Burma's rulers, whoever they may be after the 2015 elections and beyond, don't need to venture very far to find the answer to the country's chronic poverty and creaking economy – they just have to look out the window on to the streets of downtown Yangon. Here is where Burma could learn to pick up the threads of the country's commercial past. This is where globalisation was invented, and despite successive attempts to smash those silken webs that bind these traders to the world, enough still survives. If they were all equal citizens in a new Burma, Jews and Bengalis, Rohingya and Burmese, Punjabi and Karen alike, that could be an extraordinarily rich and potent mix. Just as the plural society, with all its flaws, was born in these streets in its own time, so it is easy to imagine another society emerging from the detritus of the old, better, stronger and wealthier than before. But that would require enormous political courage from all of Burma's rulers, to surmount the country's history in the name of forging an entirely new nation.

Yangon, May 2015

NOTES

Chapter One

1. Kwasi Kwarteng, *Ghosts of Empire: Britain's Legacies in the Modern World*, Bloomsbury, 2011, p. 149. For a full account of the last years of the Burmese court and British occupation, see Thant Myint-U, *The Making of Modern Burma*, Cambridge University Press, 2001, chs 7–8.
2. For further details of these buildings, see the Association of Myanmar Architects, *30 Heritage Buildings of Yangon: Inside the City that Captured Time*, Serindia Publications, 2013. I have drawn from this work for the following paragraphs.
3. Wai Wai Myaing, *A Journey in Time: Family Memoirs, Burma 1914–1948*, Universe Inc., 2005, p. 8.
4. Ruth Fredman Cernea, *Almost Englishmen: Baghdad Jews in British Burma*, Lexington Books, 2009, p. 10.
5. See the draft paper by Noriyuki Osada, "Housing the Rangoon poor: Indians, Burmese and town planning in colonial Burma", for a fuller description of the Indians in Rangoon. This paper was read at the "Sites of Modernity" workshop organized by the Department of History, Chulalongkorn University, 2014.
6. Wai Wai Myaing, *A Journey in Time*, p. 6.
7. Christopher Bayly and Tim Harper, *Forgotten Armies: Britain's Asian Empire and the War with Japan*, Penguin, 2005, p. 92.
8. Norman Lewis, *Golden Earth: Travels in Burma*, Eland, 2003.
9. Felicity Goodall, *Exodus Burma: The British Escape Through the Jungles of Death 1942*, Spellmount, 2011, p. 38.
10. Bertil Lintner, *Burma in Revolt: Opium and Insurgency since 1948*, Silkworm Books, 2003, p. 42.
11. Wai Wai Myaing, *A Journey in Time*, p. 176.
12. Bayly and Harper, *Forgotten Armies*, p. 89.
13. Quote from a later edition of J. S. Furnivall, *Colonial Policy and Practice: A Comparative Study of Burma and Netherlands India*, New York University Press, 1956, p. 304.
14. Christopher Bayly and Tim Harper, *Forgotten Wars: The End of Britain's Asian Empire*, Penguin, 2008, p. 378.
15. Sean Turnell, *Fiery Dragons: Banks, Moneylenders and Microfinance in Burma*, NIAS Press, 2009, p. 37.
16. Quoted in Bayly and Harper, *Forgotten Armies*, p. 67.
17. J. A. Berlie, *The Burmanization of Myanmar's Muslims,* White Lotus Press, 2008, p. 61.
18. Thant Myint-U, *The Making of Modern Burma*, pp. 89–90.

Chapter Two

1. See Robert Taylor, "Refighting old battles, compounding misconceptions: The politics of ethnicity in Myanmar today", ISEAS Perspective, March 2015, p. 5, for a discussion of this.
2. See Alvin Rabushka and Kenneth A. Shepsle, *Politics in the Plural Societies: A Theory of Democratic Instability*, Longman, 2009, for a more theoretical account of government responses to the plural society.
3. Donald Seekins, *Burma and Japan since 1940*, NIAS Press, 2007, p. 1.
4. Seekins, *Burma and Japan*, p. 29.
5. Goodall, *Exodus Burma*, p. 41.
6. See Bayly and Harper, *Forgotten Armies*, pp. 171–2.
7. John Latimer, *Burma: The Forgotten War*, John Murray, 2004, pp. 4–5, for his complete list of the nationalities of the Forgotten Army.
8. Latimer, *Burma*, p. 433.
9. Michael Aung-Thwin and Maitrii Aung-Thwin, *A History of Myanmar since Ancient Times*, Reaktion Books, 2013, p. 251.
10. Seekins, *Burma and Japan*, p. 81, and Taylor, "Refighting old battles", p. 4.
11. See Berlie, *The Burmanization of Myanmar's Muslims*, p. 41.

Chapter Three

1. David Steinberg, *Burma/Myanmar: What Everyone Needs to Know*, Oxford University Press, 2010, p. 17.
2. Seekins, *Burma and Japan*, p. 80.
3. Benedict Rogers, *Than Shwe: Unmasking Burma's Tyrant*, Silkworm Books, 2010, p. 48.
4. For more information see the work of the French scholar Bénédicte Brac de la Perrière, "Nats: An Overview of the Field of Religion in Burmese Studies", Asian Ethnology, Vol. 68, No. 2, 2009, p. 201.
5. Dulyapak Preecharushh, *Naypyidaw: The New Capital of Burma*, White Lotus Press, 2009, p. 89.
6. Aung San Suu Kyi, *Freedom from Fear*, Penguin, 1991, pp. 103–4.
7. Matthew Walton, "The 'wages of Burman-ness': Ethnicity and Burman privilege in contemporary Myanmar", Journal of Contemporary Asia, 2012, p. 8.
8. Aung-Thwin and Aung-Thwin, *A History of Myanmar*, p. 25.
9. See www.pcgn.org.uk/burma%200907.pdf for an exhaustive list of the name changes. Last accessed 30 June 2015.
10. Harvard University Kennedy School, Ash Center for Democratic Governance and Innovation, David Dapice, Anthony Saich and Thomas Vallely, *Appraising the Post-Sanctions Prospects for Myanmar's Economy: Choosing the Right Path*, January 2012, p. 20.
11. Ian Holliday, *Burma Redux: Global Justice and the Quest for Political Reform in Myanmar*, Columbia University Press, 2011, p. 77.
12. Berlie, *The Burmanization of Myanmar's Muslims*, p. 61.
13. See Martin Smith, *Burma: Insurgency and the Politics of Ethnicity*, Zed Books, 1999, p. 92.
14. See report from the International Crisis Group on the army and reform, *Myanmar's Military: Back to Barracks?*, 2014.
15. Smith, *Burma*, p. 260.
16. http://www.dvb.no/uncategorized/army-using-civilians-as-minesweepers/2150.
17. This account and several others can be found in the report by the Human Rights Action Group (Northern Myanmar), *Dignity Uprooted: Denied Human Rights in the Armed Conflict in Kachin State and Northern Shan State*, 2012.
18. Desmond Ball, *Burma's Military Secrets: Signals Intelligence (SIGINT) from 1941 to Cyber Warfare*, White Lotus Press, 1998, p. 61, and private information.
19. Mary Callahan, *Making Enemies: War and State Building in Burma*, Cornell University Press, 2005, p. 183.

20. See Renaud Egreteau, "The Burmese jade trail", in *Myanmar's Transition*, ed. Nick Cheesman, Monique Skidmore and Trevor Wilson, ISEAS, 2012, p. 95.
21. Turnell, *Fiery Dragons*, p. 266.
22. See Global Witness, *A Disharmonious Trade: China and the Continued Destruction of Burma's Northern Frontier Forests*, April 2009.

Chapter Four

1. Anders Engvall and Soe Nandar Linn, "Myanmar economic update: Macro-economy, fiscal reform and development options", in *Debating Democratization in Myanmar,* ed. Nick Cheesman, Nicholas Farrelly and Trevor Wilson, ISEAS, 2014.
2. Mandy Sadan, *Being and Becoming Kachin: Histories beyond the State in the Borderlands of Burma*, The British Academy, 2013, p. 98.
3. Sadan, *Being and Becoming Kachin,* p. 214.
4. Lintner, *Burma in Revolt*, p. 69.
5. Sadan, *Being and Becoming Kachin,* p. 382.

Chapter Five

1. Harry Ignatius Marshall, *The Karen People of Burma: A Study in Anthropology and Ethnology*, White Lotus Press, 1997, p. 304.
2. Lintner, *Burma in Revolt*, p. 51.
3. Marshall, *Karen People of Burma*, p. 309.
4. See Smith, *Burma*, p. 63 and Seekins, *Burma and Japan*, p. 45.
5. Lintner, *Burma in Revolt*, p. 72.
6. See Transnational Institute report, Ashley South, *Burma's Longest War: Anatomy of the Karen Conflict*, 2014, for a recent analysis of the Karen war.
7. For some reports on the living standards and conditions of the Karen, see Burma Medical Association report, Back Pack Health Worker Team and others, *Diagnosis Critical: Health and Human Rights in Eastern Burma*, 2010, or Thailand Burma Border Consortium, *Protracted Displacement and Chronic Poverty in Eastern Burma/Myanmar*, 2010.
8. Inge Sargent, *Twilight over Burma: My Life as a Shan Princess*, University of Hawaii Press, 1994, p. 49.
9. United Nations Office on Drugs and Crime, *Southeast Asia Opium Survey, Lao PDR, Myanmar*, 2013.
10. See the Report by Transnational Institute, *Bouncing Back: Relapse in the Golden Triangle*, 2014, p. 32.

Chapter Six

1. Nick Cheesman, Monique Skidmore and Trevor Wilson, eds, *Myanmar's Transition: Openings, Obstacles and Opportunities*, ISEAS, 2012, p. 151.
2. For a full appraisal of the hapless state of Burma's economy, see Asian Development Bank, *Myanmar in Transition: Opportunities and Challenges*, August 2012.
3. Ash Center, *Appraising Myanmar's Economy*, 2012, p. 5.
4. Ash Center, *Appraising Myanmar's Economy*, p. 21.
5. Emma Larkin, *Everything is Broken*, Granta, 2010, p. 78.
6. Quoted by Turnell, *Fiery Dragons*, p. 239.

Chapter Seven

1. Quotes from Peter Popham, *The Lady and the Peacock*, Rider, 2011, Ch. 2.
2. Popham, *The Lady and the Peacock*, p. 369.

Chapter Eight

1. Turnell, *Fiery Dragons*, p. 259.
2. Cheesman, Skidmore and Wilson, *Myanmar's Transition*, p. 46.
3. See the interesting paper on the make-up of the two houses of parliament by Renaud Egreteau, "A closer look at the social and political background of MPs in Myanmar's first post-SPDC national legislature", Center for Myanmar Studies, Yunnan University, Kunming, International Workshop on "Myanmar in 2014: Re-integrating into the International Community", July 2014. The author shows that in fact few of the USDP MPs have specifically military backgrounds.

Chapter Nine

1. See Egreteau, "The Burmese jade trail", p. 105.
2. China in Burma: The increasing investment of Chinese multinational corporations in Burma's hydropower, oil and natural gas, and mining sector, Earth Rights International, September 2008 (http://www.burmalibrary.org/docs5/China_in_Burma-ERI.pdf).
3. International Crisis Group Report, *China's Myanmar Dilemma*, Asia Report No. 177, September 2009, p. 11.
4. See Holliday, *Burma Redux*, p. 111, for this and a good discussion of Burma's external relations during this period.
5. Congressional Hearing report, *US Policy Toward Burma: Its Impact and Effectiveness*, 30 September 2009, p. 6.

Chapter Ten

1. See Human Rights Watch, *All You Can Do Is Pray*, April 2013, for a fuller account of the anti-Muslim violence in 2012. See also International Crisis Group, *Myanmar: The Politics of Rakhine State*, Asia Report No. 261, October 2014.
2. See Richard Horsey, "New religious legislation in Myanmar", SSRC paper, February 2015, for a discussion of the recent proposed legislation.

SELECT BIBLIOGRAPHY

The following is a list of the books, articles, reports and websites that I found most useful for writing this book. There is a vast quantity of literature on Burma/Myanmar, some of it quite unreadable, so this is by no means a comprehensive survey. Where appropriate, I suggest which part of the book/article is most relevant to the study of modern Burma, or a particular aspect of the country's recent history. Specifically, I have chosen to highlight the best recent literature on the Rohingya and the politics of Rakhine State, a subject that had previously been neglected. Everything is listed alphabetically by author under the relevant section. The date of publication, particularly for the older books, refers to the editions that I have used rather than to the original edition.

Books

Association of Myanmar Architects, *30 Heritage Buildings of Yangon: Inside the City that Captured Time*, Serindia Publications, 2013

Aung San Suu Kyi, *Freedom from Fear*, Penguin, 1991,

Aung-Thwin, Michael, and Maitrii Aung-Thwin, *A History of Myanmar since Ancient Times*, Reaktion Books, 2013

Ball, Desmond, *Burma's Military Secrets: Signals Intelligence (SIGINT) from 1941 to Cyber Warfare*, White Lotus Press, 1998

Bayly, Christopher, and Tim Harper, *Forgotten Armies: Britain's Asian Empire and the War with Japan*, Penguin, 2005

—, *Forgotten Wars: The End of Britain's Asian Empire*, Penguin, 2008

Berlie, J. A., *The Burmanisation of Myanmar's Muslims,* White Lotus Press, 2008

Callahan, Mary, *Making Enemies: War and State Building in Burma*, Cornell University Press, 2005

—, *Political Authority in Burma's Ethnic Minority States*, ISEAS, 2007

Cernea, Ruth Fredman, *Almost Englishmen: Baghdad Jews in British Burma*, Lexington Books, 2009

Cheesman, Nick, and Monique Skidmore, and Trevor Wilson, *Myanmar's Transition: Openings, Obstacles and Opportunities*, ISEAS, 2012

Dulyapak Preecharushh, *Naypyidaw: The New Capital of Burma*, White Lotus Press, 2009,

Furnivall, J. S., *Colonial Policy and Practice: A Comparative Study of Burma and Netherlands India*, New York University Press, 1956

Ghosh, Amitav, *The Glass Palace*, Random House, 2002

Goodall, Felicity, *Exodus Burma: The British Escape Through the Jungles of Death 1942*, Spellmount, 2011

Holliday, Ian, *Burma Redux: Global Justice and the Quest for Political Reform in Myanmar*, Columbia University Press, 2011

Kwasi Kwarteng, *Ghosts of Empire: Britain's Legacies in the Modern World*, Bloomsbury, 2011 (See especially part 3 on Burma, an excellent recent account of how and why the British got involved in the country.)

Larkin, Emma, *Everything is Broken*, Granta, 2010

—, *Finding George Orwell in Burma*, Penguin, 2004

Latimer, John, *Burma: The Forgotten War,* John Murray, 2004

Lewis, Norman, *Golden Earth: Travels in Burma*, Eland, 2003

Lintner, Bertil, *Burma in Revolt: Opium and Insurgency since 1948*, Silkworm Books, 2003

—, *Aung San Suu Kyi and Burma's Struggle for Democracy*, Silkworm Books, 2011

McLynn, Frank, *The Burma Campaign: Disaster to Triumph*, Vintage Books, 2011

Marshall, Harry Ignatius, *The Karen People of Burma: A Study in Anthropology and Ethnology*, White Lotus Press, 1997

Maung Maung, *Aung San of Burma*, Unity Publishing House, 2011

Orwell, George, *Burmese Days*, Penguin, 1982

Pascal Khoo Thwe, *From the Land of Green Ghosts: A Burmese Odyssey*, Harper Collins, 2003

Popham, Peter, *The Lady and the Peacock*, Rider, 2011

Rabushka, Alvin, and Kenneth A. Shepsle, *Politics in the Plural Societies: A Theory of Democratic Instability*, Longman, 2009 (The classic theoretical account of government responses to the plural society in Asia, Africa and elsewhere.)

Rogers, Benedict, *Than Shwe: Unmasking Burma's Tyrant*, Silkworm Books, 2010

—, *Burma: A Nation at the Crossroads,* Rider Books, 2012

Sadan, Mandy, *Being and Becoming Kachin: Histories Beyond the State in the Borderlands of Burma*, The British Academy, 2013

Sargent, Inge, *Twilight over Burma: My Life as a Shan Princess*, University of Hawaii Press, 1994

Seekins, Donald, *Burma and Japan since 1940*, NIAS Press, 2007

Smith, Martin, *Burma: Insurgency and the Politics of Ethnicity*, Zed Books, 1999

Steinberg, David, *Burma/Myanmar: What Everyone Needs to Know*, Oxford University Press, 2010

Taylor, Robert, *The State in Myanmar*, 2009

Thant Myint-U, *The Making of Modern Burma*, Cambridge University Press, 2001

—, *The River of Lost Footsteps: A Personal History of Burma*, Faber & Faber, 2008

—, *Where China Meets India: Burma and the New Crossroads of Asia*, Faber & Faber, 2012

Turnell, Sean, *Fiery Dragons: Banks, Moneylenders and Microfinance in Burma*, NIAS Press, 2009

Wai Wai Myaing, *A Journey in Time: Family Memoirs, Burma, 1914–1948,* Universe Inc., 2005

Articles

Brac de la Perrière, Bénédicte, "Nats: An overview of the field of religion in Burmese studies", *Asian Ethnology*, Vol. 68, No. 2, 2009. (A good academic study of how *nats* were incorporated into mainstream Burmese religion and politics.)

Callahan, Mary, "Democracy in Burma: The lessons of history", *National Bureau of Asian Research*, Vol. 9, No. 3, 1998

Egreteau, Renaud, "The Burmese jade trail", in *Myanmar's Transition*, ed. by Nick Cheesman, Monique Skidmore and Trevor Wilson, ISEAS, 2012

—, "A closer look at the social and political background of MPs in Myanmar's first post-SPDC national legislature", Center for Myanmar Studies, Yunnan University, Kunming, International Workshop on "Myanmar in 2014: Re-integrating into the International Community", July 2014. (An interesting and original analysis of the background of MPs who took their seats in the 2011 parliament, showing that in fact few of the USDP MPs have specifically military backgrounds.)

Engvall, Anders, and Soe Nandar Linn, "Myanmar economic update: Macro-economy, fiscal reform and development options", in *Debating Democratization in Myanmar*, ed. Nick Cheesman, Nicholas Farrelly and Trevor Wilson, ISEAS, 2014

Goh, Daniel P. S., "From colonial pluralism to postcolonial multiculturalism: race, state formation and the question of cultural diversity in Malaya and Singapore", Sociology Compass 2/1, 2008, pp. 232–52

Horsey, Richard, "New religious legislation in Myanmar", SSRC paper, February 2015. (A good discussion of the recent proposed legislation attempting to regulate inter-religious marriage etc.)

Noriyuki Osada, draft paper on "Housing the Rangoon poor: Indians, Burmese and town planning in colonial Burma", for a fuller description of the South Asians in Rangoon. This paper was read at the "Sites of Modernity" workshop organized by the Department of History, Chulalongkorn University, in 2014.

Raynaud, Mael, "Burma's civil society between Nargis and the 2010 elections", June 2009 (Private paper sent to author)

—, "Nay Win Maung, Une autre histoire birmane", January 2012 (Private paper sent to author)

Taylor, Robert, "Refighting old battles, compounding misconceptions: The politics of ethnicity in Myanmar today", ISEAS Perspective, March 2015, p. 5, for a recent discussion of this subject.

—, "The armed forces in Myanmar politics: A terminating role?", ISEAS Trends in Southeast Asia, 2015

Walton, Matthew, "The 'wages of Burman-ness': Ethnicity and Burman privilege in contemporary Myanmar", Journal of Contemporary Asia, 2012, pp. 1–27. (A very good analysis of Burmanisation.)

Weiss, Meredith, "Electoral patterns in Southeast Asia: The limits to engineering", ISEAS Working Paper #3, 2014

Reports

Asian Development Bank, *Myanmar in Transition: Opportunities and Challenges*, August 2012

Back Pack Health Worker Team, Burma Medical Association (and others), *Diagnosis Critical: Health and Human Rights in Eastern Burma*, 2010

(American) Congressional Hearing report, *US Policy Toward Burma: Its Impact and Effectiveness*, 30 September 2009

Global Witness, *A Disharmonious Trade: China and the Continued Destruction of Burma's Northern Frontier Forests*, April 2009

Harvard University Kennedy School, David Dapice, Thomas Vallely and Ben Wilkinson, *Assessment of the Myanmar Agricultural Economy*, February 2009

Harvard University Kennedy School, Ash Center for Democratic Governance and Innovation, David Dapice, Anthony Saich and Thomas Vallely, *Appraising the Post-Sanctions Prospects for Myanmar's Economy: Choosing the Right Path*, January 2012

Human Rights Action Group (Northern Myanmar), *Dignity Uprooted: Denied Human Rights in the Armed Conflict in Kachin State and Northern Shan State*, 2012

Human Rights Watch, *All You Can Do Is Pray*, April 2013

International Crisis Group, *Myanmar's Military: Back to Barracks?*, Asia Briefing No. 143, April 2014

International Crisis Group, *Myanmar: The Politics of Rakhine State*, Asia Report No. 261, October 2014. (The latest analysis of the politics of Rakhine State and how this has affected politics in the country more generally.)

International Crisis Group, *The Dark Side of Transition: Violence against Muslims in Myanmar*, Asia Report No. 251, October 2013. (Particularly good on the anti-Muslim violence in Rakhine State and more generally around the country.)

International Crisis Group, *China's Myanmar Dilemma*, Asia Report No. 177, September 2009

Proximity Designs, *Myanmar Past & Present*, 2014

Thailand Burma Border Consortium, *Protracted Displacement and Chronic Poverty in Eastern Burma/Myanmar*, 2010.

Transnational Institute, Kramer, Tom and others, *Bouncing Back: Relapse in the Golden Triangle*, 2014 (A very good update on the drugs situation in east Burma.)

Transnational Institute, South, Ashley, *Burma's Longest War: Anatomy of the Karen Conflict*, 2014 (for a recent analysis of the Karen war).

United Nations Office on Drugs and Crime, *Southeast Asia Opium Survey, Lao PDR, Myanmar*, 2013

Websites

For accounts of the army using civilians as minesweepers and other such abuses, see http://www.dvb.no/uncategorized/army-using-civilians-as-minesweepers/2150

The New Mandala website often hosts the best discussion of Burma. See, for example, below for a commentary on the recent political violence in Burma: http://asiapacific.anu.edu.au/newmandala/2015/03/17/dissent-and-repression-persist-in-myanmar

INDEX